Aquinas on Matter and Form and the Elements

AQUINAS
ON
MATTER AND FORM
AND
THE
ELEMENTS

A Translation and Interpretation
of the
de Principiis Naturae and the *De Mixtione Elementorum*
of
St. Thomas Aquinas

by
JOSEPH BOBIK

University of Notre Dame Press
Notre Dame, Indiana

Library of Congress Cataloging-in-Publication Data

Bobik, Joseph, 1927-
Aquinas on matter and form and the elements: a translation and
interpretation of the De principiis naturae and the De mixtione
elementorum of St. Thomas Aquinas / by Joseph Bobik.
p.   cm.
Includes index of names and index of subjects.
ISBN O-268-00653-9 (cloth ; alk. paper). — ISBN 0-268-02000-0
(pbk. : alk. paper)
1. Thomas Aquinas, Saint, 1225?-1274. De principiis naturae.
2. Philosophy of nature. 3. Thomas, Aquinas, Saint, 1225?-1274.
De mixtione elementorum. 4. Matter. I. Thomas, Aquinas, Saint,
1225?-1274. De principiis naturae. II. Thomas, Aquinas, Saint,
1225?-1274. De mixtione elementorum. III. Title.
B765.T53D744. 1997
113—dc21
97-26521

CIP

Manufactured in the United States of America
The paper used in this publication meets the minimum requirements of the American National Standard for Information Sciences—Permanence of Paper for Printed Library Materials, ANSI
Z39.48-1984.

To Teresa

and the children,

Lucy
Joseph
Teresa Maria
Thomas Aquinas
Amy

CONTENTS

CHAPTER THREE
Agent and end; principle, cause and element

CHAPTER SIX
Sameness and difference in matter and form

PART TWO
DE MIXTIONE ELEMENTORUM

PART THREE
ELEMENTS IN THE COMPOSITION
OF PHYSICAL SUBSTANCES

PART FOUR
THE ELEMENTS IN AQUINAS
AND THE ELEMENTS TODAY

PREFACE

This book has the aim of providing an **intelligible interpretation** of the views expressed by St. Thomas Aquinas in his *De Principiis Naturae* and in his *De Mixtione Elementorum*. Together, these two brief works offer a remarkably clear, sophisticated, and in many ways convincing, account of the nature of physical things, in terms of a theory which combines composition out of matter and form with composition out of elements.

An **interpretation** is an attempt to bring out the meaning of a work by entering into it in a sympathetic way, i.e., by trying hard to understand what the **author of the work** is saying. And this, to me, means at least 1) trying to make as clear as possible the sense of the claims being made by the author, and 2) arguing as convincingly as possible either for them or against them, as each of them may require.

An interpretation is **intelligible** if it 1) squares with the observed facts, i.e., with what is given in sense observation and in introspection, 2) is free of internal inconsistencies, i.e., preserves the inter-connections among ideas as given in analysis, and 3) is in principle capable of coping with objections, and with other interpretations, thereby illuminating its own positions.

xv

The aim of this book is not a scholarly one. There will be no attempt, therefore, to take into account the countless things which countless people have had to say about Aquinas on matter and form and the elements. Nor will there be any attempt to pursue in footnotes, or in appendices, or elsewhere, the generally uninteresting, and only remotely (if at all) relevant, asides which are too often pursued, and in overwhelming detail, in books of a scholarly sort.

The aim of this book, simply put, is to do some philosophy which is as genuine and as straightforward and as unencumbered as possible, using the words of Aquinas as a point of departure.

The translation of the *De Principiis Naturae* was made from the critical text of John J. Pauson;[1] comparisons were made with the critical edition of Basil M. Mattingly,[2] and with the text of the Leonine edition.[3] The translation of the *De Mixtione Elementorum* was made from the text as it appears in Spiazzi's *Opuscula Philosophica*;[4] this too was compared with the text of the Leonine edition.[5] I have tried throughout, both in translating and in interpreting, to use ordinary and understandable English, and still keep the philosophical message intact.

Because the *De Principiis Naturae* (DPN) was a very early work of Aquinas (around 1252 or 1253) and the *De Mixtione Elementorum* (DME) a

---

[1] *Saint Thomas Aquinas, De Principiis Naturae.* Introduction and Critical Text by John J. Pauson. Textus Philosophici Friburgenses, 2. Fribourg: Societe Philosophique, 1950.
[2] Basil M. Mattingly, O.S.B. *De Principiis Naturae of St. Thomas Aquinas.* Critical Edition. Notre Dame, Indiana: University of Notre Dame. Doctoral Dissertation, 1957.
[3] *De Principiis Naturae, ad fratrem Sylvestrum;* Leonine edition, vol. 43, pp. 39-47.
[4] Divi Thomae Aquinatis, Doctoris Angelici, *Opuscula Philosophica.* Cura et Studio P. Fr. Raymundi M. Spiazzi, O.P. Romae: Marietti, 1954: *De Mixtione Elementorum ad Magistrum Philippum,* pp. 155-156.
[5] *De Mixtione Elementorum, ad magistrum Philippum de Castro Caeli;* Leonine edition, vol. 43, pp. 115-157.

considerably later one (1273), and because the DME adds to what the DPN says about the elements, one should perhaps read and study the DPN before the DME. And that is why the DPN is first in the arrangement of this book, in PART ONE, followed by the DME, in PART TWO; although my translation, and interpretation, of the DME was actually done before that of the DPN. My hope is that this will have no undesirable effects on those who read this book as arranged.

PART THREE reflects on what Aquinas has to say about matter and form and the elements, here and there throughout his many works, and in various contexts. This third part attempts to do at least the following: 1) to make as clear as possible how, according to Aquinas, these two kinds of composition, i.e., composition out of matter and form and composition out of elements, are related **to one another** and **to the physical substances in which they are found,** and 2) to see whether what he says can be accepted, i.e., to argue for or against his claims and arguments, as each of them may require.

PART FOUR looks at a mix of things from various sources, in an attempt to make clearer, to the extent that it can, **both** what *Aquinas* thought about the elements **and** what *we today* think about them: about the definition of "element," about the things that are listed as elements, about the causal role(s) of the elements, about the distinctive properties of each of the elements, about how various elements combine to form **complex** bodies (**mixed** bodies, in the languange of Aquinas), about whatever else suggests itself as important. The idea is that these two views, i.e., 1) that of Aquinas and 2) that of people today, might well, by appropriate comparisons and contrasts, shed some helpful and welcome light on one another.

ACKNOWLEDGMENTS

For many of the good things in this book, I thank many generous and giving people, colleagues and students and friends. I thank James Cushing and William Shephard, professors of physics at the University of Notre Dame, for teaching me so much about quarks and leptons and the like, and for doing it with enthusiasm, clarity, and precision. I thank Gregory MacIsaac, doctoral student in philosophy at Notre Dame, for preparing the Index of Names and the Index of Subjects, and for doing it quickly, carefully, and thoroughly. I thank Coleen J. Hoover, our philosophy department's administrative assistant, for laying out, and for making camera-ready, the table of contents, the preface, the two indeces, and the copyright page, and for doing it willingly and with great skill.

And I thank Teresa, selfless wife of many years, and best friend, for being kind and understanding. But most of all for being so patient as a writer's widow -- which no doubt she would rather not have become -- for a very long time.

PART ONE

DE PRINCIPIIS NATURAE

De Principiis Naturae[1]

Chapter one
Generation and corruption

In chapter one, Aquinas talks about many things: about what can exist, and what does exist; about what is simply (or period), and what is something or other; about matter and form; about prime matter and subject; about generation and corruption, both substantial and accidental; about form, both substantial and accidental; about privation; about art and nature. His comments seem to be aimed at making clear how to think and talk about change -- in particular about change in the natural world. Think and talk about it **this way,** he seems to be saying, because **this is the way it is.**

Being: potential and actual; substantial and accidental

> 1. **Nota quod quoddam potest esse licet non sit, quoddam vero est. Illud quod potest esse, dicitur potentia esse; illud quod iam est, dicitur esse actu. Sed duplex est esse: scilicet esse essentiale sive substantiale rei, ut hominem esse, et hoc est esse simpliciter; est aliud esse accidentale, ut hominem esse album, et hoc est esse aliquid.**

> **Take note that some things can exist, though they do not, whereas others do indeed exist. Those which can exist are said to be potentially. Those which already do exist are said to be actually. And this in two ways. There is first the essential or**

1   The title of this work could just as well have been *De Principiis Generationis* or *De Principiis Rerum Naturalium*. See below pp. 11-14, the section entitled, **The meaning of "nature" in the title:** *De Principiis Naturae*, especially p. 14.

substantial existence of a thing, as for a man to be; and this is to be simply. There is secondly accidental existence, as for a man to be white; and this is to be something or other.

In **1.**, he observes that some things can exist, though they do not; and these are said to be potentially. Others things do exist; and these are said to be actually. What is the point of these remarks? one might ask. Aren't they frustratingly obvious, and singularly uninformative? What intellectual advance, of even a minimally clarifying sort, is made by noting that **what can exist** *is said* (dicitur) **to be potentially?** Or that **what does exist** *is said* (dicitur) **to be actually?** Is "what is potentially" any clearer that "what can exist"? Is "what is actually" any clearer that "what does exist"? And does "dicitur" mean: is said *in the ordinary, everyday language* into which one is born? Or does it mean: is said *in philosophical language,* for philosophical purposes? And what difference, if any, would that make?

The point of these remarks seems to be to set the stage for a philosophical account of the observed fact of change in the physical or natural world. One way, perhaps the clearest and easiest way, to begin to think about physical or natural change is to think in terms of **what can be** and **what is.** For, a thing which is undergoing change both **is** and **can be.** It **is** or **exists** (and of course, since it **is**, it also is **what it is**); and simultaneously **can be,** though it yet **is not,** that which it is becoming. It could not be undergoing change if it did not exist (and exist as **what it is**); nor if it were not true to say of if that it can be (but is not) **what it is becoming.** To be (to be actually -- what it is), to be able to be (to be potentially -- what it is becoming), and not to be (not to be actually -- what it is becoming) -- these three provide a clear and easy way of beginning to think and to talk about matter **(can be)**, form **(is)**, and privation **(is not)**. These three, i.e., matter, form, and privation -- as Aquinas sees it, and as truth has it -- are the three principles of nature, the three beginning points *(principia),* or sources, of the process of generation by which natural things are brought into existence.

Aquinas observes further, in **1.**, that the existence of a natural thing is of two sorts. There is, first, its essential or substantial existence; and this is only **one**. There is, secondly, its accidental existence; and this is **more than one**. For example, I exist -- as what I am, i.e., a rational animal. This is my **one** essential or substantial existence. This is **what I am** (essential) as an **ultimate existing subject** (substantial). But, I am also five feet eight inches tall; white, knowledgeable, and virtuous; a father and a son, and taller than my daughter; I am being carried to my son's house; before that I was at home, sitting on the sofa, at noon, and wearing comfortable slacks. These are among my **many** accidental existences. None of these is included in what I am essentially, i.e., in my one existence as an ultimate existing subject. They are, one and all of them, added to, over and above, it. The ultimate existing subject is I -- this rational animal. My being five feet eight inches tall, and white, and knowledgeable, etc. -- no one of these is what I am as an ultimate existing subject. Neither is the collection of them what I am as an ultimate existing subject. Furthermore, no one of them, nor the collection of them, is itself an ultimate existing subject.

Matter: prime matter and subject

> **2. Ad utrumque esse est aliquid in potentia. Aliquid enim est in potentia ut sit homo, ut sperma et sanguis menstruus; aliquid est in potentia ut sit album, ut homo. Et tam illud quod est in potentia ad esse substantiale, quam illud quod est in potentia ad esse accidentale, potest dici materia; sicut sperma hominis et homo albedinis. Sed in hoc differunt, quia materia quae est in potentia ad esse substantiale, dicitur materia ex qua; quae autem est in potentia ad esse accidentale, dicitur materia in qua. Item, proprie loquendo, quod est in potentia ad esse substantiale, dicitur materia prima; quod vero est in potentia ad esse accidentale, dicitur subiectum. Unde dicitur quod accidentia sunt in subiecto; non autem dicitur quod forma substantialis sit in subiecto. Et secundum hoc differt materia a subiecto, quia**

subiectum est quod non habet esse ex eo quod advenit, sed per se habet esse completum; sicut homo non habet esse ab albedine. Sed materia habet esse ex eo quod sibi advenit, quia de se habet esse incompletum. Unde, simpliciter loquendo, forma dat esse materiae, accidens autem non dat esse subiecto, sed subiectum accidenti, licet aliquando unum ponatur pro alio, scilicet materia pro subiecto, et e converso.

There is something in potency to each of these ways of being. For example, there is something in potency to being a man, like sperm and menstrual blood; and there is something in potency to being white, like man. Both what is in potency to substantial existence, and what is in potency to accidental existence, can be called matter; like sperm, the matter of man; and man, the matter of whiteness. But they differ in this: the matter which is in potency to substantial existence is called the matter *out of which;* and that which is in potency to accidental existence is called the matter *in which.* Properly speaking, however, what is in potency to substantial existence is called prime matter; whereas what is in potency to accidental existence is called a subject. Whence it is said that accidents are in a subject; but it is not said that a substantial form is in a subject. And, it is according to this that matter differs from a subject: a subject does not have existence from that which comes to it; rather it has existence, complete existence, of itself; man, for example, does not have existence from whiteness. Matter, on the other hand, does have existence from that which comes to it, for of itself it has an incomplete existence. Whence, simply speaking, form gives existence to matter; whereas an accident does not give existence to a subject, but the subject to the accident; although at times one is used for the other, that is, matter for subject, and conversely.

In 2., Aquinas pursues the opening sentence of 1. "Take note," he had said as he opened 1, "that some things can exist, though they do not, whereas others do indeed exist." He points out here, as he begins 2., that just as there are two sorts of actual existence, there are correspondingly two sorts of potential existence. "There is something in potency to each of these ways of

4

being," i.e., 1) to essential or substantial existence, or to being simply, like sperm and menstrual blood (it is really the ovum, as we know today, not the menstrual blood) to being a man; and 2) to accidental existence, or to being additionally something or other, like man to being white. And both of these can be called matter. Sperm can be called the matter of man, and man the matter of whiteness. But each is a different sort of matter. This is why the matter which is in potency to substantial existence is called the matter *out of which,* to indicate that this matter is an *ingredient* of the ultimate existing subject; and why the matter which is in potency to accidental existence is called the matter *in which,* to indicate that this matter is not an ingredient of the ultimate existing subject, but rather the ultimate existing subject itself. The difference between the two matters can be made clearer by calling the first *prime matter,* to indicate that there is nothing prior to it (since it is prime, i.e., first) which is related to it as its matter, that of itself it has no substantial form, and that therefore it does not exist of itself; and by calling the second *a subject,* to indicate that there is something prior to it, namely prime matter, which is related to it as its matter, that it has a substantial form, and that it does indeed exist of itself. This is why it is said that accidents, i.e., accidental forms, are in a subject (an ultimate existing subject); and why it is **not** said that substantial forms are in a subject. Rather, substantial forms are in prime matter, which does not exist of itself, not being an ultimate **existing** subject, though it is an ultimate **subject.** Prime matter, having an incomplete existence, has existence from that which comes to it, i.e., from the substantial form. But the subject, having a complete existence, does not have existence from the accidental forms which come to it. Rather the accidental forms have existence from the subject. Though "matter" is most properly used to designate what is in potency to substantial existence, and "subject" to desginate what is in potency to accidental existence, sometimes one is used for the other, i.e., "matter" for "subject," and vice versa.

Aquinas had said above both 1) that sperm and ovum are in potency to being a man, i.e., in potency to substantial existence; and 2) that the matter which is in potency to substantial existence is prime matter. Is one to

conclude, therefore, that sperm and ovum are the same as prime matter? --
It seems that not; for prime matter of itself is absolutely formless, has no
form of any sort; whereas sperm and ovum, both, do indeed have a form.
Besides, though prime matter is in potency to all substantial forms, it is in
potency to them in a certain order. Prime matter is in potency, first of all, to
the lowest of the substantial forms, i.e., to the substantial forms of the
elements, and through these to the substantial forms of mixed bodies, some
of which become the food which is appropriate for human consumption.
Human bodies produce sperm and ova out of some of this food, and the
sperm and ova, in turn, via fertilization and gestation, become new human
beings.   In some way, the elements remain in mixed bodies, including
human bodies. How they remain will be considered later on, at a more
opportune point.

Form: substantial and accidental

3. Sicut autem omne quod est in potentia potest dici materia, ita
omne a quo aliquid habet esse, sive substantiale sive accidentale,
potest dici forma; sicut homo, cum sit potentia albus, fit actu
albus per albedinem, et sperma, cum sit potentia homo, fit
actu homo per animam.   Et quia forma facit esse in actu, ideo
forma dicitur esse actus. Quod autem facit actu esse substantiale,
dicitur forma substantialis, et quod facit actu esse accidentale,
dicitur forma accidentalis.

Now just as everything which is in potency can be called matter,
so too everything from which something has existence, whether
substantial or accidental, can be called form. For example, man,
being potentially white, becomes actually white because of
whiteness; and sperm, being potentially man, becomes actually
man because of the soul. Now, because form causes actual
existence, form is said to be an act. What causes actual
substantial existence is called a substantial form; and what
causes actual accidental existence is called an accidental form.

Having talked about matter, i.e., about what is in potency, in **2.**, Aquinas turns in **3.** to talk about form. Form is the actuality of the potentiality which is matter. Whereas matter is that in a changing thing by which that thing **can be** what it is becoming; form is that, in a thing which has come to be, by which that thing **is actually,** now, what it was, before, only potentially (in its matter). The soul is that, in a human being which has come to be, by which the human being is a human being, i.e., by which the human being differs from the sperm and ovum out of which it came to be. To be sure, something of the sperm and ovum (i.e., prime matter, and certain elements, and certain accidental forms) survives and remains in some way in the human being which has come to be. And certain of these remaining ingredients, namely prime matter and the elements, together with the soul, constitute the **essence** of the human being which has come to be, and this essence differentiates that human being from nothingness. Not only does the human being differ from the sperm and ovum, the matter out of which it came to be, by reason of the human soul (this is the substantial form, the *forma partis);* but it differs from nothingness as well, by reason of its essence, i.e., by reason of the composition of what survives in it (from that out of which it came to be) and the human soul (this composite is the essence, the *forma totius).* Form differentiates. The substantial form, the *forma partis,* differentiates from matter. The essence, the *forma totius,* differentiates from nothingness.

Generation: substantial and accidental

4. **Et quia generatio est motus ad formam, duplici formae respondet duplex generatio: formae substantiali respondet generatio simpliciter; formae accidentali generatio secundum quid. Quando enim introducitur forma substantialis, dicitur aliquid fieri simpliciter, sicut dicimus: homo fit vel homo**

generatur. Quando autem introducitur forma accidentalis, non dicitur aliquid fieri simpliciter, sed fieri hoc; sicut quando homo fit albus, non dicimus simpliciter hominem fieri vel generari, sed fieri vel generari album.

Because generation is a motion to form, there are two kinds of generation corresponding to the two kinds of form. There is generation simply, which corresponds to substantial form. And there is generation with respect to something or other, and this corresponds to accidental form. When a substantial form is introduced, something is said to come to be simply. We say, for example, that a man comes to be, or that a man is generated. But when an acccidental form is introduced, it is not said that something comes to be simply, but that it comes to be this. When a man comes to be white, for example, we do not say simply that the man comes to be, or that he is generated; but that he comes to be, or is generated as, white.

In 3., Aquinas had talked briefly about form, and about its two types, substantial and accidental. In 4., he turns to talk about generation, the way to form. And he begins by pointing out that generation is a certain sort of motion, or movement, which terminates in form. This implies, of course, that generation begins with, departs from, matter and privation. Generation is the passage, the change, from matter and privation to form. There are two kinds of generation, one with respect to each kind of form. There is 1) generation simply, the way to substantial form; in which case a thing comes to be as an ultimate existing subject, e.g., as a human being. There is 2) generation as something or other, the way to accidental form; in which case a thing, already an ultimate existing subject, becomes this or that, e.g., white or hot.

5. Et huic duplici generationi opponitur duplex corruptio, scilicet simpliciter et secundum quid. Generatio vero et corruptio simpliciter non sunt nisi in genere substantiae, sed generatio et corruptio secundum quid sunt in omnibus aliis generibus. Et quia generatio est quaedam mutatio de non esse ad esse, e converso autem corruptio de esse ad non esse, non ex quolibet non ente fit generatio, sed ex non ente quod est ens in potentia; sicut idolum ex cupro quod est idolum in potentia, non in actu.

There are two kinds of corruption opposed to these two kinds of generation. There is corruption simply, and there is corruption with respect to something or other. Now, generation and corruption simply are found only in the genus of substance, whereas generation and corruption with respect to something or other are found in all the other genera. And although generation is a kind of change from non-existence to existence, and corruption conversely from existence to non-existence, generation does not take place from just any kind of non being, but from the non being which is being in potency. A statue, for example, comes to be from bronze which is a statue in potency, not in act.

In 5., Aquinas notes that there are two kinds of corruption, corruption being opposed to generation, just as there are two kinds of generation. There is first corruption simply, which along with generation simply, occurs only in the genus of substance. There is secondly corruption with respect to something or other, which along with generation with respect to something or other, takes place in all the other genera. Not only is generation a motion to form; but, because of that, it is also a certain sort of passage or change from non-existence to existence, inasmuch as form causes existence, as was pointed out above. The generation of a human being, for example, is the motion which terminates in the human soul, and it is because of the human soul that a human being begins, and continues, to exist. This motion begins in (departs from) non-being, but not from just any non-being; rather from that non-being which is being in potency, i.e., from an appropriate matter with an appropriate privation. And the corruption of a human being is the opposite motion, the motion which terminates in the removal of the human soul, and through that in the discontinuance of existence for the human being. Whatever causes form, causes existence. Whatever removes form, removes existence.

Generation requires matter, form and privation

6. Ad hoc ergo quod sit generatio, tria requiruntur: scilicet ens potentia, quod est materia; et non esse actu, quod est privatio; et id per quod fit actu, scilicet forma. Sicut quando ex cupro fit idolum, cuprum quod est in potentia ad formam idoli, est materia; hoc autem quod est infiguratum sive indispositum, est privatio; figura autem a qua dicitur idolum, est forma; non autem substantialis, quia cuprum ante adventum illius formae habet esse in actu, et eius esse non dependet ab illa figura, sed est forma accidentalis. Omnes enim formae artificiales sunt accidentales. Ars enim non operatur nisi supra id quod iam constitutum est in esse a natura.

In order, therefore, that there be generation, three things are required: namely, being in potency, which is matter; non-being in act, which is privation; and that through which a thing comes to being in act, namely form. When, for example, a statue is made out of bronze, the bronze which is in potency to the form of the statue is the matter; the unshaped, or the unarranged, is the privation; and the shape from which the statue gets to be called a statue is the form. But this form is not a substantial form because the bronze, before the coming of that form, already has actual existence, and its existence does not depend on that shape. This form is, rather, an accidental form. All artificial forms are accidental forms. For art works only on what has already been put into existence by nature.

10

In **6.**, Aquinas puts together, into a kind of brief summary, the requirements for generation. Three things are required, namely matter, form, and privation. Two of these, namely matter and privation, are required in that from which generation begins or departs, i.e., in the *terminus a quo*. The third, namely form, is required in the end result, or product, of the generation, i.e., in the *terminus ad quem*. Suppose that a statue is being made out of bronze. Before the change begins, the bronze is in potency to the shape of the statue (this is **ens potentia,** i.e., the matter); it is also without that shape (this is **non esse actu,** i.e., the privation). After the change, however, the bronze actually has the shape in virtue of which it both is, and is called, a statue (this is **id per quod fit actu,** i.e., the form). But this particular form, i.e., the *shape* of the bronze, Aquinas reminds the reader, is not a substantial form. And he gives two reasons: 1) the bronze is already in existence, as an ultimate existing subject, before it acquires that particular shape, and 2) that particular shape is the work of human hands, i.e., a product of human artistic activity. Human art works only on materials which have come into existence by the work of nature. Nothing can be man-made through and through. Human art presupposes nature; and God as well, one might add. What man creates, in his way, presupposes both what nature creates, in its way, and what God creates, in His.

The meaning of "nature" in the title: *De Principiis Naturae*

One might ask at this point: What exactly is this brief work of Aquinas about? That is, what exactly is the meaning of its title: *De Principiis Naturae?* What does "principium" mean? But, more especially, what does "natura" mean? That is, what exactly is this **natura** of which these principles are the principles? -- Aquinas makes clear in chapter three what "principium" means, by way of contrast with "causa" and "elementum," and in terms of the distinction between intrinsic cause and extrinsic cause. But, nowhere in this work does he give an account of what "natura" means.

The meaning of "principium" will be taken up in chapter three. But the meaning of "natura" will be taken up now, with help from what Aquinas writes elsewhere. In his commentary on the *Metaphysics* of Aristotle (*In V Metaph.*, lect. 5, nn. 808-823), Aquinas notes, following Aristotle, that "natura" has a number of related meanings. First, it means the generation of generated things (*generatio generatorum*). The **natura** of a generated thing, its **naturing** so to say, is the **process** by which it is brought into existence. By a kind of extension from "natura" to "nativitas" and then to "nascentia," Aquinas observes, "natura" is also used to mean, more specifically, the generation, or being born (*nascentia*), of living things (*generatio viventium*). Secondly, "natura" means that out of which a living thing comes to be as out of a *primary intrinsic* principle (... *[id] ex quo illud quod nascitur, generatur primo, sicut ex intrinseco principio*). It is not at all clear what this means, nor does Aquinas give an example to help remove the unclarity. Could this be a reference to the **seed** out of which living things come into existence? Isn't an acorn, for example, that out of which an oak tree comes to be as out of a primary, i.e., initiating, principle; and one which remains in the oak tree, in some way, as the primary ingredient which directs its development? Thirdly, "natura" means, generally, the intrinsic principle of the motion, whether growth or alteration or local motion (or whatever), of any natural thing as such (as different from, and prior to, something artificial or man-made). Fourthly, "natura" means, more specifically, the matter out of which a natural thing comes to be, and which remains in it as an ingredient, matter being an intrinsic cause of motion. Fifthly, "natura" means, again more specifically, the form of a natural thing, i.e., the substantial form or *forma partis*, since the motion of natural things is caused more by their form than by their matter. Sixthly, "natura" means prime matter, or first matter, i.e., matter which has no matter of itself, whether absolutely first, as in the case of the matter of **all** ultimate existing

12

subjects which have come to be in substantial change; or with respect to **some given genus** of them, e.g., water might be said to be the first matter of all liquefiable natural things.   Seventhly, "natura" means the essence of a natural thing, including both matter and form; and this is called the form of the whole, the *forma totius.*

The **process** of generation, generally, and that of being born, more specifically, continues Aquinas *(In V Metaph.,* lect. 5, nn. 824-826), got called **natura** before the substantial form did, since these processes are observable by sense, at least up to a point, whereas the form is not.   Then the word "natura" was extended to substantial form, because these processes have a relation to it, i.e., they terminate in it.   And since a substantial form is more real than a process, to have a **natura** came to mean primarily: to have a **substantial form.**   Then matter was said to be a **natura,** inasmuch as it is receptive of substantial form.   Then generation and being born were said to be, each of them, a **natura,** inasmuch as they are motions proceeding from, and terminating in, substantial form.

As regards the question posed just a bit above, namely: What exactly is this **natura** of which these principles (in the title: *De Principiis Naturae)* are the principles?, the following seems to be an acceptable answer, at least for the time being.   Taking the opening sentence of **6.,** namely: "Ad hoc ergo quod sit **generatio,** tria requiruntur: scilicet . . . materia, . . . privatio, . . . [et] forma . . .," and putting it together with the opening sentence of chapter 2, namely: "Sunt igitur tria principia **naturae,** scilicet materia, forma, et privatio," it seems not unreasonable to conclude that "natura" here means **generatio,** the **process** of coming to be.   Moreover, matter, form and privation are explicitly identified as the **principles** of nature. From which one can conclude that, though both matter and form are **natura,** each in its own way; they are not what "natura" designates in the title, *De Principiis Naturae.*   A thing cannot be its own principle, its own source, that out which it itself originates.   *De Principiis **Generationis*** would seem to be a helpful rendering of *De Principiis **Naturae.***

13

Nonetheless, one might ask, what is one to make out of the fact that, in some of its very early printed versions, the *De Principiis Naturae* gets the title *De Principiis Rerum Naturalium?*[2]   Should one say that "natura" means **res naturalis**?   Or, should one say that (though "natura" does not mean **res naturalis**) matter, form, and privation are the principles of a **res naturalis** as well as of **generatio**, i.e., of the **process** whereby a **res naturalis** comes to be?   This second suggestion seems the more reasonable one. For, as a matter of fact, "natura" does **not** mean **res naturalis**. Secondly, matter and form are the **intrinsic composing ingredients**, or principles, indeed causes, of a **res naturalis**; and privation, though only an accompaniment of matter, and **not** an intrinsic composing ingredient of the **res naturalis**, is nonetheless a necessary principle of the **res naturalis**, though a *per accidens* one.   And thirdly, as Pauson points out, variations in title, especially in the earlier manuscripts, seem "to indicate that originally there was no exact title, but each scribe affixed the title he thought suitable."[3]

---

[2]   See *Saint Thomas Aquinas, De Principiis Naturae,* Introduction and Critical Text by John J. Pauson, Textus Philosophici Friburgenses, 2; Fribourg: Societe Philosophique, 1950; p. 65, and pp. 36-39.
[3]   Pauson, *op cit.*, p. 65.

Chapter two
Matter, form and privation

In chapter two, Aquinas talks about a number of things: about privation as a principle *per accidens;* about how privation differs from negation; about principles of coming to be and principles of being; about prime matter, both absolutely prime and relatively prime; about the ingenerability and the incorruptibility of matter and form; about the sort of numerical oneness which belongs to prime matter; about prime matter as *of itself* without form or privation, yet as *in fact* never without either. His comments are aimed at making clear both 1) how matter, form and privation differ from one another, and 2) how they are related to one another -- as principles of nature, i.e., of the process of natural (as different from artificial) generation.

Privation is a principle *per accidens,* but necessary for generation

7. Sunt igitur tria principia naturae, scilicet materia, forma et privatio; quorum alterum, scilicet forma, est id ad quod est generatio, alia duo sunt ex parte eius ex quo est generatio. Unde materia et privatio sunt idem subiecto, sed differunt ratione. Illud enim idem quod est aes, est infiguratum ante adventum formae; sed ex alia ratione dicitur aes et ex alia infiguratum. Unde privatio dicitur principium non per se, sed per accidens, quia scilicet coincidit cum materia; sicut dicimus quod per accidens medicus aedificat. Medicus enim aedificat non ex eo quod est medicus, sed ex eo quod est aedificator, quod coincidit cum medico in uno subiecto. Sed duplex est accidens: scilicet necessarium quod non separatur a re, ut risibile ab homine; et non necessarium quod separatur, ut album ab homine. Unde licet privatio sit principum per accidens, non sequitur quod non sit necessaria ad generationem, quia materia a privatione numquam denudatur; inquantum enim est sub una forma, habet privationem alterius et e converso, sicut in igne est privatio aeris et in aere privatio ignis.

There are therefore three principles of nature, namely matter, form and privation. The second of these, namely form, is that toward which generation moves; the other two lie on the side of that from which generation departs. Whence, matter and privation are the same in subject, but they differ in description. The thing which is bronze is the very same thing which is unshaped, before the coming of the form. But it is said to be bronze for one reason, and unshaped for another. Whence, when privation is said to be a principle, it is not said to be a principle *per se* (i.e., because of itself), but *per accidens* (i.e., because of something other than itself), i.e., because it happens to be found together with matter. As when we say that it is *per accidens* that a medical doctor builds. For a medical doctor builds not because he is a medical doctor, but because he is a builder. Being a builder and being a medical doctor happen to be found together in the same subject. But there are two kinds of accident. There is, first, the necessary accident, which does not get separated from the thing of which it is an accident; for example, risible does not get separated from man. There is, secondly, the accident which is not necessary; and such an accident does get separated; for example, white from man. And so, though privation is a principle *per accidens,* it does not follow that it is not necessary for generation; because matter is never without privation. For insofar as it is under one form, it is with the privation of another, and conversely. For example, in fire, there is the privation of air, and in air the privation of fire.

Of the three principles of nature, begins Aquinas in 7., form is found in the *terminus ad quem*. Form is that toward which generation moves. The other two, i.e., matter and privation, on the other hand, are found in the *terminus a quo*. Matter and privation are that from which generation proceeds; and in such a way that, though they are the same in subject, they are different in description. That which can be (what it is becoming), and that which is not (what it is becoming), are one and the same thing. But that which can be, and that which is not, are conceptually different *(differunt ratione)*. The thing which is bronze, and the thing which is unshaped, are one and the same thing. But to be bronze and to be unshaped are quite different. The former is the matter, and the latter the privation.

Bronze is bronze, one ought to note, whether unshaped (as before the change, in the *terminus a quo)* or shaped (as after the change, in the *terminus ad quem)*. And the shape of the shaped bronze is not, now, an ingredient of the nature of the bronze, just as the unshapedness of the unshaped bronze was not, then, an ingredient of the nature of the bronze. Bronze has its own form, as well as its own matter, by both of which it is both actually bronze and potentially a statue. And just as its own form is not an ingredient of the nature of its own matter, neither is its own matter an ingredient of the nature of its own form. Generally speaking, matter and form are ingredients of that which is composed out of them, and neither is an ingredient of the nature of the other. Moreover, the bronze is said to be *in potency to* the shape it now has *(in the terminus ad quem,* after the change), just as it was said to be *in potency to* that shape when it did not yet have it (in the *terminus a quo,* before the change) -- but in a different sense. In the *terminus a quo,* it **was** in potency as determin**able** or perfectib**le**; in the *terminus ad quem,* it **is** in potency as determin**ed** or perfec**ted**. And this is so because after the change, as well as before the change, the shape is something **over and above**, something in addition to, the nature of the bronze; something which *can* perfect or *can* determine the bronze, the matter, in the *terminus a quo;* something which *is* determining or *is* perfecting the bronze, the matter, in the *terminus ad quem.*

Though privation is a principle of nature, Aquinas continues, privation is not a principle *per se* (i.e., because of itself), but rather *per accidens* (i.e., because of something else), namely because of the matter to which it attaches, or which it accompanies. Matter, in the *terminus a quo,* exists because of the form which it has. And whatever the form which matter has, it has also some privation or other, the character of the privation being determined by the character of the form. A thing is just what it is by reason of its matter and its form. Just what it is, and not **what it is not** (but is about to become). What it is, is real; both its matter and its form are real. What the thing is not (i.e., the privation), while the thing itself is still just what it is, in the *terminus a quo*, is not real. And this is why it is said that privation is not a principle *per se*. Privation does not exist of itself; it exists only because of the existing matter to which it attaches.

To clarify what he has been saying, Aquinas compares privation to the building activity of a medical doctor. It is not *per se*, i.e., not because he is a medical doctor, that the medical doctor builds. Rather, it is *per accidens*, i.e., because of something other than being a medical doctor. It is because the medical doctor is also a builder. One and the same thing -- in this case, the same individual person -- is both a medical doctor and a builder. Similarly, one and the same thing -- in this case, the *terminus a quo* of the change -- is both bronze (what **can be** a statue) and unshaped (what **is not** a statue). But, whereas it is not necessary that the medical doctor be a builder as well (each is a separable accident, or concomitant, of the other); it **is** necessary that matter have a privation (matter and privation are inseparable concomitants). What **can be** what it is about to become (matter), **is not** what it is about to become (privation), and necessarily. It cannot not be what it is about to become. Otherwise, it could not become that; for, it would already be that. What can receive a given form (matter) cannot now have that given form (privation). For example, in fire, which can be what it is about to become, namely air, there is, must be, the privation of air. And in air, which can be what it is about to become, namely fire, there is, must be, the privation of fire. If this were not so, then air could not become fire, because air would already be fire.

When Aquinas said above, "Sed duplex est accidens," what exactly did he mean by the world "accidens"? His example of **white** in relation to man might suggest that he was talking about a predicamental accident, i..e, about that which exists in a substance as in an ultimate existing subject. For, white is just such an accident. But he gave another example, namely **risible** in relation to man. And risibility is not a predicamental accident; it is rather a property of man, a property in the category of substance. Man is risible, because man is rational; and rational is the specific difference of man. Since white and risible, in relation to man, have this in common, namely that neither is of the conceptual content *(ratio)* of man; this suggests that "accidens" in the claim that "duplex est accidens" means: that which is found together with another without being of the conceptual content of that other. This suggestion fits the relation between matter and privation. They are found together, but neither is of the conceptual content of the other. Matter, the conceptual content of which is **can be**, is found together with privation, the conceptual content of which is **is not**. Furthermore, privation, like risibility, is a necessary accident; that is, just as risibility cannot be separated from man, neither can privation be separated from matter. For, what **can be** necessarily **is not**.

Privation, not negation

> 8. Et est sciendum quod, cum generatio sit ex non esse, non dicimus quod negatio sit principium, sed privatio, quia negatio non determinat sibi subiectum. Non videre enim potest dici etiam de non entibus, ut 'chimaera non videt;' et iterum de entibus quae non sunt nata habere visum, sicut de lapide. Sed privatio non dicitur nisi de determinato subiecto, in quo scilicet natus est fieri habitus, sicut caecitas non dicitur nisi de his quae sunt nata videre. Et quia generatio non fit ex non ente simpliciter, sed ex non ente quod est in aliquo subiecto, et non in quolibet, sed in determinato, -- non enim ex quolibet non igne fit ignis, sed ex tali non igne, circa quem nata sit fieri forma ignis, -- ideo dicitur quod privatio sit principium.

> Although generation is from non-being, we do not say, it must be understood, that negation is a principle, but privation; because negation does not determine a subject for itself. For the negation, "They do not see," can be said even of things which do not exist. For example, "Chimeras do not see." And again, even

of things which are not meant by nature to see, as of a stone. But a privation is not predicated except of a determined subject, namely of a subject which is meant by nature to come to have a certain capacity. For example, blindness is not predicated except of things which are meant by nature to see. And because generation does not take place from non-being simply, but from the non-being which is in some subject; and not in just any subject, but in a determined one -- fire, for example, does not come to be from just any non-fire, but from the sort of non-fire in which the form of fire is meant by nature to come to be -- this is why it is said that privation [not negation] is a principle.

In 8., Aquinas observes, and emphasizes, that though generation proceeds from non-being -- which might lead one to think that negation is a principle of nature -- it is privation, not negation, which is the principle. This is so, explains Aquinas, because negation does not pick out, or select, or designate a subject from which generation can appropriately depart. Negations can be predicated of anything at all, even of things which do not exist. For example, we can say, "Stones do not see" or "Mountains do not see;" and even, "Nothingness does not see" or "Chimeras (monsters of my fantasizing mind) do not see." But privations cannot be predicated except of things which, for some reason or other, do not have some capacity, or perfection, which they are meant by nature to have. For example, we can say, "This man is blind" or "This dog is blind;" but not, "Nothingness is blind" or "Stones are blind" or "Mountains are blind." For men and dogs are meant by nature to have the capacity of sight; but nothingness and stones and mountains are not.

Moreover, generation is never from absolute nothingness; for that is creation. Generation is always from something which exists, and is of a given kind (the *terminus a quo*), to something else which exists, and is of another given kind (the *terminus ad quem*). The given kind of the *terminus a quo* is rooted in its form, and is the source of the potency (matter) and of the non-being (privation) which are required for that particular sort of generation. The given kind of the *terminus ad quem* is rooted in the newly acquired form. Fire, exemplifies Aquinas, does not come to be from just any sort of non-fire, but from the sort of non-fire in which it makes sense to say there is a privation of the form of fire, i.e., the sort of non-fire which is meant by nature to receive the form of fire. Just as the privation designated by "is blind" requires an appropriate subject, for example a man or a dog; so too, the privation designated by "is not on fire" requires an appropriate subject, i.e., some combustible material, for example a piece of paper, but not a stone. Whereas paper can burn, can come to be "on fire," a stone cannot. Similarly, whereas sperm and ovum can come to be a human being, a piece of paper cannot.   "Is not a human being," as said of sperm and ovum (which are the *terminus a quo* of the generation of a human being), designates the privation which is appropriate for that generation. "Is not a human being," as said of a stone, designates only a negation. For a stone is not meant by nature to come to be a human being; the sperm and the ovum are. And this is why privation, concludes Aquinas, is one of the principles of nature, and negation is not.

Privation is a principle of coming to be, but not of being

> 9. **Sed in hoc differt ab aliis, quia alia sunt principia et in esse et in fieri. Ad hoc enim quod fiat idolum, oportet quod sit aes, et quod ultimo sit figura idoli; et iterum quando iam idolum est, oportet haec duo esse. Sed privatio est principum in fieri et non in esse; quia dum fit idolum, oportet quod non sit idolum. Si enim esset, non fieret; quia quod fit non est, nisi in successivis, ut tempus et motus. Sed ex quo iam idolum est, non est ibi privatio idoli; quia affirmatio et negatio non sunt simul, similiter nec privatio et habitus. Item privatio est principium per accidens, ut supra expositum est; alia duo sunt principia per se.**

> Privation differs from the other principles in this: the others are principles both in being and in coming to be. For in order that a statue come to be, there must be the bronze [to begin with], and ultimately there must be the shape of the statue. And again,

when the statue is already in existence, these two [the bronze and the shape] must be there. But privation is a principle in coming to be and not in being; because while the statue is coming to be, it must be that the statue is not yet in existence. For, if it were in existence, it would not be coming to be; because what is coming to be does not yet exist, unless it is something successive, like time and motion. But, as soon as the statue is in existence, the privation of statue is no longer there, because affirmation and negation are not found together; neither are privation and the form of which it is the privation. Again, privation is a principle *per accidens*, as was explained above; the other two are principles *per se*.

In 9., Aquinas points out that though matter, form and privation -- all three -- are principles of **coming to be,** only matter and form are principles of **being.** To make his meaning clear, one must note that, when Aquinas points this out, his focus is on the nature, or essence, of the newly generated thing, the *terminus ad quem.* The matter which was in the *terminus a quo* before the change began -- that matter survives in the *terminus ad quem* as an ingredient of what it is, i.e., as an intrinsic principle of its being. The form which the surviving matter receives, that too is an ingredient of the nature of the *terminus ad quem,* another intrinsic principle of its being. But the privation does not survive in the *terminus ad quem* as an ingredient of its nature; it does not survive at all. The privation is there only in the *terminus a quo,* and during the process of generation. But once that process is terminated, matter has received form (the form of which the privation had been the privation), and that particular privation is no longer there. Thus, that particular privation was there as a principle of the **coming to be** of the *terminus ad quem,* but is not there as a principle of the **being** of the *terminus ad quem.* To be sure, just as matter was there throughout the process of generation, so too was some form or other. Otherwise the matter could not have been in existence, nor therefore could any privation have been in existence. Matter cannot exist without form; and privation cannot exist without matter. And so, matter, form and privation -- all three -- are principles of the coming to be *(fieri)* of the *terminus ad quem;* but only

22

matter and form are principles of the being *(esse)* of the *terminus ad quem.*
What is in process of coming to be, does not yet exist. This is why privation is
there during the coming to be, but not beyond.   And this is why privation
(the privation, that is, which is a principle of nature) can be likened to
successive realities, like time and motion, which, qua successive, both are (in
one respect) and are not (in another respect).   Privation is a **non-being** which
is, as well as a **being** which **is not** -- in a *terminus a quo* which is meant by
nature (in a given appropriate process of generation) to receive the form of
which the privation is a privation.

Matter and privation

10. Ex dictis igitur patet quod materia differt a forma et a
privatione secundum rationem.   Materia enim est id in quo
intelligitur forma et privatio; sicut in cupro intelligitur figura et
infiguratum.   Quandoque enim materia denominatur cum
privatione, quandoque sine privatione; sicut aes, cum sit materia
idoli, non importat privationem, quia ex hoc quod dico 'aes,'
non intelligitur indispositum sive infiguratum. Sed farina, cum
sit materia respectu panis, importat in se privationem formae
panis, quia ex hoc quod dico 'farina,' significatur indispositio
sive inordinatio opposita formae panis.   Et quia in generatione
materia sive subiectum permanet, privatio vero non, neque
compositum ex materia et privatione, ideo materia quae non
importat privationem, est permanens, quae autem importat, est
transiens.

It is clear, therefore, from the things which have been said, that
matter differs in description [definition] from form and from
privation. For matter is that in which form and privation are
understood; as, for example, the shape and the unshaped in
bronze. Sometimes indeed matter is denominated as with a
privation, sometimes as without a privation.   Bronze, for
example, as the matter of a statue, does not include a privation;
because when I call it bronze, it is not understood to be
unarranged or unshaped.   But flour, as the matter of bread, does
include in itself the privation of the form of bread, because when
I call it flour, what is signified is the lack of arrangement, or the

disorder, which is opposed to the form of bread. And because in generation the matter, or subject, is there throughout, whereas the privation is not, and neither is the composite of matter and privation; the matter which does not include a privation is something permanent, whereas the matter which does, is something transient.

In **10.**, Aquinas reflects a bit more on the difference between matter and privation. He begins by noting that though matter differs from privation, it differs from form as well. And it differs from both of them in description , or definition *(secundum rationem).* Matter is that in which both form and privation can be found. Bronze, for example, is that in which both shape and lack of shape can be found. And sometimes matter is designated by a word which connotes the privation which is in it. For example, the word "flour" designates something which has the role of matter with respect to bread, and in such a way that "flour" connotes the privation of the form of bread. "Flour" means, whatever else it means: **that which is not bread.** "Flour" connotes the state of indisposition or disorder which is opposed to the form of bread. But sometimes matter is designated by a word which does not connote the privation which is in it. The word "bronze," for example, designates something which functions as matter with respect to a statue, but in such a way that its lack of shape is not connoted. Whatever "bronze" means, or does not mean, it does not mean: **what is not a statue.** Whereas "flour" says **not yet bread,** "bronze" does not say **not yet statue.** Still, just as "flour" says **can be bread,** so too "bronze" says **can be a statue.** And whereas the bronze survives in the statue as bronze, since "bronze" does not connote the privation which does not survive; flour does not survive in bread as flour, since "flour" does connote the privation which does not survive. The bronze is there throughout, as bronze *(est permanens).* The flour is not there throughout, as flour *(est transiens).* Matter and **privation** are radically different, since matter survives and privation does not. Similarly, matter and **form** are radically different, since matter survives and form does not. But, whereas to say that the privation does not survive is to say that it was there (in the *terminus a quo*), then passed away (in the *terminus ad quem*); to say that the form does not survive is to say something quite different, namely that it was not there at all (in the *terminus a quo*), but came to be (in the *terminus ad quem*).

Prime matter, simply prime and relatively prime

11.   Sed est sciendum quod quaedam materia habet compositionem formae, sicut aes cum sit materia respectu idoli. Ipsum tamen aes est compositium ex materia et forma. Et ideo aes non dicitur materia prima, quia habet materiam. Illa autem materia quae intelligitur sine qualibet forma et privatione, sed subiecta est formae et privationi, dicitur materia prima propter hoc quod ante ipsam non est alia materia. Et hoc etiam dicitur 'hyle.' Et quia omnis definitio et omnis cognitio est per formam, ideo materia prima per se non potest cognosci vel definiri, sed per compositum, ut dicatur quod illud est materia prima, quod hoc modo se habet ad omnes formas et privationes sicut aes ad idolum et infiguratum. Et haec dicitur simpliciter prima.   Potest etiam aliquid dici materia prima respectu alicuius generis, sicut aqua est materia prima in genere liquabilium.   Non tamen est prima simpliciter, quia est composita ex materia et forma; unde habet materiam priorem.

Some matter, it must be understood, has in itself a composition with form, like bronze, when it is matter with respect to a statue. For, the bronze itself is something composed of matter and form. And so, bronze is not said to be prime matter, because it itself has matter.   That matter, however, which is understood without any form and privation, but is subject to form and privation, is said to be prime matter, because of the fact that there is no other matter prior to it.   And this is also called 'hyle.' And because every definition, and all knowledge, is through form, it follows that prime matter cannot be known or defined through itself, but through the composite, as when it is said that that is prime matter which is related to all forms and privations as bronze is to the statue and to the unshaped. And this matter is called

simply prime. But something can be called prime matter with respect to a given genus, as water is prime matter in the genus of watery things. But such matter is not simply prime, because it is itself composed of matter and form. And so, it has a prior matter.

In **11.**, Aquinas turns again to consider the nature of prime matter. Above in **2.**, he had pointed out a number of things about prime matter: prime matter is what is in potency to substantial existence; it is the matter *out of which* an ultimate existing subject in the natural world is made; it is not itself an ultimate **existing** subject, though it is an ultimate **subject**; of itself it has only an incomplete existence, which is completed and actualized by the substantial form which comes to it. Here in **11.**, Aquinas emphasizes two aspects of the nature of prime matter, namely 1) that it is not something composed of matter and form, and so there is no matter prior to it; and 2) that it is of itself unknowable and indefinable.

The first aspect. Prime matter is called prime, or first, precisely because there is nothing prior to it (it is first) which is related to it as its matter; precisely, in another way of saying it, because unlike natural substance, it is not composed of matter and form. If there were a matter prior to it, prime matter could not be prime. Prime matter *of itself* has no matter, and that is why *of itself* it can have neither a form nor a privation. Nonetheless, it is that in which, as in a subject, both form and privation are found.

But, there are matters other than prime matter. And, not being prime, these others are such that each of them is composed of matter and form, each of them has matter as an intrinsic ingredient. Bronze, for example, is matter with respect to a statue. But bronze itself is composed of matter and form. Bronze, therefore, is not prime matter, because it has a prior matter. Or, sperm and ovum are matter with respect to a human being; but both sperm and ovum, in turn, have a **prior** matter, a matter out of which each has come to be. Sperm and ovum, therefore, are not prime matter. There are nonetheless matters which are prime matters in relation to a given genus of things, like water in relation to all watery things, or oil in relation to all oily things, or wood in relation to all wooden things. For whereas wood is an intrinsic ingredient of all wooden things, wood itself is not made out of wood. Wood which is prior to wood could not itself be wood. Nor could water which is prior to water be water. Nor oil, prior to oil, oil.

The second aspect. Prime matter, continues Aquinas, is such *in itself* that it is unknowable, indefinable, *through itself.* This is so because every definiton, indeed all knowledge, is through form, and form is not a component of the nature of prime matter. Form comes to prime matter, form exists in prime matter as in a subject; but form is not, not ever, an intrinsic ingredient of the nature of prime matter. Nonetheless, prime matter can be defined -- or *can be known,* if one would rather not speak of *defining* prime matter -- *through the form* which comes to it. It can be said that what prime matter is, is a potency for substantial form; or better, that prime matter is related to all substantial forms in the way in which bronze is related to all statue-shapes. Better still, it can be said that prime matter is related to all substantial forms, and to all privations of substantial form **as well,** in the way in which bronze is related to all statue-shapes (forms), and to the lack of these statue-shapes **as well** (privations).

Prime matter has neither matter nor form nor privation. And although it is the subject in which form and privation are found, there is nothing which can be a subject in which it can be found. It cannot be known *through itself* since it has no form; nonetheless, it can be known *through the form* which is *in it* without being *of it.*

Why, someone might ask, did Aquinas say that, although prime matter cannot be known *through itself,* since it has no form as an intrinsic ingredient, it can be known *through the composite (per compositum)?* That is, why did he say "through the composite," and not, "through form," since he had just said that all knowledge is **through form?** His example, too, seems to be a bit puzzling. For he says, "as when it is said that that is prime matter which is related to all forms and privations as bronze is to the statue and to the unshaped." The **unshaped** to which bronze is related seems to coincide with the **privations** to which prime matter is related; but **the statue** to which bronze is related does not seem to coincide with **the forms** to which prime matter is related. The statue is a composite -- a composite of bronze and the shape. But forms are not composites; a form is but one ingredient of the composite, the other ingredient being matter. And since matter is an ingredient of the composite, doesn't saying that matter is knowable *through the composite* amount to saying that matter is in some way, at least in part, knowable *through itself,* precisely because it is a part (an ingredient) of the composite through which it is said to be knowable?

What is to be said? Perhaps this. When Aquinas says that prime matter can be known through the composite, he ought to be taken to mean: through that in the composite by which the composite is actual. And that, of course, is the substantial form. For a natural substance **to be actual** is for it to be different from the **terminus a quo** from which it was generated. And this difference is rooted in the substantial form. But, for a natural substance **to be actual** is also for it to be different from **non-being.** And this difference ie rooted in its essence, only part of which is the substantial form, the other part being matter. To be sure, the natural substance comes to differ from non-being (by its essence) only when it comes to differ (by its substantial form) from the *terminus a quo* from which it was generated. And it differs from that *terminus a quo,* it is to be emphasized, by its substantial form. And so, the substantial form is fundamentally that by which a natural substance, as well as the matter which is an intrinsic component of it, both **is** and **is knowable.**

12. Et sciendum est quod materia prima, et etiam forma, non generatur neque corrumpitur, quia omnis generatio est ex aliquo ad aliquid. Illud autem ex quo est generatio, est materia; illud vero ad quod est, est forma. Si igitur materia vel forma generetur, materiae esset materia et formae forma in infinitum. Unde generatio non est nisi compositi, proprie loquendo.

It must be understood that prime matter, and form as well, is neither generated nor corrupted, because every generation is from something to something. Now that from which generation proceeds is matter, and that to which it proceeds is form. So that, if matter or form were generated, there would be a matter for matter and a form for form, endlessly. Whence, there is generation only of the composite, properly speaking.

In 12., Aquinas continues reflecting on the nature of prime matter. Prime matter, he points out, is neither generable nor corruptible, because every generation is from something to something -- from matter to form. Thus, if prime matter were generated, there would be a matter in it, out of which it came to be. There would, therefore, be a matter prior to prime matter, and so prime matter would not be prime. There would also be a form in it, by which prime matter would differ from that out of which it came to be. But, prime matter of itself is without any form. Similarly, if prime matter were corrupted, then again -- since the generation of one thing is the corruption of another, both of which are composed of matter and form -- prime matter would have in itself both a matter and a form. But, prime matter has neither. Lastly, if prime matter were generated or corrupted, there would be a matter for matter, and a form for matter, *ad infinitum*. And so, generation and corruption would be impossible.

Like prime matter, the substantial form too is both ingenerable and incorruptible. If it were generated or corrupted, then -- since the generation of one thing is the corruption of another, both of which are composed of matter and form -- substantial form would have in intself both a matter and a form. But, substantial form has neither. Again, if substantial form were generated or corrupted, there would be a form for form, and a matter for form, *ad infinitum*. From which it would follow that there could be no ultimate existing subjects which come to be in change. Generation and corruption would be impossible.

The numerical oneness of prime matter

13. Sciendum est etiam quod materia prima dicitur una numero in omnibus. Sed unum numero dicitur duobus modis: scilicet quod habet unam formam determinatam in numero, sicut Socrates. Et hoc modo materia prima non dicitur una numero, cum in se non habeat aliquam formam. Dicitur etaim aliquid unum numero, quod est sine dispositionibus quae faciunt differe secundum numerum. Et hoc modo materia prima dicitur una numero, quia intelligitur sine omnibus dispositionibus a quibus est differentia in numero.

It should also be understood that prime matter is said to be one in number in all [natural] things. But, being one in number is said in two ways. First, that is said to be one in number which has a form which is determinately one in number, like Socrates. Prime matter is not said to be one in number in this way, since it has no form at all in itself. Secondly, a thing is said to be one in number if it is without the dispositions which cause things to differ in number. And prime matter is said to be one in number in this way, because it is understood to be without any of the dispositions from which difference in number arises.

In 13., Aquinas considers what it means to say that prime matter is one in number, or numerically one (one when it is counted), in all things. "All things," of course, means: all things which have prime matter as an ingredient of their essences. To be numerically one means, primarily, to be countably one as a result of the division of matter -- matter being divisible only because of the quantity which it has, because of the substantial form which it has. But, only that which has a **substantial form** can be numerically one in this way, and prime matter has no substantial form. Or, only that which has **matter** can be numerically one in this way, and prime matter has no matter. Secondly, to be numerically one means to be such in itself that there is no way in which it can be divided so as to yield a numerical plurality, i.e., to be such, as Aquinas puts it here in **13.**, that it is without the dispositions which can bring about numerical difference. Prime matter of itself has neither matter nor substantial form nor quantity, and so is without any of the requirements for the possibility of numerical plurality.

And so, to be numerically one means: **to be one among many of a same type;** which many have resulted from a division, division presupposing divisibility, divisibility being based on quantity, quantity arising out of substantial form, and substantial form inhering in prime matter as in an ultimate subject. But, to be numerically one means also: **to be one, but *not* among many of a same type;** because there is no possibility of many of a same type. Prime matter is numerically one in this way.

To be numerically one means: there are others like it. Prime matter is not numerically one in this way. To be numerically one means also: there cannot be others like it. Prime matter is numerically one in this way.

Though prime matter exists, it does not exist *through itself*

> **14. Et est sciendum quod, licet materia prima non habeat in sua ratione aliquam formam vel privationem, sicut in ratione aeris neque est figuratum neque infiguratum, tamen numquam denudatur a forma et privatione. Quandoque enim est sub una forma, quandoque sub alia. Sed per se numquam potest esse, quia -- cum in ratione sua non habeat aliquam formam, non habet esse is actu, cum esse in actu non sit nisi a forma. Sed est solum in potentia. Et ideo quidquid est in actu, non potest dici materia prima.**

Lastly, it should be understood that, although prime matter has in its nature neither any form nor any privation, just as bronze has in its nature neither to be shaped nor to be unshaped, it is nonetheless never without a form and a privation. For it is sometimes under one form, and sometimes under another. But through itself matter can never exist. Since it has no form as an ingredient of its nature, prime matter does not have actual existence, since actual existence is only from a form. Prime matter exists only in potency. And so, whatever has actual existence cannot be called prime matter.

In **14.**, Aquinas returns to a point he had made above, in **2.**, about the nature of prime matter, namely that it does not exist through itself. Neither form nor privation, notes Aquinas, are of the nature of prime matter, yet matter is never without some form and some appropriate privation. Sometimes prime matter has this form, sometimes that form; for example, sometimes the form of a dog, sometimes the form of a tree, depending on the nature of the agent cause(s) which have been exerting their causality. And so, prime matter cannot exist **through itself,** since it has no substantial form as an ingredient of what it is. Nonetheless, prime matter does exist -- **through the form** which happens to be **in it** without being **of it,** whether it is the form of a dog or of a tree or of whatever.

Thus, only that is real **through itself,** or exists **through itself,** which has a substantial form as an ingredient of what it is; and that is the substance, the ultimate existing subject, which has come to be. Whatever else is real, or exists, exists in some way **through another.** And that is how prime matter is real, or exists -- **through another,** i.e., through the substantial form which is **in it,** but is *not* an ingredient of what it is. That, too, is how accidental forms exist, i.e., through another -- through the substantial form of the substance of which they are the accidental forms.

To be real is to be different from nothingness. But real things differ from nothingness differently -- some **through themselves,** some **through another.** Now, some things are **substances,** or ultimate existing subjects, and these differ from nothingness **through themselves.** Other things are either principles of a substance, or accidents of a substance, and these differ from nothingness **through another,** i.e., through the substance of which they are the principles or the accidents. Prime matter is not a substance; it is a principle of a substance. And so, prime matter is real **through another,** i.e., through substance, which is real **through itself.**

Although prime matter and the accidents have it in common that they are real through another, i.e., through substance; they differ in how they are related to the substantial form of the substance. Whereas prime matter is the subject in which the substantial form inheres, the substantial form is the subject (in some cases along with prime matter) in which the accidents inhere.

Chapter three
Agent and end; principle, cause and element

In chapter three, Aquinas considers a number of things: the need of an agent for generation, in addition to matter, form and privation; the need of an end; the difference between a voluntary agent and a natural agent; what it means to intend an end; the four causes, namely material, efficient, formal and final; the difference between a principle and a cause; intrinsic causes and extrinsic causes; *per se* causes and *per accidens* causes; how an element differs from a principle and from a cause. His comments seem to be aimed primarily at 1) making clear that there are four kinds of cause, and 2) at making clear, in some detail, what an element is. Elements survive in the *terminus ad quem* of a change in a way which is both like, and quite unlike, the way in which prime matter survives. It is important, Aquinas seems to be saying, to note both the likeness and the difference.

In addition to matter and form, there must be an agent

15. Ex dictis igitur patet tria esse principia naturae, scilicet materia, forma et privatio. Sed haec non sunt sufficientia ad generationem. Quod enim est in potentia non potest se reducere ad actum; sicut cuprum quod est in potentia idolum, non facit se idolum, sed indiget operante, qui formam idoli extrahat de potentia in actum. Forma autem non potest se extrahere de potentia in actum. Et loquor de forma generati quam diximus esse terminum generationis. Forma enim non est nisi in facto esse; quod autem operatur est in fieri, idest dum res fit. Oportet igitur praeter materiam et formam esse aliquid principium quod agat, et hoc dicitur esse efficiens, vel movens, vel agens, vel unde est principium motus.

It is clear, therefore, from the things which have been said, that there are three principles of nature, namely matter, form and privation. But these are not sufficient for generation. For what is in potency cannot bring itself into a state of actuality. Bronze, for example, which is a statue in potency, does not make itself be a statue. It needs something actively working, which brings out the form of the statue from potency into act. Neither can the form bring itself out of potency into act; I am speaking of the form of the generated thing, the form which we have said is the end-point of generation. For the form is not there until the thing has been made to be; and what is actually working is there during the coming to be, i.e., while the thing is being made. It is necessary, therefore, that there be in addition to the matter and the form some principle which does something; and this is said to be what makes, or moves, or acts, or that from which the motion begins.

In **15.**, Aquinas begins by noting that matter, form and privation -- the three principles of nature -- are not sufficient for generation. In generation, what is in potency is brought to a state of actuality; matter receives form. But, since actuality is not of the nature of potentiality, matter cannot receive form from itself. A piece of bronze, for example, cannot make itself be a statue; because the bronze, as bronze, is only in potency to the shape of the statue. There is need for an actively working cause, a sculptor in this case; a cause which has it in its active power to give the bronze the shape of a statue, thereby bringing what is in potency into a state of actuality. Whereas the bronze is that *out of which* the statue is made, and *not* that which makes the statue; the sculptor is *that which makes* the statue, and *not* that out of which the statue is made.

Just as matter cannot bring itself to a state of actuality, neither can the form, continues Aquinas. Just as matter cannot be the *operans*, for one reason, i.e., because it is in potency; neither can the form, for another reason, i.e., because it does not yet exist. And he makes it very clear that he is talking about the form of the thing about to be generated, the form which is about to appear in the *terminus ad quem* -- *et loquor de forma generati quam diximus esse terminum generationis.* The form of the generated thing is not there until **after** the thing has been generated. The *operans* -- i.e., the thing which has it in its active power to give form to matter -- must be there **before** the thing is generated, i.e., during the process in which the thing comes to be, or while the thing which comes to be is being made.

And so, concludes Aquinas, in addition to the matter, by which something (the *terminus ad quem)* **can be** actual; and in addition to the form, by which something (the *termiunus ad quem)* **will be** actual; there is need for a third principle, something which acts -- *aliquod principiuim quod agat* -- a principle by the active power of which something (the *terminus ad quem)* **is made to be** actual. In addition to matter and form, there must be an agent.

In addition to the agent, there must be an end

> **16. Et quia, ut dicit Aristoteles in** *II Metaphysicae,*[4] **omne quod agit non agit nisi intendendo aliquid, oportet esse aliud quartum, id scilicet quod intenditur ab operante, et hoc dicitur finis. Et est sciendum quod, licet omne agens tam naturale quam voluntarium intendat finem, non tamen sequitur quod omne agens cognoscat finem vel deliberet de fine. Cognoscere enim finem est necessarium in his, quorum actiones non sunt determinatae, sed se habent ad opposita, sicut se habent agentia voluntaria; et ideo oportet quod cognoscant finem, per quem suas actiones determinent. Sed in agentibus naturalibus sunt actiones determinatae, unde non est necessarium eligere ea quae sunt ad finem. Et ponit exemplum Avicenna**[5] **de citharaedo quem non oportet de qualibet percussione chordarum deliberare, cum percussiones sint deliberatae apud ipsum; alioquin esset**

---

4   Aristotle, *Metaph.,* Bk, II, ch. 2, 994 b 9-16. -- Footnote references to authors cited by Aquinas will be of the briefest sort. For more extended footnotes, which include goodly portions of the text of the authors whom Aquinas cites, see Pauson, *op. cit.*

5   *Liber Secundus Physicorum Avicennae,* "*Sufficientia,*" c. 10:   Sicut qui scribit aut qui tangit cytharam; si incipiens discernere unamquamque litterarum aut unumquodque tonorum et voluerit scire numerum eorum, hebetabitur et impedietur et non procedet suo ordine in singulis quae incipit agere nisi in eo quod facit sine deliberatione. Quamvis initium illius operis et appetitus non fuerit nisi ex deliberatione; sed exercere illud primum in principio est sine deliberatione.   (Ex. Cod. Paris. Nat. Lat. 6443, fol 22r-v).   -- From Basil M. Mattingly, O.S.B., *De Principiis Naturae of St. Thomas Aquinas,* Notre Dame, Indiana: University of Notre Dame, Doctoral Dissertation, 1957; p. (-18-).

inter percussiones mora, quod esset absonum. Magis autem videtur de agente voluntarie quod deliberet quam de agente naturali, et ita patet per locum a maiori, quod si agens voluntarie, de quo magis videtur, non deliberet aliquando, ergo nec agens naturale. Ergo possibile est agens naturale sine deliberatione intendere finem; et hoc intendere nihil aliud est quam habere naturalem inclinationem ad aliquid.

And because everything which acts, acts only by intending something, as Aristotle says in book two of the *Metaphysics*, there must be some fourth thing, namely that which is intended by that which is doing the work. This is said to be the end. And it should be understood that, although every agent, both natural and voluntary, intends an end, it does not follow nonetheless that every agent knows, or deliberates about, the end. To know the end is necessary in the case of those things whose actions are not determined, but are open to opposites, as are voluntary agents. And so, these things must know the end, through which they determine their actions. But in the case of natural agents, the actions are determined. Whence it is not necessary for them to choose the means to the end. And Avicenna offers the example of the one who sings while playing the cithara, who does not have to deliberate each time he strikes the strings, because he has deliberated about the strikings beforehand; otherwise there would be a delaying pause between strikings, which would be dissonant. Moreover, it seems more appropriate for a voluntarily acting agent to deliberate, than it does for a natural agent. And so, it seems clear by arguing *a maiori*, that if a voluntarily acting agent, for whom deliberation seems more appropriate, does not deliberate at least at times, neither therefore does a natural agent. It is possible, therefore, that a natural agent intend an end without deliberating about it. And this intending is nothing other than having a natural inclination toward something.

In **16.**, Saint Thomas reflects on the need for an end. Since everything which acts, he observes, acts only by intending something, there must be some fourth thing -- in addition to these three: matter, form and agent -- which moves the agent. Matter cannot give itself a form. The form cannot bring itself into existence. It is the agent which gives form to matter. But, if the agent were not inclined, either by its own choice or by its own nature, to do some work, to perform some activity; no work would be done, no activity would be performed. And so, no form would be given to matter. And this is why, as Aquinas notes elsewhere, the end is said to be the cause of causes, i.e., the cause of the causality of the causes. The end causes the agent to function as an agent, i.e., to give form to matter, thereby causing the form and the matter to function, respectively, as form and matter.

But, there is a difference, observes Aquinas, between a voluntary agent and a natural agent. A voluntary agent knows, and deliberates about, the end; knows, and deliberates about, the various means to the end; then freely selects an end, thereupon freely choosing the means thereto. A natural agent, on the other hand, is not open to considering pursuing different means to previously selected ends. A natural agent neither selects its ends, nor chooses the means thereto. The actions of a natural agent are set or determined by its nature, just as, and because, the ends which it pursues are determined by that same nature.

Thus, both voluntary agents and natural agents act for an end. And both intend the end. But this -- that both intend the end -- does not mean, points out Aquinas, that both know and deliberate about the end and about the means thereto. For, whereas the actions of a voluntary agent are not determined by its nature, those of a natural agent are. And so, it is necessary for the voluntary agent to know and to deliberate, but not for the natural agent. To say that a natural agent intends a given end is to say simply that it is inclined by its nature to perform the activities by which it achieves that end. Avicenna, points out Aquinas, proposes the example of the person who sings while playing the cithara. This person, though a voluntary agent, does not have to stop to think and deliberate each time he strikes the strings, because he has thought out and planned and practiced the strikings many times beforehand, so much so, that his playing has become a habit, a kind of second nature. Thus, by an argument *a maiori*, since a voluntary agent --

for whom deliberation seems more appropriate than for other sorts of agents -- does not, **at least at times,** have to deliberate about ends and the means thereto -- neither should a natural agent have to. And so, concludes Aquinas, it is possible for a natural agent to intend an end without deliberating either about that end or about the means thereto. To say that a natural agent intends an end is simply to say that it has a natural inclination to perform the activities by which that end can be achieved.

Four causes, three principles

17. Ex dictis igitur patet quod sunt quatuor causae, scilicet materialis, efficiens, formalis et finalis. Licet autem principium et causa dicantur quasi convertibiliter, ut dicitur in *V Metaphysicae,*[6] tamen Aristoteles in libro *Physicorum*[7] ponit quatuor causas et tria principia. Causas autem accipit tam pro extrinsecis quam pro intrinsecis. Materia et forma dicuntur intrinsecae rei, eo quod sunt partes constituentes rem; efficiens et finalis dicuntur extrinsecae, quia sunt extra rem. Sed principia accipit solum causas intrinsecas. Privatio autem non nominatur inter causas, quia est principum per accidens, ut dictum est. Et cum dicimus quatuor causas, intelligimus de causis per se, ad quas tamen causae per accidens reducuntur, quia omne quod est per accidens, reducitur ad id quod est per se.

It is clear, therefore, from the things which have been said, that there are four causes, namely material, efficient, formal and final. And although "principle" and "cause" are used as though they were convertible, as is said in book five of the *Metaphysics,* nonetheless Aristotle in his book the *Physics* writes that there are four causes and three principles. He takes the causes to be both extrinsic and intrinsic. Matter and form are said to be intrinsic to a thing, because they are parts constituting the thing. The efficient and the final are said to be extrinsic, because they are outside the thing. But, as principles he takes only the intrinsic causes. And privation is not named among the causes, because it is a principle *per accidens,* as has been said.

---

6   Aristotle, *Metaph.,* Bk. V, ch. 1, 1013 a 16-17.
7   Aristotle, *Physics,* Bk. I, ch. 6, 189 b 16-18; ch. 7, 191 a 20-21; Bk. II, ch. 3, 195 a 15.

And when we say there are four causes, we understand this to refer to the *per se* causes, to which the *per accidens* causes are reduced, because everything which is *per accidens* is reduced to that which is *per se*.

In **17.**, Aquinas makes it his concern to begin to clarify the difference between cause and principle. He continues this clarifying concern in **18.**.

"Principle" and "cause" are used in different ways. Sometimes they are used convertibly, notes Aquinas, so that whatever is called a principle is called a cause, and whatever is called a cause is called a principle. When used convertibly, it is obvious that both "principle" and "cause" mean what "cause" means, i.e., that from which the **existence** of something else follows. For example, the sculptor and the bronze are "principles," or "causes," of the statue in this sense; for both contribute something to the **existence** of the statue. This seems to be the point of the reference to book five of the *Metaphysics*, where Aristotle notes that "principle" and "cause" are used "quasi convertibiliter," as Aquinas puts it, i.e., as though they were convertible.

But, sometimes "principle" and "cause" are not used convertibly. And when this happens, whatever is said to be a cause is said to be a principle, but not vice versa. For there are, in this usage, principles which are not causes; for example, **unshaped** in the change from bronze to statue. Unshaped is a principle of this change, meaning that it counts as **something from which the change begins,** "principle" (from the Latin *"principium"*) meaning simply **a beginning point;** but **not** a beginning point from which the **existence** of something else follows. The existence of the statue does not follow from the unshaped; though it does follow from the bronze and the sculptor and the shape and the intended end. And these, of course, are causes. The unshaped contributes nothing to the existence of the statue.

Moreover, continues Aquinas, sometimes "cause" is used to refer to both the intrinsic causes (matter and form) and the extrinsic causes (agent and end), "intrinsic" naming those causes which are ingredients of the nature of the effect, and "extrinsic" naming those which are not ingredients of the nature of the effect. The bronze and the shape, for example, are ingredients of the nature of the effect, i.e., of the statue, whereas the sculptor and his intended end are not. By way of difference, "principle" is sometimes used to refer to the **intrinsic** causes **only,** e.g., to the bronze and to the form. Thus, matter and form are both principles and causes, because both are **intrinsic** causes. But, privation is not listed among the causes, because it is a *per accidens* principle, i.e., a principle which attaches to, or accompanies, matter, which is a *per se* principle, a principle through itself, as explained above. And so, when it is said that there are four causes, the reference is to *per se* causes. Privation, thus, is not counted among the causes, because it is **of itself** neither a cause, nor a principle (and what is not a principle cannot be a cause). This seems to be the point of the reference to the *Physics* of Aristotle, where Aristotle notes that there are four causes, but three principles.

Aquinas concludes **17.** with the observation that *per accidens* causes are reduced to *per se* causes, "because everything which is *per accidens* is reduced to that which is *per se.*" What exactly does this mean?, one might ask. That is, what does "reduced" mean in the claim that "everything which is *per accidens* is reduced to that which is *per se*"? And what exactly is the point of observing that *per accidens* causes are reduced to *per se* causes?

The meaning of "reduced"

"Reduced" means literally: **brought back to,** or **led back to.** To what? To something (the *per se*) without which it could not be, or could not be understood. The *per accidens* is whatever it is (or is said to be) -- whether a cause, or a principle, or something real -- through, or because of, something other than itself, simply because it cannot be whatever it is (or is said to be)

41

through, or because of, itself, since it lacks something, or is somehow deficient or incomplete. An accident, like quantity or quality or relation, for example, is something real *per accidens,* i.e., through, or because of, something other than itself, namely because of the substance of which it is an accident. An accident cannot be real because of itself, simply because it is an accident; as an accident, it lacks something, is deficient, is incomplete. It is such of itself that it is real only because of something other than itself, because of that in which it inheres, namely substance. And substance is such of itself that it is real because of itself. Of itself, a substance is an ultimate existing subject. -- Similarly, privation is a principle (and a cause) *per accidens,* i.e., because of the matter to which it attaches, which it accompanies, in which it is found. And matter is a principle *per se.* Privation is lacking, is deficient, is incomplete, in a way in which matter is not; though matter itself is lacking, deficient, incomplete, in a way in which a substance is not. Matter, along with form, is an ingredient of the **essence** of a substance, whereas privation is not. Matter has something in it (**an essence** of sorts) whereby it differs from nothingness, though it cannot assert this difference unless it has a form. Privation has nothing in it whereby it differs from nothingness; so that, even though privation is found only in a matter which has a form, it cannot, even so, assert itself as different from nothingness. Whereas matter has an essence of sorts, privation has no essence of any sort at all.

Similarly, again, the medical doctor who builds a house is a *per accidens* efficient cause of the house. For he builds the house not because he is a medical doctor, but because he is also a builder. Being a medical doctor is something which attaches to, accompanies, is found together with, being a builder. Again, the man who marries a virtuous and beautiful woman, who is also wealthy beyond measure, can be said to be motivated *per accidens* by her wealth, *per se* by her virtue and her beauty. He marries her not because she is wealthy, but because she is virtuous and beautiful; just as the medical doctor builds a house not because he is a medical doctor, but because he is a builder.

42

Accidents are real *per accidens,* i.e., because of substance. Privations are principles (and causes) *per accidens,* i.e., because of matter. The medical doctor builds *per accidens,* i.e., because of being a builder. The man marries the wealthy woman *per accidens,* i.e., because of her virtue and beauty. -- Substance is real *per se,* i.e., because it is an ultimate existing subject. Matter is a principle (and a cause) *per se,* i.e., because it is matter. The builder builds *per se,* i.e., because he is a builder. The virtuous and beautiful woman is the motivating (final) cause *per se,* i.e., because she is virtuous and beautiful.

The point of observing that *per accidens* causes are reduced to *per se* causes

The point, now, of the observation that *per accidens* causes are reduced to *per se* causes should be clear. It is simply this. If there were no *per se* causes, there could be no *per accidens* causes either. Indeed, there would be no causes at all. Similarly, with respect to principles. And absolutely universally, if there were nothing whatever which is *per se* -- whether a cause, or a principle, or something real, or an item of knowledge -- there would be absolutely nothing at all.

Principle and cause defined

18. **Sed licet principia ponat Aristoteles pro causis intrinsecis in** *I Physicorum,*[8] **tamen, ut dicitur in** *XI Metaphysicae,*[9] **principium proprie dicitur de causis extrinsecis, elementum de**

---

8   The reference is to what Aristotle does in the **whole** of Bk. I of the *Physics,* but in particular to his **own** account of the **intrinsic** principles in ch. 7, and to his response to the difficulties of earlier thinkers in ch. 8.

9   Aristotle, *Metaph.,* Bk, XII, ch. 4, 1070 b 22-27. This point is not very clear in Aristotle, notes Mattingly (*op. cit.,* p. (-20-), footnote 2). Aristotle says: Since not only the elements present in a thing are causes, but also something external, i.e., the moving cause, clearly while 'principle' and 'element' are different, both are causes, and 'principle' is divided into these **two** kinds [intrinsic and extrinsic?] . . .   But Aquinas comes to a clarifying rescue: . . . nam principium proprie dicitur **quod est extra** sicut movens . . .   Elementum proprie dicitur causa **intrinseca** ex qua constituitur res . . . (*In XI Metaph.,* lect. 4, nn. 2468-2469).

causis quae sunt partes rei, idest de causis intrinsecis. Causa autem dicitur de utrisque, licet quandoque unum ponatur pro altero; omnis enim causa potest dici principium et omne principium causa. Sed tamen causa videtur addere supra principium communiter dictum, quia id quod est primum, sive ex eo consequatur esse posterioris sive non, potest dici principium, sicut faber dicitur principium cultelli, quia ex eius operatione est esse cultelli; sed quando aliquid movetur de nigredine ad albedinem, dicitur quod nigredo est principium illius motus, et universaliter omne id a quo incipit esse motus dicitur principium, tamen nigredo non est id ex quo consequitur esse albedinis. Sed causa dicitur solum de illo primo, ex quo consequitur esse posterioris. Unde dicitur quod causa est id ex cuius esse sequitur aliud. Et ideo illud primum a quo incipit esse motus non potest dici causa per se, etsi dicatur principium. Et propter hoc, privatio ponitur inter principia et non inter causas, quia privatio est id a quo incipit generatio. Sed potest etiam dici causa per accidens, inquantum coincidit cum materia, ut supra expositum est.

But, although Aristotle uses "principles" to refer to intrinsic causes in book one of the *Physics;* nonetheless, as is said in book eleven of the *Metaphysics,* "principle" is said properly of extrinsic causes, and "element" of causes which are parts of a thing, i.e., of intrinsic causes. "Cause," moreover is said of both; even though one is sometimes used for the other, for every cause can be called a principle, and every principle a cause. Still, however, cause seems to add something to principle taken commonly, because that which is first, whether the existence of a posterior follows from it or not, can be said to be a principle. For example, the maker is called a principle of the knife, because the existence of the knife comes from his work. But when something is changed from black to white, black is said to be a principle of that change; and universally everything from which a change begins is said to be a principle. Black, however, is not something from which the existence of white follows. "Cause" is said of something which is first only if the existence of a posterior follows from it. Whence it is said that a cause is that from the existence of which another follows. And so, something first from which a change begins cannot be called a cause just because it is something first, even though it is called a principle. And this is why privation is placed among the principles and not among the causes, because privation is that from which generation begins. But it can also be called a cause *per accidens,* inasmuch as it is an accompaniment of matter, as was explained above.

In **18.,** continuing the concern of **17.,** Aquinas makes clear exactly how cause differs from principle. He points out what the two have in common. He also gives a definition of each.

"Principle," begins Aquinas, can be used to refer to **intrinsic** causes **only** (to matter and form), as Aristotle does in book one of the *Physics,* where he uses "principle" to refer, as well, to privation, which accompanies matter as a kind of **intrinsic** attachment. For he speaks there of **three** principles of nature -- matter and form (*per se* principles), and privation (a *per accidens* principle).

But "principle"can be used, **and properly,** to refer to **extrinsic** causes as well (to agent and end), as Aristotle notes in book eleven of the *Metaphysics.* Moreover, "element" can be used, though not properly, to refer to any sort of **intrinsic** cause. When used properly, however, "element" refers to intrinsic causes of a special sort, i.e., of the sort which are the **material** parts of some whole, but are themselves made up of a matter and a form. And "cause" can be used to refer to both, i.e., to the extrinsic as well as to the intrinsic. Still, "cause" and "principle" are used at times for one another, as has been said. Nonetheless, there is a sense of "cause" in which it adds to the meaning of "principle." "Principle," taken commonly, means something first (a **primum**) from which something else, a posterior, begins or takes its origin, whether the **existence** of the posterior follows from it or not (this is a **definition** of principle which **can** be predicated of a cause). But "principle,"

45

taken less commonly, and "cause" have this in common: each is something first (a **primum**), from which something else, a posterior, begins, or takes its origin. If the **existence** of the posterior follows from the **primum**, i.e., if the **primum** contributes something to the **existence** of the posterior; the **primum** is a principle which is also a cause (this is the definition of cause). Matter, form, agent and end are principles which are also causes. If, on the other hand, the **existence** of the posterior does **not** follow from the **primum**, the **primum** is simply a principle, without being also a cause (this, too, is a **definition** of principle, but a definition which cannot be predicated of a cause). In the change, for example, in which something black becomes white, the **primum** black is a principle, but without being a cause. Black is neither the matter, nor the form, nor the agent, nor the end of the effect, i.e., of the white thing. So, too, privation is a principle which is a principle **only**. Privation contributes nothing to the existence of the effect. What contributes to the existence of the effect is either a **part** of the **essence** of the effect, i.e., either its **matter** or its **form**; or something which is **productive** of the **essence** of the effect, i.e., the **agent** which by its activity gives form to matter (thereby constituting the **essence**), because it has been motivated by some **end**. Essence is that, intrinsic to a thing, whereby the thing has existence. Privation is neither a **part** of essence; nor an agent or a motivating end, which are **productive** of essence. And this is why privation, concludes Aquinas, is placed among the principles, for privation is, indeed, something from which generation takes its origin; but not among the causes, for it contributes nothing to the **existence** of the effect. Nonetheless, a privation can, without harm and without risk to truth, be called a cause, so long as it is called a cause *per accidens*, i.e., because of the matter to which it attaches, or in which it inheres, matter being a cause *per se*. Every *per accidens* is the *per accidens* which it is only because of the appropriate *per se* to which it is related, on which it depends, without which it would not be anything at all.

19. Elementum autem non dicitur proprie nisi de causis ex quibus est compositio rei, quae proprie sunt materiales. Et iterum non de qualibet causa materiali, sed de illa ex qua est prima compositio; sicut non dicimus quod membra sunt elementa hominis, quia membra etiam componuntur ex aliis. Sed dicimus quod terra et aqua sunt elementa, quia haec non componuntur ex aliis corporibus; sed ex ipsis est prima compositio corporum naturalium. Unde Aristoteles in *V Metaphysicae*[10] dicit quod "elementum est id ex quo componitur res primo, et est in ea, et non dividitur secundum formam." Expositio primae particulae, scilicet "ex quo componitur res primo," patet per ea quae diximus. Secunda particula, scilicet "et est in ea," ponitur ad differentaim illius materiae quae ex toto corrumpitur per generationem; sicut panis est materia sanguinis, sed non generatur sanguis nisi corrumpatur panis; unde panis non remanet in sanguine, et ideo non potest dici panis elementum sanguinis. Sed elementa oportet aliquomodo remanere, cum non omnino corrumpantur, ut dicitur in libro *De Generatione*.[11] Tertia particula, scilicet "et non dividitur secundum formam," ponitur ad differentiam eorum quae habent partes diversas in forma, idest in specie; sicut manus cuius partes sunt caro et ossa, quae differunt secundum speciem. Sed elementum non dividitur in partes diversas secundum speciem, sicut aqua, cuius quaelibet pars est aqua. Non enim oportet ad esse elementi ut non dividatur secundum quantitatem, sed sufficit si non dividatur secundum speciem; et si etiam nullo modo dividatur, dicitur elementum, sicut litterae dicuntur elementa dictionum.

Element is said properly only of those causes out of which the composition of a thing arises, and which are properly material. And not of just any material causes, but of those out of which the thing's primary composition arises. We do not say, for example, that his bodily members are the elements of a man, because the members themselves are composed of other things. But we do say that earth and water are elements, because these are not composed of other bodies. Rather, it is out of them that

---

10   Aristotle, *Metaph.*, Bk. V, ch. 3, 1014 a 26-27.
11   Aristotle, *De Gen. et Corrupt.*, Bk. I, ch. 10, 327 b 29-31.

the primary composition of natural bodies arises. Whence Aristotle says in book five of the *Metaphysics* that "an element is that out of which a thing is primarily composed, which is immanent in the thing, and which is indivisible according to form." The explanation of the first part, namely "out of which a thing is primarily composed," is clear from the things we have said. The second part, namely "which is immanent in the thing," is used to differentiate an element from the sort of matter which is totally corrupted by generation. Bread, for example, is the matter of blood, but blood is not generated unless the bread is corrupted. Whence bread does not remain in blood, and so bread cannot be said to be an element of blood. Elements must remain in some way, since they are not entirely corrupted, as is said in the book *On Generation*. The third part, namely "and which is indivisible according to form," is used to differentiate an element from those material parts which have parts which are diverse in form, i.e., in species. From the hand, for example, whose parts are flesh and bones, which differ according to species. But an element is indivisible into parts which are diverse according to species; like water, each part of which is water. And it is not necessary for an element that it be indivisible according to quantity; it suffices that it be indivisible according to species. And even if it is in no way divisible, it is said to be an element, as letters are said to be the elements of speech.

Having defined principle and cause in **18.**, Aquinas turns in **19.** to make clear what an element is. An element is a special kind of principle. It is a principle which is also a cause -- but a **material** cause, and of a **special** kind.

Elements, begins Aquinas, are material causes out of which a natural body comes into existence. But an element is not just any kind of material cause (component, or ingredient). Elements are material ingredients of a **primary** sort. That is, whereas other natural bodies are composed out of them, there are no material ingredients, no natural bodies, prior to them, out of which they are composed. An element, like any principle, is a **primum**. It has been said that the elements have no elements of their own. Arms and legs, and the like, exemplifies Aquinas, are not the elements of a man, because they are, in turn, composed out of other bodies, like flesh and bones. Water and earth, however, continues Aquinas, **are** elements; for there are no prior bodily things out of which they are composed. Today, of course, we know that water and earth **are** composed out of prior bodily ingredients, and so cannot be elements. Water, for example, is composed out of hydrogen and oxygen. Hydrogen and oxygen, too, are made out of prior constituents, e.g., protons and electrons; and protons, too, out of prior constituents still -- quarks. Are quarks, then, among the elements of all natural bodies? Whether or not quarks are elements of natural bodies is something to be decided by the empirical methods of contemporary physics. This much is clear, nonetheless, about what an element is: it is a **material** ingredient of a **bodily** sort which has no such bodily ingredients of its own. It is a bodily ingredient which is a **primum**.

But there is more to what an element is, continues Aquinas, and this more is what Aristotle has in mind when he writes, in book five of the *Metaphysics*, that "an element is that out of which a thing is primarily composed, which is immanent in it, and which is indivisible according to form." The first part of this account of what an element is, of this **definition** of element, namely "out of which a thing is primarily composed," expresses the two points noted in the preceding paragraph: 1) the words "out of which" are used to indicate that an element is a **material** ingredient of a bodily sort; and 2) the word "primarily" is used to point out that the element itself has **no prior** bodily ingredients out of which it is constituted.

49

The second part, namely "which is immanent in the thing," expresses how an element differs from any and every principle which is of a **passing or transient** sort, whatever it may be, whether a privation, or a contrary, or a completely corrupted matter, or matter taken with a privation or with a contrary. These are, all of them, passing or transient, rather than **remaining**. An element must remain in some way in that of which it is an element. For example, in the change in which a green apple becomes a red apple, the **privation**, non-red, does not remain in the red apple. Neither does the **contrary**, green. Neither does the **matter taken with the contrary**, green apple, remain. Lastly, neither does the **matter taken with the privation**, non-red apple, remain. And in the change in which bread becomes blood, the bread does not remain as bread. For, when bread becomes blood, bread is completely corrupted, and so does not remain. Bread, therefore, cannot be an element of blood. Earth, water, air and fire -- in the proportion and arrangement appropriate to a red apple, or to blood -- would remain, according to Aquinas. According to what we know today, however, we would say perhaps that what remains are certain sorts of quarks, and certain sorts of leptons, in the arrangement and proportion required for being a red apple, or for being blood.

The third part, namely "and which is indivisible according to form," expresses how an element differs from those material parts which have parts which differ in kind; for example, to express how an element differs from a hand. A hand is a material part of a man, and the hand itself has material parts, e.g., flesh and bones. But flesh is a part of one kind, and bone is a part of another kind. Flesh and bones differ in kind from one another, as well as from the hand, the whole, of which they are parts. Taking water as an element, as Aquinas would, one could note that water is indeed divisible into parts; but each part of water is just water. The parts into which water is divisible are, all of them, the same in kind with one another, and with the whole of which they are the parts. Similarly, the parts into which air is divisible are, each of them, just air. Each part of air, like every other part of air, and like the whole of which each is a part, is just air. Is it the case -- if a quark is divisible -- that each of its parts, is just a quark? And, if a lepton is divisible, is each of its parts just a lepton?

But further, as Aquinas explains in his commentary on book five of the *Metaphysics,* this last part of the definition of element expresses how an element differs from prime matter, too, which has no form or species at all. An element **has** a form or species. It is, after all, a natural body. And it is indivisible into species which are diverse from its own. Prime matter cannot be an element, simply because it is not a natural body; and so, unlike an element, it cannot have a species with respect to which it is indivisible. It is clear, from the immediately preceding, that although an element, unlike other natural bodies, cannot itself be composed out of prior natural bodies; it is nonetheless something composed -- composed out of prime matter and substantial form. All natural bodies are composed out of prime matter and substantial form.

Lastly, adds Aquinas, it is not necessary for an element that it be indivisible into quantitative parts. Earth, water, air and fire, as Aquinas sees it, are elements -- yet they **are divisible** into quantitative parts (each of which, of course, is the same in kind as the element which was divided). What **is** required for an element is that it be indivisible into quantitative parts which differ in kind. (Of course, if something is indivisible into quantitative parts, it must be indivisible into quantitative parts which differ from one another in kind, or species, as well. And so, such a thing could be an element, if there could be such a thing; and if such a thing could really be a material ingredient of a bodily thing.) Letters, i.e., **spoken** letters, notes Aquinas, are in a way like earth, water, air and fire, i.e., they are elements, yet they are divisible into quantitative parts -- but of a **temporal** sort. To explain. Speech -- i.e., language **sounds** *(dictiones)* -- ranges from the complex to the simpler to the simplest. A sermon, for example, is a complex *dictio*, which is made up of paragraphs (simpler), which are made up of sentences (simpler), which are made up of words (simpler), which are made up of syllables (simpler), which are made up of letters which are either consonants or vowels (the simplest). As the simplest, neither consonants nor vowels are made up of prior language sounds. There are no prior language sounds. And so, spoken letters, i.e., consonants and vowels, are the elements of speech. They cannot be divided into quantitative parts which differ in kind from one another, and from the consonants and vowels themselves. When divided, they are divided into parts each of which is the same in kind as all the others, and as the whole which was divided. That is, when a vowel sound is divided, each of its parts is a vowel sound -- temporally shorter, but a vowel sound nonetheless. And when a consonant sound is divided, each of its parts is a consonant sound -- temporally shorter, but a consonant sound nonetheless. It is to be emphasized that this is a division **with respect to time**; and that each of these parts is a **temporal** part, each becoming temporally shorter as the division proceeds. And this is why Aquinas observes, at the end of **19.**, that letters (sounded or spoken) are elements which are in no way divisible, i.e., not only with respect to species, but with respect to quantity as well. For, spoken or sounded letters are **not** three dimensional.

At this point, one might raise the question: Are there natural bodies which are indivisible into quantitative parts, and so indivisible into quantitative parts which differ in kind? A molecule of water, we know today, is divisible, resolvable, into hydrogen and oxygen; and hydrogen and oxygen into protons, neutrons, and electrons; and protons and neutrons, in turn, into quarks. Are quarks indivisible into quantitative parts, and so incapable of division into quantitative parts which differ in kind? (What does it mean to say, as physicists at times say today, that a quark is dimensionless?) Or, are quarks **divisible** into quantitative parts? And if so, do these parts differ in kind from one another, and from the divided quark itself? Or, are they the same in kind with one another, and with the divided quark itself? Does physics have an answer to these questions? They are certainly not questions which philosophy can answer.

In his commentary on the *Metaphysics*, Aquinas adds an interesting and helpful clarification as regards how **indivisibility according to species** is to be understood. When it is said that an element is indivisible into parts which are diverse according to species, both from one another and from the whole which has been divided; this is not to be understood of parts which result from a **simple** quantitative division, but of parts which result from a division **because of alteration**. Each quantitative part of a piece of wood is just wood, yet wood is not an element. One simply takes a saw, or a knife, and cuts the wood up into quantitative parts. This is a **simple** quantitative division. But hydrogen and oxygen are, neither of them, water. Nor can one simply take a knife to water, and cut it up into hydrogen and oxygen. Hydrogen and oxygen are indeed parts of water (quantitative parts); but they come into being from water **because of a decomposing alteration.**   There is a way to decompose water, to alter water, so as to retrieve the hydrogen and oxygen out of which it came to be.   But the way is not a simple quantitative division. One does not cut it up with a knife. One **alters** the water by using the agent causality of sulfuric acid and electricity.

Similarly, the two u-quarks and the one d-quark which compose a proton are not themselves protons.   Nor can one simply take a knife to a proton, and cut it up into quarks. Its three quarks are indeed parts of the proton (quantitative parts); but they would have to come into being out of it **because of a decomposing alteration**.   Is there a way to decompose a proton, to alter a proton, so as to retrieve the two u-quarks and the one d-quark out of which it came to be? The way cannot -- most certainly -- be a simple quantitative division.   One cannot cut up a proton with a knife.   Can one decompose the proton by bombarding it in an accelerator with certain appropriate subatomic particles? But, then, can quarks be retrieved at all? Physicists say that "there can be no such thing as a free quark"?   Why not?   If not, then can a quark really be an element?   Aren't elements supposed to be retrievable from the wholes of which they are parts, and thereupon capable of separate, free, existence? Were they capable of such existence in the high energy conditions "just after" the Big Bang, conditions which no longer obtain, and which physicists are trying to duplicate in their accelerator experiments?

Unlike complex bodies like wood and water, an element cannot be divided, or resolved, by alteration into **bodies** which are more simple than the element itself.   Only prime matter and substantial form are more simple than an element, and neither one nor the other is a body; neither one nor the other has a form. If the material component(s) of what we take to be an element **has a form(s)**, then what we have taken to be an element is not an element.   The material component of an element must be **absolutely formless**, i.e., must be prime matter. And its formal component, therefore, must be a form which is proportioned to absolutely formless matter, i.e., a **substantial** form; and, at this lowly, absolutely basic level, a substantial form which manifests itself in a collection of appropriately identifying features, such as mass, electric charge, color charge, spin, baryon number.

Prime matter survives in one way, the elements in another

Both prime matter and the elements survive in the *terminus ad quem* of a substantial change, but each survives differently; for what each is, is something quite different.

1) An element has a substantial form, and belongs to a species, i.e., it is a certain kind of substance. Prime matter has no substantial form.

2) An element is a natural body. Prime matter is not.

3) An element is the simplest of bodies, being composed only out of prime matter and substantial form; there are no elements in the composition of an element. Prime matter is absolutely simple, absolutely uncomposed, is not a body at all.

4) If, and to the extent that, an element can be divided (quantitatively), each resulting part must be of the same nature as the divided whole; otherwise it would not be an element. Prime matter, of itself, cannot be divided at all.

5) An element has a material component, an **absolutely formless** material component, i.e., prime matter. Prime matter has no material component(s); there is nothing of a material (potential, receptive) nature which is prior to prime matter.

6) An element has a **formal** component which is proportioned to its material component, i.e., to prime matter; its formal component is a substantial form. Prime matter has no formal component; prime matter is of itself pure potency for substantial form.

7) An element has certain active **powers** by which it performs its proper activities. Prime matter has no active powers at all.

Given what each is, i.e., what prime matter is and what an element is; given, secondly, that the *terminus ad quem* of a substantial change is a substance; and given, thirdly, that a substance can have only one substantial form, its own; it follows that prime matter survives in the newly generated substance in one way, and the elements in another way. Prime matter survives as just what it is, completely unchanged, a pure potentiality for substantial form. True, prime matter is never without a substantial form (at least that of an element); nonetheless that substantial form never becomes an ingredient of the nature of prime matter. The elements, by way of contrast, do **not** survive as just what they are. **They** do not survive, i.e., **not** with their substantial forms, **not** as the substances that they are. What survives is precisely their **powers**; but as changed into powers which are **a kind of mean**, appropriate to the newly generated substance, changed by reason of an alteration brought about by a conjunction of 1) an interaction among the relevant elements, and 2) the required agent causality of certain other things. Moreover, these mean powers are **sustained in being** by the substantial form of the newly generated substance, and function as the **instruments** through which that substance performs its proper activities. More is said about this below, on pp. 120-126, pp. 131-133, and pp. 137-143.

55

Concluding reflection

20. Patet igitur ex dictis quod principium aliquomodo est in plus quam causa, et causa in plus quam elementum; et hoc est quod dicit Commentator in V *Metaphysicae*. [12]

It is clear, therefore, from the things which have been said, that "principle" applies in some way to more things than does "cause," and "cause" to more things than does "element." And this is what the Commentator says in his comments on book five of the *Metaphysics*.

In 20., Aquinas reflects briefly on what he has said about principle (taken commonly) and cause and element; and notes that "principle" has a meaning which is more universal than that of "cause," and "cause" than that of "element." A cause is a kind of principle, for what "principle" means is part of what "cause" means. And an element is a kind of cause, for what "cause" means is part of what "element" means. And so, what "principle" means is also part of what "element" means. Every element is a cause and a principle. Every cause is a principle. But there are principles which are neither causes nor elements; and causes which are not elements.

---

[12] Elementum enim non dicitur de causis extrinsecis, sed dicitur de intrinsecis, et dignius de materia. Principium autem est dignius dici de causis extrinsecis, et causa est maior principio in hoc. Principum etiam est quasi universalius causa, cum dicatur principium de principiis transmutationis et de quatuor causis. (Averroes, *Metaph. V*, c. 3, com. 4, fol. 50a, 11.49 ss.). -- From Mattingly, *op. cit.*, p. (-25-).

56

Chapter four
Relations among the four causes

In chapter four, St. Thomas points out many things about the four causes: the same thing can have several causes; the same thing can be the cause of contraries; the same thing can be both cause and effect in relation to a same other thing; the final cause is the cause of causes; matter is prior to form in generation and in time; form is prior to matter in substance and in completed existence; the agent is prior to the end in generation and in time; the end is prior to the agent in substance and in completed existence; matter and agent are causes which are prior in generation; form and end are causes which are prior in perfection; absolute necessity proceeds from causes which are prior in generation, that is from matter and agent; conditional necessity proceeds from causes which are posterior in generation, that is from form and end; the form, the agent and the end can coincide in some ways, because each has a measure of actuality; matter, however, cannot coincide with any of the other causes, because matter is potentiality. His comments are aimed at making clear a number of things which follow from the fact that the causes are **four** in number, and that each of the four is just what it is, i.e., matter: potentiality; form: actuality; agent: the active or working cause of change; end: what is intended by the agent.

An effect can have more than one cause; and a cause, more than one effect

21.   Viso igitur quod quatuor sunt causarum genera, sciendum est quod non est impossibile ut idem habeat plures causas, ut idolum cuius causa est cuprum et artifex, sed artifex ut efficiens, cuprum ut materia. Non est etiam impossibile ut idem sit causa contrariorum, sicut gubernator est causa salutis navis et submersionis; sed huius per absentiam, illius per praesentiam.

Having seen, therefore, that there are four genera of causes, it should be understood that it is not impossible that a same thing have a number of causes; like a statue, the cause of which is the bronze, and the sculptor, but the sculptor as efficient cause, and the bronze as matter. Also, it is not impossible that a same thing be the cause of contraries. The helmsman, for example, is the cause of a ship's safety and of its sinking; of its sinking by his absence, of its safety by his presence.

In **21.**, Aquinas begins by observing that it is not impossible for a same thing to have more than one cause. Indeed, one should add, it is **necessary** for a same thing to have more than one cause. The example of Aquinas is an artifact, namely a statue, of which the bronze is the material cause, and the sculptor the efficient cause. But a natural thing, too, must have more than one cause. For example, the sperm and the ovum are the material cause of the newly conceived dog; and the parents, Lassie and King, are the efficient cause. But a thing cannot have a material cause without also having a formal cause; nor can it have an efficient cause without having a final cause. The formal cause, the canine soul (in this example), differentiates the *terminus ad quem* from the matter, i.e., the sperm and the ovum in this example, as that matter was found in the *terminus a quo*. And the final cause, a newly conceived dog, moves Lassie and King to exercise their agent causality. Without all four causes, it is not possible for an effect to come to be. Matter cannot receive form except from an appropriate agent. And the agent cannot give form to matter without the intended end.

Moreover, continues Aquinas, neither is it impossible for a same thing to be the cause of more than one effect, e.g., of contraries. The helmsman, exemplifies Aquinas, is the cause of the **safety** of his ship, by being present at his post and skillfully guiding the ship through a treacherously difficult and narrow passage. But he can also be the cause of the **sinking** of his ship -- by leaving his post and letting the wind and the churning waters dash the ship against a rocky reef. Not only can a same thing be the cause of contrary effects, like safety and sinking, it can also be the cause of a plurality of effects which are not contraries. Fire, for example, can melt ice, boil water, and make one comfortable on a cold day; water can slake one's thirst, revive a drooping plant, cool the air on a hot and humid day. The sun can illuminate the air, and warm it as well. Indeed, it is not possible for a same thing not to have more than one effect, simply because of the variety of affectable things within the reach of its causality -- one fire, close enough to ice to melt it, close enough to water to bring it to a boil, close enough to a cold person to make him comfortably warm.

An agent can be both cause and effect in relation to an end; so too matter in relation to form

22. Sciendum est etiam quod possibile est ut idem sit causa et causatum respectu eiusdem, sed diversimode; ut deambulatio est causa sanitatis ut efficiens, sed sanitas est causa deambulationis ut finis; deambulatio enim est aliquando propter sanitatem. Et etiam corpus est materia animae, anima vero est forma corporis.

Efficiens enim dicitur causa respectu finis, cum finis non sit in actu nisi per operationem agentis; sed finis dicitur causa efficientis, cum non operetur nisi per intentionem finis. Unde efficiens est causa illius quod est finis, ut puta deambulatio ut sit sanitas, non tamen facit finem esse finem, et ideo non est causa causalitatis finis, idest non facit finem esse causam finalem; sicut medicus facit sanitatem esse in actu, non tamen facit quod sanitas sit finis. Finis autem non est causa illius quod est efficiens, sed est causa ut efficiens sit efficiens. Sanitas enim non facit medicum esse medicum, et dico sanitatem quae fit operante medico, sed facit ut medicus sit efficiens. Unde finis est causa causalitatis efficientis, quia facit efficiens esse efficiens; et similiter facit materiam esse materiam, et formam esse formam, cum materia non suscipiat formam nisi propter finem, et forma non perficiat materiam nisi propter finem. Unde dicitur quod finis est causa causarum, quia est causa causalitatis in omnibus causis.

Materia etiam dicitur causa formae, inquantum forma non est nisi in materia; et similiter forma est causa materiae, inquantum materia non habet esse in actu nisi per formam. Materia enim et forma dicuntur relative ad invicem, ut dicitur in *II Physicorum*. [13] Dicuntur enim ad compositum sicut partes ad totum, et simplex ad compositum.

It should be understood, also, that it is possible for a same thing to be both a cause and the thing caused, with respect to a same thing, but in diverse ways. Walking, for example, is the cause of health as an efficient cause, but health is the cause of walking as an end. For a walk is sometimes taken for the sake of health. Also, the body is the matter of the soul, whereas the soul is the form of the body.

For the efficient cause is said to be a cause with respect to the end, since the end does not become something actual except through the work of the agent; whereas the end is said to be the cause of the efficient cause, since the efficient cause does not do its work except through the intention of the end. Whence the efficient cause is the cause of that which is the end; walking for example, of health. But the efficient cause does not make the end be the end. It is therefore not the cause of the causality of the end; that is, it does not make the end be the final cause. The medical doctor, for example, makes health actually be, but he does not make health be the end. The end, moreover, is not the cause of that which is the efficient cause, but rather is the cause of the fact that the efficient cause is an efficient cause. For health does not make the medical doctor be a medical doctor (I am speaking of the health which comes about by the work of the medical doctor); rather, health makes the medical doctor be an efficient cause. Whence the end is the cause of the causality of the efficient cause, because it makes the efficient cause be an efficient cause. And similarly, the end makes the matter be the matter, and the form be the form, since the matter does not acquire a form except on account of the end, and the form does not perfect the matter except on account of the end. Whence it is said that the end is the cause of causes, because it is the cause of the causality in all the causes.

Likewise, matter is said to be the cause of the form, inasmuch as the form does not exist except in matter; and similarly the form is the cause of matter, inasmuch as matter does not have actual existence except through the form. For matter and form are related to one another as mutual causes, as is said in book

---

[13] Aristotle, *Physics*, Bk. II, ch. 2, 194 b 9-10.

two of the *Physics;* and to the composite, as parts to a whole, and as the simple to the composed.

In **22.**, Aquinas points out that it is possible for a same thing to be both cause and effect in relation to a same other thing, so long as it is cause with respect to one kind of causality and effect with respect to another kind of causality. This would not be possible with respect to the same kind of causality. Clearly, it would not be possible for a thing to be the efficient cause of its own efficient cause; for example, a son could not possibly be the father of his own father. Similarly, it would not be possible for a thing to be the material cause of its own material cause; for example, a statue could not possibly be the matter out of which its own matter (e.g., marble) was made.

But this **is** possible with respect to a different kind of causality. Walking, exemplifies Aquinas, is both the cause of, and caused by, health. Or, perhaps more clearly, walking is the cause of health, and health is the cause of walking. But, whereas walking is the **efficient** cause of health, health is **not** the efficient cause of walking. It is rather the **final** cause of walking. Similarly, continues Aquinas, the body is both the cause of, and caused by, the soul. Or, the body is the cause of the soul, and the soul is the cause of the body. But, whereas the body is the matter in which the soul exists, the soul is not the matter in which the body exists. It is rather the form which vivifies the body. Whereas the body is cause **as matter**, the soul is cause **as form**. And this does not mean that the body is the matter of the soul, as though it were a part of the nature of the soul. Nor does it mean that the soul is the form of the body, as though it were a part of the nature of the body. Rather, the body and the soul are the matter and the form, respectively, of the nature of the composite, i.e., of the whole which is the living thing, e.g., a human being.

Moreover, the reciprocal or mutual causal connection between the efficient cause and the final cause must be properly understood. The efficient cause is the cause of **the thing** which is the end, e.g., walking is the cause of **health**.

But the efficient cause does not cause the end to be the end. That is, it is not the cause of the causality of the end. The medical doctor, for example, causes the health which is the end, but he does not cause the health to be the end. Further, the end is not the cause of the thing which is the efficient cause; it is rather the cause of the fact that the thing which is the efficient cause is the efficient cause. For example, health does not cause the medical doctor to be a medical doctor -- Aquinas is speaking here explicitly of the health which comes about by the efforts of the medical doctor; rather, health causes the medical doctor to be an efficient cause. And so, the end is the cause of the causality of the efficient cause, inasmuch as it makes the thing which is the efficient cause to be precisely that, i.e., the efficient cause. And beyond that, the end makes the matter (material cause) to be the material cause, and the form (formal cause) to be the formal cause. And this is so because the matter acquires the form only for the sake of the end, just as the form perfects the matter only for the sake of the end. This is why it is said that the end is the cause of causes, meaning that the final cause causes the causality in all the causes, i.e, in the other three causes.

But what, one might ask, causes the causality of the end? What is it that makes the end to be the end? The efficient cause does not make the end to be the end, as already noted. And since that is so, neither does the matter cause the causality of the end; and neither does the form; since it is the end which causes **their** causality. Shall we say, then, that the causality of the end is an **uncaused** causality? This seems the right thing to say. For, from one point of view, there are no other causes besides the other three, which could possibly cause the causality of the end; and the other three cannot, as just noted. And, from another point of view, the final cause would be the cause of its own causality, by circularity. That is, the end would cause the agent to be the agent, which would cause the matter to be the matter, which would cause the form to be the form. And the form would have to cause the end to be the end; for there is no other kind of cause. But nothing can be the cause of its own causality.

23. Sed quia omnis causa, inquantum est causa, naturaliter prior est causato, sciendum est quod prius dicitur duobus modis, ut dicit Aristoteles in XVI *De Animalibus*, [14] per quorum diversitatem potest aliquid dici prius et posterius respectu eiusdem et causa causatum. Dicitur enim aliquid prius altero generatione et tempore, et iterum in substantia et complementum. Cum ergo operatio naturae procedat ab imperfecto ad perfectum et ab incompleto ad completum, imperfectum est prius perfecto secundum generationem et tempus, sed perfectum est prius imperfecto substantia; sicut potest dici quod vir est ante puerum in substantia et complemento, sed puer est ante virum in generatione et tempore. Sed, licet in rebus generabilibus imperfectum sit prius perfecto et potentia prior actu, considerando in aliquo eodem quod prius est imperfectum quam perfectum et in potentia quam in actu, simpliciter tamen loquendo oportet actum et perfectum prius esse; quia quod reducit potentiam ad actum, actu est et quod perficit imperfectum, perfectum est. Materia quidem est prior forma generatione et tempore; prius enim est cui advenit, quam quod advenit. Sed forma est prior materia in substantia et completo esse, quia materia non habet esse completum nisi per formam. Similiter efficiens est prius fine generatione et tempore, cum ab efficiente fiat motus ad finem; sed finis est prior efficiente inquantum est efficiens in substantia et complemento, cum actio efficientis non compleatur nisi per finem. Igitur istae duae causae, scilicet materia et efficiens, sunt prius per viam generationis; sed forma et finis sunt prius per viam perfectionis.

Every cause, insofar as it is a cause, is naturally prior to what is caused. This is why it should be understood that "prior" is said in two ways, as Aristotle says in book sixteen of *On Animals*. And it is through the diversity of these two ways that something can be said to be prior and posterior in relation to a same thing,

---

[14]   Aristotle, *De Gen. Animal.*, Bk. II, ch. 6, 742 a 19-22. -- As Pauson (*op. cit.*, p. 69) points out, Aquinas' reference to **chapter XVI** indicates that he was using the Arab-Latin translation, usually entitled *De Animalibus*, in which the order of the books is: *De Historiis Animalium*, I-X; *De Partibus Animalium*, XI-XIV; and *De Generatione Animalium*, XV- XIX.

and a cause can be said to be something caused. For a thing is said to be prior to another in generation and time, and again in substance and completeness. Since, therefore, the operation of nature proceeds from the imperfect to the perfect and from the incomplete to the complete, the imperfect is prior to the perfect in generation and time, but the perfect is prior to the imperfect in substance. It can be said, for example, that the man is before the boy in substance and completeness, whereas the boy is before the man in generation and time. But, although in generable things the imperfect is prior to the perfect, and potency is prior to act (considering that *in one and the same thing* the prior is imperfect rather than perfect, and in potency rather than in act); nonetheless, *absolutely speaking,* it is necessary that what is in act and perfect be prior; because what brings potency to act is itself in act, and what perfects the imperfect is itself perfect. Matter, indeed, is prior to form in generation and time; for that to which something comes, is prior to that which comes to it. But form is prior to matter in substance and completeness of existence, because matter has completeness of existence only through form. Similarly, the efficient cause is prior to the end in generation and time, because the motion toward the end comes from the efficient cause. But the end is prior to the efficient cause, insofar as it is the efficient cause, in substance and completeness, since the action of the efficient cause is completed only through the end. These two causes, therefore, namely the matter and the efficient cause, are prior in the way of generation; but the form and the end are prior in the way of perfection.

In **23.**, St. Thomas begins by observing that although a cause, as cause, is prior by nature to what it causes; nonetheless, because the word "prior" has two different uses, one and the same thing can be both prior and posterior, and both cause and effect, in relation to a same other thing. The two uses of the word "prior" are these: 1) with respect to generation and time, which can be taken to mean: with respect to **coming into existence**, and 2) with respect to substance and completeness, which can be taken to mean: with respect to **existence**. The operation of nature, it is easy to observe, moves from what is imperfect and incomplete to what is perfect and complete. To speak of the operation of nature is to speak of generation; and generation takes time, i.e., it begins and ends. For example, the boy comes to be before the man comes to be; and so, the boy is prior to the man with respect to generation and time. But the man is perfect and complete in a way in which the boy is not; and so, the man is prior to the boy with respect to human substance and completeness of being.

In **one and the same generable thing,** continues Aquinas, the imperfect and potential is observed to be prior to the perfect and actual. Indeed, this is how it must be. But, absolutely speaking, i.e., outside the context of one and the same generable thing, what is perfect and in act is prior to what is imperfect and in potency. And this is so because only what is perfect and actual can bring what is imperfect and potential to a state of perfection and actuality. Matter, thus, in the context of one and the same generable thing, is prior to form with respect to generation and time; for form comes to matter, and that to which something comes is already in existence, i.e., prior in time to that which comes to it. But, the form is prior to matter in substance and completeness of existence; that is, matter acquires completeness of existence only through the form.

Similarly, continues Aquinas, the efficient cause is prior to the end in generation and time; that is, the motion toward the end comes from the efficient cause which is already in operation, temporally before the end comes into existence. But, the end is prior to the efficient cause in substance and completeness of existence. This must be properly understood. It is not being said that the completely existing end is prior, as actually existing, to the action of the efficient cause. The statue which the sculptor is about to make, for example, does not actually exist before the sculptor begins to make it. For this would be to say that the statue exists before it exists; which is clearly impossible. What **is** being said is that the completion of the action of the efficient cause is found only in the actually existing statue; that is, that the action of the efficient cause continues until the end has begun to exist. And so, the actual existence of the end is the completion of the efficient causality of the agent; just as the actual existence of the form is the completion of the material causality of the matter.

Why this concern, one might ask, to point out that the matter and the efficient cause are prior in generation and time, whereas the form and the end are prior in substance and perfection (or completeness of existence)? The answer, it appears, is provided in **24.** (to which we now turn), where Aquinas reflects on the kinds of necessity found in the physical world, i.e., absolute necessity and conditional necessity.

Absolute necessity and conditional necessity

24. Et notandum quod duplex est necessitas, scilicet absoluta et conditionalis. Necessitas quidem absoluta est, quae procedit a causis prioribus in via generationis, quae sunt materia et efficiens; sicut necessitas mortis quae provenit ex materia, scilicet ex dispositione contrariorum componentium; et haec dicitur absoluta, quia non habet impedimentum. Haec etiam dicitur necessitas materiae. Necessitas autem conditionalis procedit a causis posterioribus in generatione, scilicet a forma et fine; sicut dicimus quod necessarium est esse conceptionem, si debeat generari homo. Et ista dicitur conditionalis, quia hanc mulierem concipere non est necessarium simpliciter, sed sub hac conditione, scilicet si debeat generari homo. Et haec dicitur necessitas finis.

It should be noted that necessity is of two sorts, namely absolute and conditional. Now absolute necessity is the necessity which proceeds from causes which are prior in the way of generation, which are the matter and the efficient cause. The necessity of death, for example, derives from matter, i.e., from the disposition of the composing contraries. And this necessity is said to be absolute, because it has no impediment. It is also called the necessity of matter. Conditional necessity, however, proceeds from causes which are posterior in generation, namely from the form and the end. We say, for example, that conception is necessary, if a man is to be generated. And this necessity is said to be conditional, because it is not simply necessary that this woman conceive, but under this condition, namely if a man is to be generated. And this necessity is called the necessity of the end.

In **24.**, Aquinas points out that there are two kinds of necessity. There is 1) **absolute** necessity when something **must** come to be because something else **has preceded** -- unless (Aquinas adds elsewhere, as in *In VI Metaph.*, lect 3, n. 1193 and n. 1217) something else is there to prevent it, like a freely acting human agent. There is 2) **conditional** necessity when something **must** come to be because without it something else cannot follow, i.e., if -- indeed **only if** -- that something else is to follow. There is no reason, other than the following of the posterior, why the prior has to come to be. Absolute necessity, he observes, derives from causes which are prior in generation, i.e., from the matter and the agent; but it resides in what is posterior. Conditional necessity derives from causes which are posterior in generation, i.e., from the form and the end; but it resides in what is prior. Given such and such a matter, or such and such an agent, something (i.e., some form or some end) must follow. But, if -- **only if**, hence under a condition -- this form is to come to be, or this end is to be achieved, then there must be (beforehand) such and such a matter, or such and such an agent. But, apart from that condition, there is no need at all for that matter or for that agent to have preceded.

Having noted that absolute necessity derives from causes which are prior in generation, namely matter and agent, Aquinas offers an example of necessity deriving **from matter**, i.e., the necessity of death. Death is absolutely necessary, because of the **disposition** of the **contraries** which compose the body of a living thing, i.e., because of the tendency of the composing contraries to act in a certain way under certain conditions. But he gives **no** example of absolute necessity deriving from the **agent**. Is there a reason for not giving such an example? Similarly, having noted that conditional necessity derives from causes which are posterior in generation, namely form and end, Aquinas offers an example of necessity deriving **from the end**, i.e., the necessity of conception. Conception is conditionally necessary, because of the generation of a man, i.e., if a man is to be generated. But he gives **no** example of necessity deriving from the **form**. Is there a reason for not giving such an example? Can it be that absolute necessity derives somehow from the matter and the agent together? And that conditional necessity derives somehow from the end and the form together?

This might well be the case. Consider that the end of the agent is to act in such a way as to confer a certain sort of form on a certain sort of matter. And so, the end **is** the form. Thus, the necessity which is said to derive from the end, can be said to derive from the form as well. To say: if this **end** is to be achieved, is the same as to say: if this **form** is to come to be. Thus, form and end together are the source of conditional necessity, but not as though the form were one thing and the end another; the form and the end are one and the same thing.

Consider, further, that a certain sort of matter must receive a certain sort of form, when a certain sort of agent is acting on it. And so, although the matter and the agent are not the same thing (though the form and the end are the same thing), given such an agent acting on such a matter, such a form must be the result. The necessity, for such a form, which derives from the matter, derives from it only in conjunction with the appropriate agent. The source of absolute necessity is the matter, indeed, but together with, and as being affected by, the agent. -- And so, given such a matter being affected by such an agent, such a form (such an end) **must** follow, out of absolute necessity. And, **if (only if)** such a form (such an end) is to come to be, then such a matter, being affected by such an agent, **must** precede, out of conditional necessity.

The necessity of death

It will be helpful at this point to reflect a bit on Aquinas' **example** of absolute necessity. This may help to make clearer exactly what absolute necessity is. His example, recall, was the necessity of death, a necessity deriving from matter, i.e., from the fact that a living thing is made up of components which are contraries: . . . **sicut necessitas mortis quae provenit ex materia, scilicet ex dispositione contrariorum componentium . . ..** It is quite clear that when Aquinas says "composing **contraries**," he means "composing **elements**." Now, each of the elements has a distinguishing quality or property. Fire is hot; heat is the distinguishing property of fire. Air is dry, water wet, and earth cold. Hot and cold are contraries. Wet and dry are contraries. When the cold and the dry overcome the hot and the wet, death occurs. Life needs the hot and the wet. So that when a living thing is not hot (warm) enough, nor wet (moist) enough, it dies. Hypothermia alone, as well as dehydration alone, can bring on death. The two together can bring on death all the more quickly and certainly. Similarly, when the hot and the wet overcome the cold and the dry, death occurs. Life needs the cold and the dry. So that when a living thing is not cold enough, i.e., when it is too hot; or when it is not dry enough, i.e., when it is too wet, it dies. Hyperthermia (e.g., high fever) alone, as well as hyperhydration (too much water) alone, can bring on death. And the two together can bring on death all the more quickly and certainly.

Furthermore, the elements are intrinsically, and so necessarily, corruptible, because they are composed of prime matter and substantial form. It follows, therefore, that mixed bodies too, i.e., bodies composed of the elements, are intrinsically, and so necessarily, corruptible. For, as Aquinas puts it: . . . **corruptis componentibus, corrumpitur compositum . . .** (*In II Sent.*, d.16, q.1, a.1 ad 3).

Again, it is necessary for a human being, indeed for any living thing, to die, because matter is in potency to another form: . . . **homini . . . convenit**

69

necessitas moriendi, ex hoc scilicet quod materia est in potentia ad aliam formam . . . (*De Malo*, q.5, a.5, ad 13). And matter is in potency to other forms, precisely because it is first in potency to the forms of the elements, i.e., the contraries, which compose the body of a living thing.

Moreover, when one element overpowers another with its distinguishing quality or property, what follows is the corruption of the overpowered one and the generation and/or augment of the overpowering one. It is only when the powers of the elements have been rendered, and continue to be, more or less equal to one another (when they more or less balance one another, or are more or less in a state of equilibrium) that there comes to be, and continues to be, a mixed body, either a living one or a non-living one.

Someone might say that being composed of elements does **not** make corruption (which is death for a living thing) necessary, but only **possible**. It is quite clear that what is composed **can** fall apart. But **must** it fall apart? If something must, it can. But, is it true that if something can, it must? -- By way of response, one must note that the necessity of death, according to Aquinas, derives "from the disposition of the composing contraries." Not simply from the fact that there is a composition, nor even from the fact that the composition is out of contraries (elements). Rather, from the **disposition** (ex dispositione) of the composing contrary elements. And "disposition" means a tendency or inclination to act or behave in a certain way under certain conditions. Under certain conditions, the heat of fire can overcome the cold of earth; and when it does, death occurs. Or the dryness of air can overcome the wetness of water; and when it does, death occurs. Thus the nature or essence of a **living** mixed body, inasmuch as it is composed of elements, is such that it is **necessarily** corruptible, necessarily **capable** of death. And **under certain conditions**, it **does** corrupt, it **does** die. Thus, to speak of the necessity of death, . . . **necessitas mortis** . . . , is to speak of the necessity of the **possibility** of death, and **not** of the actual fact of death. Aquinas puts it clearly and explicitly for the careful reader: . . . sicut dicimus animal **necesse esse** corruptibile [notice: **necessarily** corruptible], quia hoc consequitur eius materiam inquantum ex contrariis componitur . . .   (*In V Metaph.*, lect. 6, n. 833).

Again, someone might ask why Aquinas says here that absolute necessity **has no impediment.**   Elsewhere he observes that an effect follows necessarily because its cause has preceded, **unless there is an impediment:**   . . . necesse est, . . . **causa posita,** sequi effectum, **nisi sit impedimentum** . . . (*In VI Metaph.*, lect. 3, n. 1193).   --   By way of response, one must note that there is no possibility of an impediment to the necessity of the possibility of death for a living mixed body **once constituted in being,** for such a body has such a necessity by its very essence, inasmuch as it is composed out of contraries (elements). And its being composed out of contraries is the **causa posita.** But there is the possibiliy of an impediment to the **actual** death, at some given time, of a living mixed body, inasmuch as there are any number of agent causes in the physical world which can at a given time prevent its death: . . . **unde. . . [etiam causis] positis, adhuc potest impediri effectus, propter occursum . . agentis . . ..** (*In VI Metaph.*, lect. 3, n. 1191).

Three of the causes -- form, end, agent -- can coincide with one another; the fourth, i.e., matter, cannot coincide with any of the other three

25. Et est sciendum quod tres causae possunt incidere in unum, scilicet forma, finis et efficiens, sicut patet in generatione ignis. Ignis enim generat ignem, ergo ignis est causa efficiens inquantum generat; et iterum ignis est forma inquantum facit esse actu quod prius erat potentia; et iterum est finis inquantum est intentus ab agente, et inquantum terminatur ad ipsum operatio agentis.

Sed duplex est finis, scilicet finis generationis et finis rei generatae, sicut patet in generatione cultelli; forma enim cultelli est finis generationis, sed incidere quod est operatio cultelli, est finis ipsius generati, scilicet cultelli.

Finis autem generationis coincidit cum duabus dictis causis aliquando, scilicet quando fit generatio a simili in specie; sicut homo generat hominem, et oliva olivam, quod non potest intellegi de fine rei generatae. Sciendum tamen est quod finis incidit cum forma in idem numero, quia illud idem numero quod est forma generati, est finis generationis. Sed cum efficiente non incidit in idem numero, sed in idem specie. Impossibile enim est ut faciens et factum sint idem numero, sed possunt esse idem specie; ut quando homo generat hominem, homo generans et generatus sunt diversi numero, sed idem specie.

Materia autem non coincidit cum aliis, quia materia ex eo quod est ens in potentia, habet rationem imperfecti; sed aliae causae, cum sint actu, habent rationem perfecti; perfectum autem et imperfectum non coincidunt in idem.

It should be understood that three of the causes -- namely the form, the end, and the efficient cause -- can coincide in a thing in some way one, as is clear in the generation of fire. For fire generates fire. And so, fire is the efficient cause, insofar as it generates. Fire is also the form, insofar as it makes that which was formerly in potency to be in act. It is also the end, insofar as it is intended by the agent, and insofar as the operation of the agent terminates in it.

But there are two sorts of end, namely the end of generation, and the end of the generated thing, as is clear in the generation of a knife. For the form of the knife is the end of generation; but cutting, which is what the knife does, is the end of the generated thing, namely of the knife.

At times the end of generation coincides with the other two mentioned causes [namely the form and the efficient cause]. This happens when generation takes place from a thing which is alike in species; as when a man generates a man, and an olive tree an olive tree. But this cannot be the case with respect to the end of the generated thing. It should be understood, nonetheless, that the end [of generation] coincides with the form, in a thing one in number, because the numerically one thing which is the form of the generated thing is the end of generation. But the end [of generation] does not coincide with the efficient cause in a thing the same in number; rather in a thing the same in species. For it is impossible for the maker and the thing made to be the same in number, but they can be the same in species. When a man generates a man, for example, the man generating and the man generated are diverse in number, but the same in species.

Matter, however, does not coincide with the others; because matter, by the fact that it is a being in potency, has the nature of something imperfect, whereas the other causes, since they are in act, have the nature of something perfect. The perfect and the imperfect do not coincide in a same thing.

In **25.**, Aquinas points out that something one and the same (one and the same, in some sense or other) can be the agent and the end and the form -- all three. He begins with the example of the generation of fire. Fire generates fire. And so, as generating, fire is the efficient cause. And as generated, fire is both the form and the end. Inasmuch, as generated, it makes **what can be** on fire, i.e., some combustible material, **to be actually** on fire, it is the form. Inasmuch, as generated, it is also what is intended by the agent, and is that in which the work of the agent is terminated, it is the end.

Having given the example of fire, Aquinas notes next that there are two kinds of end: 1) the end of the process of generation, and 2) the end of the thing which has been generated. To clarify, he uses the production of a knife as an example. The form of the knife is the end of the process of generation, i.e., of the process of the production of the knife; whereas cutting is the end of the thing generated, i.e., of the knife itself. He makes this distinction in order to be able to point out that when something the same is the agent and the form and end, all three; it is the end in the sense of the end of the process of generation, and only when like is generated by like, as man by man, or an olive tree by an olive tree, or fire by fire. This cannot happen when like is not generated by like, as in the case of a knife by the knife maker. Clearly, the end of the process of generation, e.g., the form which is the sharpness of the blade of the knife, cannot in any way be the same as the knife maker himself. Neither can this happen when the end is the end of the generated thing. The cutting to be done by the knife, for example, cannot in any way be the same as the knife maker himself.

Moreover, continues Aquinas, the end of generation is the same in number as the form, i.e., the very thing which is the form of the generated thing is the same, numerically the same, as the end of generation. But, the end of generation is not the same, not numerically the same, as the efficient cause. Indeed, this is not possible; the maker, for example, cannot be numerically identical with the thing made. They can, however, be identical in species, as when a man generates a man. The man generating and the man generated are diverse in number, emphasizes Aquinas, but the same in species.

Lastly, concludes Aquinas, matter cannot coincide with any of the other three causes, simply because matter has the nature of something imperfect; it is a being in potency. The agent, the form, and the end, by way of difference, are beings in act, and so have the nature of something perfect. It is impossible for the perfect and the imperfect to coincide so as to be a same thing. Or, one and the same thing cannot be both perfect and imperfect in the same respect. Or, that which can be, cannot be that which is; just as that which is not, cannot be that which is.

Chapter five
Divisions within each of the four causes

In chapter five, St. Thomas points out, and makes clear, a number of ways in which each of the four kinds of cause -- efficient, material, formal, final -- can be divided. A cause can be a cause in a prior sense or in a posterior sense; a cause can be remote or proximate, *per se* or *per accidens*, simple or composite, actual or potential, universal or singular. His comments are aimed at making clear how effects can be acceptably explained by their causes. That is, not just any cause can be used to explain an effect; a cause ought to be proportioned to its effect. For example, actual effects are to be explained by actual causes, universal effects by universal causes, singular effects by singular causes. Above all, every explanatory attempt should seek the first cause -- ". . . semper debemus reducere quaestionem ad primam causam . . . ". An explanation which does not include the first cause is not a complete explanation; for one must still ask: Why? This is so because a cause which is not a first cause is also an effect, and as an effect, needs to be explained.

Prior causes and posterior causes

> 26. Viso igitur quod sunt quatuor causae, scilicet efficiens, materialis, formalis et finalis, sciendum est quod quaelibet istarum causarum dividitur multis modis. Dicitur enim aliquid causa per prius et aliquid per posterius, sicut dicimus quod ars et medicus sunt causa sanitatis, sed ars est causa per prius, medicus per posterius; et similiter in causa formali et in aliis causis. Et nota quod semper debemus reducere quaestionem ad primam causam, ut si quaeratur: quare iste est sanus? respondendum est: quia medicus sanavit; et iterum: quare medicus sanavit? propter artem sanandi quam habet.

> Having seen therefore that there are four causes, namely efficient, material, formal and final, it should be understood that each of these causes is divided in many ways. For some

things are called causes in a prior sense, others in a posterior sense. We say, for example, that art and the medical doctor are causes of health; but art in a prior sense, and the medical doctor in a posterior sense. And similarly with respect to the formal cause, and the other causes. Note, too, that we should always take a question all the way back to the first cause. If it be asked, for example, "Why is this person healthy "? one should answer, "Because the medical doctor has restored him to health." And, asking further, "Why did the medical doctor restore him to health?" one would answer, "Because of the art of healing which he has."

Aquinas begins **26.** by observing that each of the four causes can be divided in a number of ways. Having made that observation, he points out a first division, that into causes in a prior sense and causes in a posterior sense. Then he uses the efficient cause as an example. Both art and the medical doctor are efficient causes of health; but the medical doctor in a posterior sense, he notes, and art in a prior sense. Aquinas does not make explicit, however, the sense of "prior" and "posterior" which he has in mind. Does he mean prior and posterior **in time? in power? in universality?** In some other sense? In what sense of "prior" is the art of healing, which the medical doctor has, a cause which is **prior** to the medical doctor himself? It would seem that there is no priority here, since the medical doctor is a medical doctor precisely by reason of the art of healing which is **in him.** Moreover, as in him, the art of healing seems to be a formal cause rather than an efficient cause. But, if it is an efficient cause, then it is something **in the medical doctor,** i.e., that **in the medical doctor** by which he can perform as a medical doctor; and so, again, not prior to him.

Remote causes and proximate causes: the same as prior causes and posterior causes, respectively

27.   Sciendum est etiam quod idem est dictu causa propinqua quod causa posterior, et causa remota quod causa prior. Unde ista duae divisiones: causarum alia per prius, alia per posterius,

et causarum alia remota, alia propinqua, idem significant. Hoc autem observandum est quod semper illud quod universalius est, causa remota dicitur; quod autem specialius, causa propinqua; sicut dicimus quod forma hominis propinqua est sua definitio, scilicet animal rationale mortale; sed animal est magis remota et iterum substantia remotior. Omnia enim superiora sunt formae inferiorum. Et similiter materia idoli propinqua est cuprum, sed remota est metallum, et iterum remotior corpus.

It should be understood that to speak of a proximate cause is the same as to speak of a posterior cause, and of a remote cause the same as of a prior cause. Whence these two divisions: some causes are prior, others posterior; some causes are remote, others proximate, come to the same thing. Moreover, it should be observed that the cause which is more universal is always called the remote cause, whereas the one which is more particular, the proximate cause; as when we say that the proximate form of man is his definition, namely rational mortal animal; whereas animal is more remote, and substance more remote still. For all the superiors are forms of the inferiors. Similarly, the proximate matter of a statue is bronze, whereas a remote matter is metal, and a more remote matter still is body.

In 27., Aquinas moves on to a second division, that into remote causes and proximate causes. He begins by pointing out that proximate causes are the same as the posterior causes considered in 26., and remote causes the same as the prior causes of 26.. And so, the first two divisions of cause come to the same thing.

Then he explains that the cause which is more universal is always called the remote cause. And having already observed that a remote cause is the same as a prior cause, Aquinas has in effect answered the question raised above (p. 76) about exactly what he means by "prior" and "posterior." It is clear now that he means prior and posterior in **universality**. His examples confirm this: **substance,** in the realm of the *formal* cause (with respect to man), is more universal than **animal**, which is in turn more universal than rational mortal animal; **body,** in the realm of the *material* cause (with respect to statue), is more universal than **metal,** which is in turn more universal than **bronze.** Similarly, one might add, **one who works by an art which is in him (artifex),** in the realm of the *efficient* cause (of health), is more universal than **medical doctor.** Which suggests that Aquinas might better have said "artifex" than "ars." **Artifex** -- but not **ars** -- is related to **medicus** as the more universal (hence, as the prior or the more remote) to the more particular or less universal (hence, as the posterior or the more proximate). A **medicus** is a kind of **artifex,** but not a kind of **ars.**[15]

Having given **ars** and **medicus,** in **26.,** as examples of efficient causes related as the prior to the posterior, Aquinas had added, ". . . et similiter in causa formali et in aliis causis. . .". In **27.,** he gave an example of formal causes related as the prior to the posterior, namely **substantia, animal,** and **animal rationale mortale;** and of material causes similarly related, namely **corpus, metallum,** and **cuprum.** He did not give an example of **final** causes so related. For the sake of a kind of completeness, the following example might be acceptable, namely **qualitas, dispositio, sanitas,** moving from the prior to the posterior, as the goal or final cause of the work of the medical doctor. And as an example of form, or formal cause, in the sense of **forma partis,** one might suggest **forma substantialis, anima, anima rationalis,** moving from the prior to the posterior, as the formal cause of man.

Semper debemus reducere quaestionem ad primam causam

It is not wholly clear what Aquinas means by saying that "we should always take a question all the way back to the first cause" (p. 69, **26.**); though it is clear **why** one should do this, namely to have a **complete explanation.** For a cause which is not a first cause is also an effect, and as an effect, needs to be explained -- as was said above (p. 69).

---

[15]   See Pauson, *op. cit.,* footnote 1, pp. 98-99.

On first reading, it seems he has in mind a series of **different things,** each of which is **both** the same kind of cause -- either efficient, or formal, or final, or material, depending on the sort of explanation being given -- **and** is more universal than its predecessor in the scope of its causal power, so that the first cause is a thing with the most universal possible causal scope. But, a consideration of his examples seems to indicate something different. As Aquinas' examples move from the proximate (posterior, less universal) cause to the remote (prior, more universal) cause, one sees that the series is **not** a series of **different things** at all, but rather that **one and the same thing** is being designated at different levels of universality. Bronze, which is the proximate material cause of the statue, can be called metal and body. And it is not the case that metal is the material cause of bronze, and body the material cause of metal, in the same sense in which bronze is the material cause of the statue. Rather, body and metal and bronze -- all three -- are the one material cause of the statue. They are not three different material causes in series; they are the same material cause, though differently described, i.e., body describes the material cause in a more universal way than metal does, and metal in turn in a more universal way than bronze does.

The same thing is the case in Aquinas' example of **substantia, animal** and **animal rationale mortale** as the formal causes (in the sense of **forma totius**) of man. The same thing is also the case in the example of **artifex** and **medicus** as the efficient causes of health; in the example of **qualitas, dispositio,** and **sanitas** as the final causes of the work of the medical doctor; and in the example of **forma substantialis, anima,** and **anima rationalis** as the formal causes (in the sense of **forma partis**) of man. In all these examples, it is quite clear that the universals, the more and the lesser as well, are **predicable** universals, i.e., universals **in praedicando,** and not **causal** universals, i.e., not universals **in causando.** And, on first reading, one would have expected them to be just that, i.e., universals **in causando.**

In what sense, if any -- one might ask -- do more universal **predicable** universals serve to complete the explanation given by less universal predicable universals? That is, what is more complete about saying that metal is the material cause of the statue than saying that bronze is; and what is more complete still about saying that body is the material cause of the statue than saying that metal is? Metal, as was said above, is not that out of which bronze is made, in the sense in which the statue is made out of bronze. Nor is body that out of which metal is made, in that same sense. Rather, the **concept** of metal is a material component of the **concept** of bronze, and the **concept** of body is a material component of the **concept** of metal -- material component in the sense of a concept which is open to, potential to, specification by a differentiating concept. The concept of body is open to being specified by a differentiating concept which, when added to the concept of body, provides the concept of metal. Similarly, the concept of metal is open to being specified by a differentiating concept which, when added to the concept of metal, provides the concept of bronze.

If one goes the other way now, i.e., from the less universal to the more universal, beginning with the question, "What is the material cause of the statue?" one will be able to see how a more universal **predicable** universal completes the explanation given by a less universal one. The completion amounts to **clarification**, by way of **explicit additions** of superior genera and their differences. Having answered that bronze is the material cause of the statue, one then asks, "What exactly is bronze?" And one answers that bronze is a kind of metal, metal being a genus of bronze. Then one asks, "What is metal?" One answers that metal is a kind of body, body being another, and more universal, genus of bronze. Then, "What **kind** of metal is bronze?" The answer here will provide the specific difference of bronze. Then, "What is a body?" The answer, "A body is a kind of substance," provides the genus of body. Then, "What **kind** of body is metal?" The answer here will provide the specific difference of metal. -- One can see that

80

the movement here is a movement up the Tree of Porphyry; and that when one has come to the top of the tree, one has a **complete** answer, i.e., an **explicitly clarified answer**, to the question, "What is bronze?" which is also a complete answer, i.e., an explicitly clarified answer, to the question, "What is the statue made out of?" or, "What is the material cause of the statue?" One has given an explicitly clarified account of the nature of bronze.

Now, there is another way to answer the question, "What is the material cause of the statue?" or, "What is the statue made out of?" a way which asks for material causes of material causes, rather than asking for more universal predicable universals whose function is to clarify. The material cause of the statue is bronze, or the statue is made out of bronze. Bronze is made out of copper (Cn) and tin (Sn). Copper (tin, too) is one of the elements, and an atom of copper (of tin, too) is made out of neutrons, protons, and electrons. And these in turn are made ultimately out of quarks. And here, in quarks, we have come -- at least as far as our present knowledge takes us -- to the **first** material components of physical things. If the quark is, indeed, the **first** material component, the question, "What is a quark?" will be answered by saying that it is something made out of **prime matter** and a **substantial form** of a certain sort, to be described in terms of a reference to what a quark does.

Causes *per se* and causes *per accidens*

> 28. **Item causarum alia est per se, alia per accidens. Causa per se dicitur, quae est causa alicuius rei inquantum huiusmodi; sicut aedificator est causa domus et lignum materia scamni. Causa per accidens dicitur illa quae accidit causae per se, sicut cum dicimus quod grammaticus aedificat. Grammaticus enim dicitur causa aedificationis per accidens, non enim inquantum grammaticus, sed inquantum aedificatori accidit quod sit grammaticus. Et similiter est in aliis causis.**

> **Again, some causes are causes because of themselves (per se), and others are causes because of something which has happened**

to them (per accidens). A cause is said to be a cause *per se* when it, precisely as such, is a cause of something. For example, a builder [precisely as such, i.e., as a builder] is the cause of a house, and the wood [precisely as such, i.e., as wood] is the matter of the bench. A cause is said to be a cause *per accidens* when it happens to be conjoined to that which is a cause *per se,* as when we say that the grammarian builds. The grammarian is said to be the cause of the building *per accidens,* i.e., not inasmuch as the grammarian is a grammarian, but inasmuch as it happens to the builder that the builder is a grammarian. And similarly for the other causes.

In **28.**, Aquinas reflects briefly on a third division of causes, that into **per se** causes and **per accidens** causes. A **per se** cause is a cause such that its effect depends on that cause taken precisely as such, i.e., according to what it is. For example, a builder taken precisely as such, that is, according to what he is, i.e., a builder, is the **efficient** cause of the houses he builds. And wood taken precisely as such, that is, according to what it is, i.e., wood, is the **material** cause of the statues which have been made out of wood. A **per accidens** cause, on the other hand, is a cause such that what is said to be its effect can be said to depend on it, but not taken as such -- taken rather according to some conjoined characteristic which it happens to have, and by reason of which it is the **per se** cause of that effect. For example, a medical doctor can be said to be the efficient cause of the houses he builds, but these houses do not depend on the medical doctor taken precisely as such, that is, according to what he is, i.e., a medical doctor. Rather, these houses depend on the medical doctor only, and precisely, because the medical doctor is also, happens to be **(accidit)**, a builder. This man is a man with at least two skills or arts, that of a medical doctor and that of a builder. And there is no reason why one cannot say that the medical doctor is the efficient cause of the houses he builds, so long as he is also a builder, and so long as it is understood that he is the efficient cause precisely as builder, and **not** as medical doctor. -- As another example, this **hot thing**, or this **cold thing**, can be said to be the material cause of the statue which has been made out of it. But the statue does not depend on this hot thing (or on this cold thing), taken as such, that is, according to what each is, i.e., a hot thing or a cold thing. Rather, the statue depends on the hot thing, or the cold thing, precisely because each is also, each happens to be (accidit), wood. This piece of material is a piece of material with at least two features or attributes: 1) that of being wood, and 2) that of being hot (or cold). And there is no reason why one cannot say that this hot thing (or this cold thing) is the material cause of the statue, so long as it is also a piece of wood, and so long as it is understood that it is the material cause precisely as wood, and **not** as hot thing (or cold thing).

One can see quite readily that effects are properly explained only by their **per se** causes; not by their **per accidens** causes. The **per accidens** causes are irrelevant, and possibly countless in number. One can also see that, when one speaks of such-and-such as being the cause of such-and-such other, one always means **per se** cause, even though he does not explicitly say that he means **per se** cause. One can also see that it is important to keep in mind the distinction between **per se** cause and **per accidens** cause, in order to avoid being misled in one's atttempt at an explanation. If one gets drunk on **water** mixed with bourbon on Monday, on **water** mixed with scotch on Tuesday, on **water** mixed with rye whiskey on Wednesday, on **water** mixed with gin on Thursday, on **water** mixed with vodka on Friday, one most be careful not to conclude that it is water which has caused the drunkenness as a **per se** cause.

Simple causes and composite causes

> 29. Item causarum quaedam est simplex, quaedam composita. Simplex causa dicitur quando solum dicitur causa illud quod per se est causa, vel etiam solum illud quod est per accidens; sicut si dicamus aedificatorem esse causam domus, et similiter si dicamus medicum esse causam domus. Composita autem dicitur quando utrumque dicitur causa, ut si dicamus: aedificator medicus est causa domus. Potest etiam dici causa

simplex, secundum quod exponit Avicenna:[16] illud quod sine adiunctione alterius est causa, sicut cuprum idoli -- sine adiunctione enim alterius materiae ex cupro fit idolum -- et sicut dicitur quod medicus facit sanitatem, vel quod ignis calefacit. Composita autem causa dicitur quando oportet plura advenire ad hoc quod sit causa; sicut unus homo non est causa motus navis, sed multi; et sicut unus lapis non est materia domus, sed multi.

Further, some causes are simple, others are composite. A cause is said to be a simple cause when that alone, which is the *per se* cause, is said to be the cause, as if we were to say that the builder is the cause of the house; or that alone which is the *per accidens* cause, as if we were to say that the medical doctor is the cause of the house. A cause is said to be a composite cause when both are said to be the cause, as if we were to say that the *builder-medical doctor* is the cause of the house. -- A cause can also be called a simple cause, according to the account given by Avicenna, when it is such that it is a cause without anything else being added to it; as bronze is the cause of the statue, for the statue is made out of bronze without the addition of any other matter; and as when it is said that the medical doctor brings about health, or that fire heats. A cause is said to be a composite cause, on the other hand, when a number of things must come together in order that there be a cause; one man, for example, is not the cause of the motion of a ship, but many; and one stone is not the matter of a house, but many.

In **29.**, Aquinas considers briefly a fourth division of causes, the division into simple causes and composite causes. This division has been taken in **two** different ways. In the first way, a simple cause is one which is said to be a cause **by itself alone**, whether a *per se* cause by itself alone, or a *per accidens* cause by itself alone. The builder, for example, is the **simple** *per se* cause of the house; and the medical doctor is the **simple** *per accidens* cause of

---

[16]   Avicenna, *"Sufficientia,"* II, 8: . . . simplex est cum opus provenit ex una virtute, ut attrahere et expellere a virtutibus corporalibus. Sed compositum est cuius opus provenit ex multis virtutibus quae sint una in specie, ut multi homines cum movent navem, aut diversam speciem [sc. quae sint diversa in specie], sicut fames quae fit ex virtute activa et sentiente. (Ex. Cod. Paris. Nat. Lat. 6443, fol. 51r). -- From Mattingly, *op. cit.,* p. (-38-).

the house. A cause is a composite cause when **both together** are said to be the cause, i.e., both the *per se* cause and the *per accidens* cause; as when the **builder-medical doctor** is said to be the cause of the house, or of health. Or, as when this **cold thing-piece of wood** is said to be the material cause of the statue; or of the head board of a bed.

The second way of taking this division is a way suggested by Avicenna. A cause is a simple cause, if it is said to be the cause **by itself alone,** but in the sense of **one** thing rather than **many**. There is no need here for many things to come together in order that there be a cause. For example, when a piece of wood suffices as the material cause of a statue, as opposed to the case in which a statue requires, say, wood and bronze and glass and iron, as its multiple material cause. The wood alone is a **simple** material cause; the wood plus bronze plus glass plus iron is a **composite** material cause. In these examples, both the simple cause and the composite cause are *per se* material causes. But both can just as well be *per accidens* material causes. For example, this hot thing (which is also a piece of wood) is a **simple** *per accidens* cause of the statue. And this hot thing (which is also a piece of wood) plus this cold thing (which is also a piece of bronze) plus this very heavy thing (which is also a piece of glass) plus this rusty thing (which is also a piece of iron) is a **composite** *per accidens* cause of the statue. Similarly with respect to the other kinds of cause -- formal and efficient and final; both the simple cause and the composite cause can be either *per se* causes or *per accidens* causes.

Causes in act and causes in potency

> 30. Item causarum quaedam est actu, quaedam potentia. Causa in actu est quae actu causat rem, sicut aedificator cum aedificat, vel cuprum, cum ex eo est idolum. Causa in potentia est quae, licet non causet rem in actu, potest tamen causare, sicut aedificator dum non aedificat. Et sciendum quod loquendo de

causis in actu, necessarium est causam et causatum simul esse,
ita quod si unum sit et alterum. Si enim sit aedificator in actu,
oportet quod aedificet; et si sit aedificatio in actu, oportet quod
sit aedificator in actu. Sed hoc non est necessarium in causis,
quae sunt solum in potentia.

Further still, some causes are causes in act, others are causes in
potency. A cause in act is a cause which is actually causing a
thing; a builder, for example, while he is building, or bronze,
when the statue has been made out of it. A cause in potency is a
cause which, though it is not actually causing a thing, can cause
it; the builder, for example, while he is not building. And it
should be understood that, speaking of causes in act, it is
necessary that the cause and the thing caused exist
simultaneously, in such a way that if one exists so does the
other. For, if there is a builder in act, he must be building; and if
there is building going on in act, there must be a builder in act.
But this is not necessary in the case of causes which are causes
only in potency.

In 30., Aquinas turns to a brief consideration of a fifth division of
causes, the division into causes in act, or actual causes, and causes in potency,
or potential causes. "A cause in act," he writes, "is a cause which is actually
causing a thing." One might object that this is a very unilluminating way to
try to make something clear; or more strongly, that it is an unacceptable
way. For it seems to be saying nothing more than that an actually causing
cause is an actually causing cause. And this contributes nothing at all to
clarification. -- But, if one considers this rightly, one can see that sometimes
we refer to things as causes whether they are actually performing as causes or
not. And it is to this that Aquinas is calling our attention. For example, we
call a sculptor a cause of the statue whether he is actually engaged in
exercising his causality, i.e., actually wielding hammer and chisel, or not.
When he is so engaged, he is said to be a cause in act. When he is not, he is
said to be a cause in potency, meaning that he can, or is able to, be so engaged.
And so, a cause in act is an actually causing cause; a sculptor sculpting, a

builder building, a medical doctor doctoring,   A cause in potency is a cause which is not, but can be, an actually causing cause.

One can see very readily that effects are properly explained only by their **actual** causes.   Potential causes are unacceptable.   To say that this is **now** an effect of something which **can**, but is **not now** causing it, is unacceptable; or at least very misleading.   As Aquinas emphasizes, in the case of causes in act, the cause and the effect must exist simultaneously; if one exists so does the other.   Sunlight is the actual effect **right now** of a simultaneously existing, and **right now** efficiently causing, sun.   The statue is the actual effect **right now** of a simultaneously existing, and **right now** materially causing, bronze. The motion of a physical thing in motion is the actual effect **right now** of a simultaneously existing, and **right now** moving, mover.   This quite clearly, one might like to note, is how Aquinas intends his First Way to be understood.   The **motion** of the thing observed to be in motion -- which (motion) is the point of departure of the First Way -- as well as the **moved movers**, however many there may be -- the existence of which (moved movers) is inferred from the fact of motion -- and the **Unmoved Mover Itself** -- the existence of which is the conclusion of the argument --   must **all of them** exist simultaneously.   This observed motion is the actual effect **right now** of a simultaneously existing, and right now moving, number of moved movers in series, and of a simultaneously existing, and **right now** moving, Unmoved Mover.   If there is a mover in act, it must be moving; and if there is moving going on in act, there must be a mover in act.   This, however, is not necessary in the case of movers which are movers only in potency.   For a mover in potency is a mover which is not, but can be, an actually moving mover.   A mover which is not actually a mover need not, indeed cannot, have an actually, and simultaneously, existing effect.   A cause which is not actually a cause can have, so to say, only an effect which is not actually an effect.   Or, such a cause cannot have an effect which is actually an effect.

31. Sciendum est autem quod causa universalis comparatur causato universali, causa vero singularis comparatur causato singulari; sicut dicimus quod aedificator est causa domus, et hic aedificator huius domus.

Lastly, it should be understood that a universal cause goes with a universal effect, whereas a singular cause goes with a singular effect. We say, for example, that a builder is the cause of a house, and that this builder is the cause of this house.

In 31., Aquinas touches on a sixth division of causes, the division into universal causes and singular causes. A universal cause, he notes, *comparatur*, "goes with," a universal effect, and a singular cause with a singular effect. And though he does not take time to make explicit what he means by the word "comparatur," one can surely take him to have in mind both 1) explanation and 2) definition.

As regards explanation, universal effects are properly explained only by appropriately universal causes, and singular effects by appropriately singular causes.   Whereas a builder is the appropriately universal cause which explains the building of a house; **this** builder is the appropriately singular cause which explains the building of **this** house.   Similarly, whereas wood is the appropriately universal material cause which explains the existence of a statue; **this** wood is the appropriately singular material cause which explains the existence of **this** statue.   Similarly for final and formal causes. -- For more on how to explain effects properly, see above pp. 78-81, the section entitled **Semper debemus reducere quaestionem ad primam causam.**

As regards definition, a universal cause can be defined as a cause with a universal effect; a singular cause, as a cause with a singular effect.   For example, whereas what a builder is, is an efficient cause whose effect is the building of a house; what this builder is, is an efficient cause whose effect is the building of this house. Similarly, whereas wood can be defined as a material cause whose effect is a statue; this wood can be defined as a material cause whose effect is this statue. Similarly, for final and formal causes.

Chapter six
Sameness and difference in matter and form

In chapter six, Aquinas turns his attention to matter and form, the intrinsic causes of physical things which come to be in substantial change, in order to point out, and make clear what it means to say, that 1) what is numerically the same has a matter and a form which are numerically the same, 2) that things which are specifically the same have a matter and a form which are specifically the same, 3) that things which are generically the same have a matter and a form which are generically the same, and 4) that things which are the same only according to an analogy have a matter and a form which are the same only according to an analogy. Then, in order to make these things clear, he finds it helpful, indeed necessary, to talk about univocal, equivocal and analogical predication.

Things: the same in number, the same in species, the same in genus, and the same only according to an analogy

32. Sciendum est etiam quod loquendo de principiis intrinsecis, scilicet materia et forma, secundum convenientiam et differentiam principiatorum est convenientia et differentia principiorum. Quaedam enim sunt idem numero sicut Socrates et hic homo, demonstrato Socrate. Quaedam sunt diversa numero, sed idem in specie, sicut Socrates et Plato, qui, licet conveniant in specie humana, differunt tamen numero. Quaedam autem differunt specie, sed sunt idem genere; sicut homo et asinus conveniunt in genere animalis. Quaedam autem sunt diversa in genere, sed sunt idem solum secundum analogiam; sicut substantia et quantitas, quae non conveniunt in aliquo genere, sed conveniunt solum secundum analogiam. Conveniunt enim solum in eo quod est ens; ens autem non est genus, quia non praedicatur univoce, sed analogice.

It should also be understood that, speaking of the intrinsic principles matter and form, there is a sameness and a difference of principles according to the sameness and difference of the things derived from these principles. For some things are

90

the same in number, like Socrates and this man, Socrates being pointed out. Some things are diverse in number, but the same in species, like Socrates and Plato, who, although they agree in the human species, differ nonetheless in number. Others, differ in species, but are the same in genus; a man and an ass, for example, agree in the genus of animal. Others, still, are diverse in genus, but are the same only according to an analogy, like substance and quantity, which do not agree in any genus, but only according to an analogy. For they agree only in being. And being is not a genus, because it is not predicated univocally, but analogically.

In **32.**, Aquinas begins by observing that **the matter and the form** of things which are both the same and different in different ways, are both the same and different in correspondingly different ways. Then, he points out a number of ways in which **things** are both the same and different. **Socrates** and **this man** are the same in number, i.e., one when counted, though they are different in name or designation. Being called by the name "Socrates" is different from being designated by the expression "this man." **Socrates** and **Plato**, however, though the same in species (both of them are human beings), are not the same in number, i.e., not one when counted. They differ in number; they are two when counted. Each has his own **designated matter**, which is the principle of individuation. **A man** and **an ass**, though the same in genus (both of them are animals), are not the same in species. An ass is one kind of animal, a man quite another kind. Each has its own **specific difference**, which is the principle of the species. **Substance** and **quantity**, lastly, are the same only according to an analogy. They are the same neither in number, nor in species, nor in genus. They are the same only in this, that both are beings. But each has its own **way of being**. Moreover, a way of being is not a genus, cannot be a genus; because unlike a genus, being is not predicated univocally. Being is predicated analogically.

91

33. Ad huius autem intelligentiam sciendum est quod tripliciter aliquid praedicatur de pluribus: univoce, aequivoce et analogice. Univoce praedicatur quod praedicatur secundum idem nomen et secundum eamdem rationem, idest definitionem, sicut animal praedicatur de homine et de asino. Utrumque enim dicitur animal, et utrumque est substantia animata sensibilis, quod est definitio animalis. Aequivoce praedicatur quod praedicatur de aliquibus secundum idem nomen et secundum diversam rationem, sicut canis dicitur de latrabili et de caelesti, quae conveniunt solum in nomine et non in definitione sive significatione; id enim quod significatur per nomen est definitio, sicut dicitur in *IV Metaphysicae*.[17] Analogice dicitur praedicari quod praedicatur de pluribus, quorum rationes sunt diversae, sed attribuuntur alicui uni eidem, sicut sanum dicitur de corpore animalis et de urina et de potione, sed non ex toto idem significat in omnibus. Dicitur enim de urina ut de signo sanitatis, de corpore ut de subiecto, de potione ut de causa; sed tamen omnes istae rationes attribuuntur uni fini, scilicet sanitati.

For an understanding of this, it should be kept in mind that there are three ways in which something is predicated of many things: univocally, equivocally and analogically. That is predicated univocally which is predicated according to the same word and according to the same meaning, or definition, as "animal" is predicated of man and of ass. For each is said to be an animal, and each is an animated substance capable of sensing, which is the definition of animal. That is predicated equivocally which is predicated of a number of things according to the same word and according to a diverse meaning, as "dog" is said of what is capable of barking and of the heavenly body, which have in common only the word, but not the definition or signification; for that which is signified by a word is the definition, as is said in book four of the *Metaphysics*. That is said to be predicated analogically which is predicated of many things so that the meaning is different for each, but so that there

---

[17]   Aristotle, *Metaph.*, Bk. IV, ch. 7, 1012 a 22-24.

is an attribution to some one and the same thing, as "healthy" is said of the body of an animal and of urine and of a drink, but does not mean wholly the same thing with respect to all of them. For it is said of urine as of a sign of health, of the body as of the subject of health, and of the drink as of a cause of health. Nonetheless, all of these meanings include an attribution to one end, namely health.

In **33.**, Aquinas makes clear what it means to say that a word is predicated analogically, by showing how analogical predication differs from univocal predication and from equivocal predication. In **34.**, he continues his consideration of analogical predication. His remarks in **33.** and **34.**, taken together, are ordered toward explaining his concluding observations in **32.**, namely: 1) that there are things which, though different, are nonetheless **the same in a special way,** i.e., according to an analogy; 2) that in such cases the word, a same word, used to designate this sameness is not predicated univocally, but analogically; 3) that substance and quantity are the same in this special analogical way, and 4) that the word "being" which is used to designate this sameness is not predicated univocally, but analogically.

In most predications, one should note, there are words and meanings and things (referents). The words are predicated of these things with certain intended meanings. In a univocal predication, a same word is predicated of many different things with a meaning which is **wholly the same.** For example, the word "animal" is predicated of men and dogs and horses (and of many other things as well) with this same meaning, namely **sensing organism;** or, the word "organism" is predicated of trees and dogs and men (and of many other things besides) with this same meaning, namely **living body.** In an equivocal predication, a same word is predicated of many different things, but of each with a meaning which is **wholly different.** For example, the word "pen" is predicated of this thing with the meaning **writing instrument,** and of that thing with the meaning **enclosure for animals;** or, the word "bank," of this thing with the meaning **money saving and lending institution,** and of that thing with the meaning **the rising ground bordering a** river. In an analogical predication, a same word is predicated of many different things with a meaning which is both the same and different, partly the same and partly different. To explain. There is a first meaning, and a number of posterior meanings. Part of the first meaning is retained as part of each of the posterior meanings. The posterior meanings differ from the first meaning, and from one another as well, by adding a different relation to the retained part of the first meaning. The word "healthy," for example, is predicated of many things in this way. Its first meaning is the meaning predicated of things, living organisms, which are appropriate **subjects** of the bodily disposition which is health. We say that this man is healthy, or that this dog is healthy, and we mean that they have, or are subjects of, the bodily disposition which is health. Then we extend the word "healthy" to other things because these other things have a relation (other than that of being a subject) to the bodily disposition which is health (this disposition is the retained part of the first meaning). Urine, for example, is said to be healthy because it is **a sign of** the bodily disposition which is health. Food is said to be healthy, because it is **preservative of** the bodily disposition which is health. Medicine is said to be healthy, because it is **restorative of** the bodily disposition which is health. The meaning **bodily disposition which is health** is part of each of the several meanings of the word "healthy." The posterior meanings differ from the first meaning, and from one another, by adding a different relation to the retained part of the first meaning, i.e., to **bodily disposition which is health**; one meaning (said of urine) adds the relation **sign of**, another (said of food) the relation **preservative of**, still another (said of medicine) the relation **restorative of**. And health is the **one end**, or goal, of which the living organism is the **subject**, of which the urine is a **sign**, and which the food **preserves**, and the medicine **restores**.

34. Aliquando enim ea quae conveniunt secundum analogiam, idest in proportione vel comparatione vel convenientia, attribuuntur uni fini, sicut patet in praedicto exemplo; aliquando uni agenti, sicut medicus dicitur et de eo qui operatur per artem et de eo qui operatur sine arte, ut vetula, et etiam de instrumentis, sed per attributionem ad unum agens quod est medicina. Aliquando autem per attributionem ad unum subiectum, sicut ens dicitur de substantia et de quantitate et qualitate et aliis praedicamentis. Non enim ex toto est eadem ratio qua substantia est ens et quantitas et alia; sed omnia dicuntur ens ex eo quod attribuuntur substantiae, quae quidem est subiectum aliorum. Et ideo ens dicitur per prius de substantia et per posterius de aliis; et ideo ens non est genus substantiae et quantitatis, quia nullum genus praedicatur per prius et posterius de suis speciebus. Sed praedicatur analogice. Et hoc est quod diximus, quod substantia et quantitas differunt genere, sed sunt idem secundum analogiam.

Now, sometimes the things which are the same according to an analogy -- that is, in a proportion or comparison or agreement -- are attributed to one end, as is clear in the example just noted. Sometimes they are attributed to one agent, as "medical" is said both of someone who works by means of his art and of someone who works without the art, as an old experienced woman, and even of instruments; and in each of these cases by an attribution to one agent which is the art of medicine. At other times, they are attributed to one subject, as "being" is said of substance and of quantity and quality and the other predicaments. For that by which substance is a being, on the one hand, and that by which quantity and the others are beings, on the other hand, are not wholly the same. All of these others are said to be beings because of the fact that they are attributed to substance, which of course is the subject of all of them. And so, "being" is said first of all of substance, and posteriorly of the others. And this is why being is not a genus in relation to substance and quantity, i.e., because no genus is predicated of its species, first of one, and posteriorly of others, and being is predicated just that way, i.e., analogically. And this is what we said above, that substance and quantity differ in genus, but are the same according to an analogy.

In 34., Aquinas adds to what he had said about analogical predication in 33., by pointing out that the diverse things, and their diverse relations, which figure in analogical predications are attributed at times to **one and the same end**, as to health in the example offered in 33.. Health, quite clearly, is the one end desired by the living organism which is the subject of health, the one end of which urine is a sign, the one end which food preserves, and the one end which medicine restores. But, at times they are attributed to **one and the same agent**, and at times to **one and the same subject**. -- To **one and the same agent**, as in the case of the word "medical," to the one who possesses the art of medicine, i.e., the medical doctor. The word "medical" is predicated **per prius** of 1) the medical doctor who does his medical work by means of the art he possesses, and **per posterius** of other things, such as 2) the old woman, perhaps a midwife, who does her medical work without the art which the medical doctor has, but rather by her years of medical experience, and 3) even of the instruments, like a syringe or a stethoscope, which are used by those who are engaged in medical work. -- The art of medicine, clearly, is in various ways the cooperating agent, or the cooperating moving cause, which assists nature, the primary agent, in its (nature's) efforts at doctoring. In one way, in the case of the medical doctor; for he possesses the art. In another way, in the case of the old woman; for she possesses the experience and the know-how, though without the art, which (experience and know-how) others have because they have the art. In still another way, in the case of the medical instruments; for they are things which are necessary, or at least helpful, for a better functioning of the art.

At times the diverse things, and their diverse relations, which figure in analogical predications are attributed to **one and the same subject**, as in the case of the word "being," to what is an ultimate existing thing, i.e., to

96

substance. The word "being" is predicated **per prius** of 1) substance, which is what has existence in and of itself, and which therefore exists in a most proper sense; and **per posterius** of other things, such as 2) quantity, 3) quality, 4) relation, and 5) the other predicaments, all of which have existence only in relation to substance, none in and of themselves, and so exist in a less proper sense.

Matter and form: the same in number, the same in species, the same in genus, and the same only according to an analogy

35. Eorum igitur quae sunt idem numero, et forma et materia sunt idem numero, sicut Tulii et Ciceronis. Eorum autem quae sunt idem specie, sed diversa numero, etiam materia et forma non est eadem numero, sed specie, sicut Socratis et Platonis. Et similiter eorum quae sunt idem genere, et principia sunt idem genere; ut anima et corpus asini et equi differunt specie, sed sunt idem genere. Et similiter eorum quae conveniunt secundum analogiam tantum, principia sunt eadem secundum analogiam tantum, sive proportionem. Materia enim et forma et privatio, sive potentia et actus, sunt principia substantiae et aliorum generum. Tamen materia substantiae et quantitatis, et similiter forma et privatio, differunt genere, sed conveniunt solum secundum proportionem in hoc quod, sicut se habet materia substantiae ad substantiam in ratione materiae, ita se habet materia quantitatis ad quantitatem. Sicut tamen substantia est causa caeterorum, ita principia substantiae sunt principia omnium aliorum.

And so, the form and the matter of what is numerically the same, are also numerically the same, for example of Tullius and of Cicero. The matter and the form of things which are the same in species, but diverse in number, for example the matter and the form of Socrates and of Plato, are likewise not the same in number, but only in species. Similarly, the principles of things which are the same in genus, are themselves the same in genus; for example, the soul and the body of an ass and of a horse differ in species, but are the same in genus. Similarly, again, the principles of things which are the same only according to an analogy, are the same only according to an analogy, or a

proportion. For, matter and form and privation, and potency and act as well, are principles of substance and of the other genera. Nonetheless, the matter of substance and of quantity, and similarly the form and the privation, differ in genus but are the same only according to a proportion, which amounts to this, that just as the matter of substance is related to substance as its matter, so too is the matter of quantity related to quantity. Just as substance is the cause of the others, so too the principles of substance are the principles of all the others.

In 35., Aquinas takes up the main point of chapter six, namely that the matter and the form of things which are both the same and different in different ways, are both the same and different in correspondingly different ways. He begins with sameness in number, then moves to sameness in species, then to sameness in genus, and lastly to sameness according to an analogy only.

Tullius and Cicero are one and the same individual, one and the same in number or when counted, though they are different in name. That is, being called by the name "Tullius" is different from being called by the name "Cicero," though both names designate one and the same individual. The form and the matter of Tullius and of Cicero, who are one and the same in number, are one and the same in number. The soul and the body of **this** man are **this** soul and **this** body.

What is the point of this? one may ask. Is its point to note that this man is **this** man because his body is **this** body and his soul is **this** soul? Or, is its point to note that this body is **this** body and that this soul is **this** soul, because they are the body and the soul of **this** man? Does the numerical sameness of the matter and of the form cause, and by causing explain, the numerical sameness of the individual? Or, does the numerical sameness of the individual cause, and by causing explain, the numerical sameness of the matter and the form?

A not unreasonable suggestion is the following, that Aquinas' point is twofold. 1) To observe that there is a correspondence between the sameness of the matter and form, on the one hand, and the sameness of the things made out of matter and form, on the other hand; so that if the thing is numerically the same, so are its matter and its form; and if the matter and the form are numerically the same, so is the thing; and similarly for sameness in species, in genus, and according to an analogy only. 2) To observe, in accord with the underlying task of this short work as a whole (which is an attempt to become clear on the **principles** of natural things) that **matters and forms** of different sorts are the **principles** of natural things of different sorts; and not vice versa, i.e., not that things of different sorts are the principles of matters and forms of different sorts. Matter and form, and privation as well, are the principles of natural things, matter and form being principles which are also causes, privation being a principle which is **not** also a cause. Principles which are causes account for the existence of things, whereas principles which are not causes do not. Matter and form account for existence because they are intrinsic components of the makeup, i.e., ingredients of the essence, of a natural substance; privation is not. Moreover, universal causes account for the existence of universal effects, less universal causes account for the existence of less universal effects, and individual causes account for the existence of individual effects. Thus, generic matter and form account for the existence of things which are the same in genus, e.g., body and soul account for the existence of an ass and of a horse; specific matter and form account for the existence of things which are the same in species, e.g., human body and human soul account for the existence of Plato and of Socrates; and individual matter and form account for the existence of what is the same in number, i.e., the individual, e.g., my body and my soul account for my existence. Lastly, analogical matter and form account for the existence of things which are the same only according to an analogy, e.g., the matter and the form of substance account, in one way (i.e., as intrinsic components), for the existence of the substance itself, but also, and in other ways (but **never** as intrinsic components), for the existence of all the accidents of the substance as well. Some accidents are caused by the form alone of the substance (as by an efficient cause, and as received by an **extrinsic** matter, or subject), e.g., the human intellect. Some are caused by the form and the matter of the substance together (as by an efficient cause, and as received by an **extrinsic** matter, or subject), e.g., the powers of sensation. No accidents, however, are caused by the matter alone of the substance (i.e., not as by an efficient cause; though matter, as ultimate subject, is what accounts for the receptivity of the substance, as a whole composed of matter and form, with respect to its **material** accidents); for matter, of itself, is just potency without any actuality at all.

PART TWO

DE MIXTIONE ELEMENTORUM

The question
How do elements remain in the physical things which are made up out of them?

> 1. Dubium apud multos esse solet quomodo elementa sint in mixto.
>
> There is a continuing uncertainty among many as regards how elements are in a mixed body.

The question being considered in this brief work, as Aquinas indicates in 1., is the question: how are elements in a mixed body?

And, this prompts one to ask: what exactly is this question asking?   It is clear that even the beginnings of an answer to the immediately preceding question require, in turn, some sort of answer to further questions, at least the following: what is an element? and, what is a mixed body?

As regards the first question, what is an element?, it should be pointed out, to begin with, that the context here is the physical world.   So that, the elements being considered are elements of things in the physical world. -- An element, generally described, as Aquinas understands it, is that (whatever) out of which something (whatever) is made, as out of a primary constituent, which remains in that something, and which is indivisible in kind. --   An element of things in the physical world, as Aquinas understands it, is a simple body, a simple physical thing, out of which a complex body, a complex physical thing, is made, as out of a primary constituent, i.e., a constituent which itself has no prior bodily constituents. An element remains in some way in the complex body (exactly how it remains, is the question of this brief work). An element is indivisible in kind, i.e., it cannot be broken down so as to yield parts which are different in kind from its own kind. Moreover, an element can exist separately, i.e., not as a constituent of a complex body, both before and after having been such a constituent. Elements can act upon, and be acted upon by, one another. They become constituents of a complex body only after they have been altered by one another, though not beyond retrievability.

As regards the second question, what is a mixed body?, it should be noted simply that a mixed body is a physical thing which is made up out of elements; a mixed body is what was called a *complex body* in the immediately preceding paragraph.

Though Aquinas thought, given his times, that water was one of the four elements, the other three being earth, air and fire -- an idea going back to ancient Greece -- today we would say that water cannot be an element. It is, rather, a mixed body; for, unlike an element, it is made up out of prior constituents, i.e., out of hydrogen and oxygen. Now, what about hydrogen and oxygen? Would they count as elements? Perhaps not. For, though both remain in water in some way; though both can exist separately, i.e, not as constituents of water, both before and after being such constituents; though both can act upon, and be acted upon by, one another; though both have been altered by one another, but not beyond retrievability, in order to become constituents of water; -- it does not seem to be the case that they are primary constituents. For they, in turn, are made up out of prior constituents, e.g., protons and electrons. Nor does it seem to be the case that they are indivisible in kind, for the constituents of oxygen, e.g., electrons and protons, are other in kind than oxygen, and those of hydrogen, similarly, are other in kind than hydrogen. Shall we say, then, that protons and electrons are the elements of mixed bodies; or that ingredients which are more simple still, are the elements of mixed bodies? Quarks, perhaps? But, can protons, electrons and quarks exist separately, i.e., not as constituents of mixed bodies, both before and after having been such constituents?

A first answer
The elements remain with their substantial forms, but their active and passive qualities have been changed into some sort of mean

> 2. Videtur autem quibusdam quod, qualitatibus activis et passivis elementorum ad medium aliqualiter reductis per alterationem, formae substantiales elementorum maneant. Si enim formae substantiales non remaneant, videbitur esse corruptio quaedam elementorum, et non mixtio.

> To some, it seems that, though the active and passive qualities of the elements are changed by alteration into some sort of mean, the substantial forms of the elements remain. For, if the substantial forms do not remain, there would seem to be a corruption of the elements, and not a mixing of them.

> 3. Rursus, si forma substantialis corporis mixti sit actus materiae, non praesuppositis formis simplicium corporum, tunc simplicia corpora amittent elementorum rationem. Est enim elementum ex quo componitur aliquid primo, et est in eo, et est indivisibile secundum speciem. Sublatis enim formis substantialibus, non sic ex simplicibus corporibus corpus mixtum componetur, quod in eo remaneant.

Again, if the substantial form of a mixed body is the act of matter in such a way that the forms of the simple bodies are not presupposed, then the simple bodies will lose the status of elements. For an element is that out of which a thing is made in a primary way, and remains in the thing, and is indivisible in kind. So that, if the substantial forms of the elements are taken away, a mixed body will not be made out of simple bodies in such a way that they remain in it.

As some see it, notes Aquinas in **2.**, the elements remain intact in the mixed body, i.e., with their respective substantial forms, though their active and passive qualities have been altered.

They argue, first, as Aquinas points out in **2.**, that the active and passive qualities of a mixed body are different from, indeed are some sort of mean between, those of each of its constituent elements; for, if they were not different, it would be impossible to differentiate the mixed body from its elements. For, a thing acts, and is acted upon, according to what it is. But the elements themselves, in a mixed body, must remain unchanged, must retain their substantial forms. For, if this were not the case, then the elements would have been corrupted. And, just as it is impossible for a whole to be made up of constituents which no longer exist; so too is it impossible to have a mixing of elements, out of elements which no longer exist.

They argue, secondly, as Aquinas notes in **3.**, that if the substantial form of a mixed body were to inform prime matter directly, so that the forms of the now-constituting simple bodies had perished, then the simple bodies would not fulfill the definition of an element. For, whatever else an element is, it is something which remains in the mixed body.

Both these arguments, i.e., the argument in **2.** and the one in **3.**, begin by supposing that the substantial forms of the simple bodies do not survive in the mixed body. But, whereas the first argument notes that, in that case, there would not be a mixing of simple bodies, but a corruption of them; the second argument notes that, in that case, the simple bodies could not be elements, because they would not remain in the mixed body. To have a mixing out of simple bodies, urges the argument in 2., one must have the simple bodies. For the simple bodies to be elements, insists the argument in 3., they must remain in the mixed body as its ingredients.

Suppose one were to apply some of these thoughts to water and oxygen and hydrogen, taking water as a mixed body, and oxygen and hydrogen as its elements. Do oxygen and hydrogen "remain intact" in water? It seems that they do, at least in some way; for they can be retrieved. Have their active and passive qualities been altered? Changed into some sort of mean? And, what are the active and passive qualities of hydrogen and oxygen -- i.e., before they became constituents of water? And what is the mean, i.e., what are the active and passive qualities of water, in terms of which water is to be differentiated from oxygen and hydrogen? What exactly is it that oxygen does to hydrogen, and vice versa, to produce this mean quality (or qualities), which is the mean quality (or qualities) proper to water?

Arguments of Aquinas against the first answer

4. **Est autem impossibile sic se habere.**

But, it is impossible that it be this way.

In **4.**, Aquinas makes the claim that the substantial forms of the simple bodies cannot possibly remain in the mixed body of which these simple bodies have become the constituents. In **5.** and in **6.**, he presents his arguments for that claim.

Before turning to those arguments, it might be helpful to consider that, if the substantial forms of hydrogen and oxygen remained in water, then water would be water throughout, yet simultaneously hydrogen in certain of its parts, and oxygen in certain other of its parts. Which is quite clearly impossible. It must be the case then that, when hydrogen and oxygen become constituents of water, they cease being hydrogen and oxygen respectively. For water is water, and just water. Nonetheless, both oxygen and hydrogen must remain in some way in the water. For, both are retrievable. But, how exactly do they remain? This is the main question being addressed by Aquinas in this brief work. Whatever the way in which they remain, they cannot remain precisely as hydrogen and oxygen, each with its appropriate substantial form. Shall we say, then, that they remain by reason of their active and passive qualities, but as altered somehow into some sort of mean qualities, which are the qualities appropriate to water? Again, what exactly are these qualities, i.e., those of hydrogen and of oxygen, as well as those of water?

5. Impossibile est enim materiam secundum idem diversas formas suscipere elementorum. Si igitur in corpore mixto formae substantiales elementorum salventur, oportebit diversis materiae partibus eas inesse. Materiae autem diversas partes accipere est impossibile, nisi praeintellecta quantitate in materia; sublata enim quantitate, substantia remanet indivisibilis, ut patet primo *Physicorum*.[1] Ex materia autem sub quantitate existente, et forma substantiali adveniente, corpus physicum constituitur. Diversae igitur partes materiae, formis elementorum subsistentes, plurium corporum rationem suscipint. Multa autem corpora impossibile est simul esse. Non igitur in qualibet parte corporis mixti erunt quatuor elementa. Et sic non erit vera mixtio, sed secundum sensum, sicut accidit in congregatione corporum, insensibilium propter parvitatem.

---

[1] Aristotle, *Physics*, Bk. I, ch. 2, 185 b 11-18; Aquinas, *In I Phys.*, lect. 3, nn. 3-4. Aristotle does **not** say explicitly that if quantity were taken away, substance would remain indivisible; but this is very clearly implied in what he does say by way of arguing against the One of Parmenides and Melissus. Notice that Aquinas says: ut **patet** primo Physicorum, and **not**: ut **dicitur** primo Physicorum.

For it is impossible for matter, the same matter, to take on the forms of diverse elements. If therefore the substantial forms of the elements survive in a mixed body, they will have to be in diverse parts of its matter. But it is impossible for matter to have diverse parts, unless quantity is understood as being in that matter. For, if quantity were taken away, substance would remain indivisible, as is clear from book one of the *Physics*. Now, it is out of a matter which exists with quantity, and a substantial form which comes to that matter, that a physical body is constituted. And so, the diverse parts of matter, each of which subsists by means of the form of some element, take on the nature of more than one body. Now, it is impossible for a body to be many bodies at the same time. The four elements, therefore, will not be found in any and every part of the mixed body. And so, there will not be a true mixing, but a mixing according to sense, as happens in the case of a collection of bodies which cannot be perceived because they are so small.

6. Amplius, omnis forma substantialis propriam dispositionem in materia requirit, sine qua esse non potest. Unde alteratio est via ad generationem et corruptionem. Impossibile est autem in idem convenire propriam dispositionem quae requiritur ad formam ignis, et propriam dispositionem quae requiritur ad formam aquae, quia secundum tales dispositiones ignis et aqua sunt contraria. Contraria autem impossibile est simul esse in eodem. Impossibile est igitur quod in eadem parte mixti sint formae substantiales ignis et aquae. Si igitur mixtum fiat, remanentibus formis substantialibus simplicium corporum, sequitur quod non sit vera mixtio, se ad sensum solum, quasi iuxta se positis partibus, insensibilibus propter parvitatem.

Furthermore, every substantial form requires a proper disposition in its matter, a disposition without which it cannot exist. This is why alteration is the way to generation and to corruption. Now, it is impossible for the proper disposition which is required for the form of fire, and for the proper disposition which is required for the form of water, to be found together in the same thing; because according to such dispositions, fire and water are contraries. And it is impossible for contraries to be found in the same thing at the same time. It is impossible, therefore, for the substantial forms of fire and water to be together in the same part of the mixed body. If, therefore, a mixed body comes to be in such a way that the substantial forms of the simple bodies remain in it, it follows that this is not a true mixing, but a mixing only to sense, as though its parts, too small to be perceptible, had simply been placed next to one another.

It would be impossible, argues Aquinas in 5., for the matter of a mixed body, because it is a same matter, to take on the forms of diverse elements. For, in that case, a thing of one kind would be simultaneously a thing of a number of different kinds. Thus, if the substantial forms of diverse elements were to survive in a mixed body, each would have to be found in a diverse quantitative part of the matter of that body. It is clear, therefore, that the four elements could not be found in each and every part of the mixed body. And so, this would not be a true mixing, but only an apparent mixing, what Aquinas calls a "mixing to sense." The wrongly called mixed body would be, rather, only a collection of bodies, a collection of four different kinds (the four elemental kinds) of juxtaposed (not mixed) bodies, each so small that neither they nor their juxtaposition could be perceived by sense.

Moreover, argues Aquinas in 6., every substantial form requires a proper disposition in its matter. Without its proper disposition, the substantial form cannot begin to exist; nor can it continue to exist. Now, it is alteration which both brings on proper dispositions and disperses them. As bringing them on, alteration is the way to generation; as dispersing them, it is the way to corruption. Now, it is impossible for contrary dispositions to be found in the same part of a mixed body, e.g., those of fire and of water. And so, it is impossible for the substantial forms of fire and water to be found in the same part of a mixed body. If, therefore, a mixed body were to come into existence, and the elements which constitute it were to retain their respective substantial forms, this would not be a true mixing, but a mixing only to sense -- and for the same reason given above in 5., i.e., because the mixed body, improperly so called, would be just a collection of juxtaposed (not mixed) parts, each of which would be an elemental substance, placed alongside other elemental substances, all of them too small to be perceptible.

What exactly, one might ask at this point, is the difference between a true mixing *(vera mixtio)* and a mixing only to sense *(mixtio ad sensum, secundum sensum, solum)*?   Is Aquinas suggesting in **5.**, by implication at least, that in a true mixing the four elements (or however many of them are required by the substantial form of the mixed body) are found in any and every quantitative part ("...in qualibet parte...") of the mixed body? For, he writes: "Non igitur *in qualibet parte* corporis mixti erunt quatuor elementa. Et sic non erit vera mixtio, sed secundum sensum... ."   If this is what he is suggesting, then it is clear that the elements cannot be in the mixed body with their respective substantial forms. For, a mixed body is just what the mixed body is, and throughout. It is certainly true that water (taking water as a mixed body) is water throughout, that every part of water is just water, and that no part of water is either hydrogen or oxygen (taking these as the constituting elements). And this clearly implies that, however it is that the elements survive in a mixed body, they cannot survive with their respective substantial forms.   In a mixing which is a mixing to sense only, on the other hand, the parts which make up the resulting body remain, each of them, with their respective substantial forms. So that, if water were a mixing only to sense, some parts of the water would be oxygen, other parts would be hydrogen, and the water itself would not be water at all, let alone throughout. Water would be only a collection of justaposed atoms of hydrogen and oxygen. Furthermore, water would not have the qualities which we know to be proper to water. Rather, some parts of it would have the qualities of hydrogen; other parts, the qualities of oxygen.

Water is water throughout. Every part of water is just water. No part of water is either hydrogen or oxygen. But hydrogen and oxygen are required to produce water. Both are retrievable from water. Both can act upon, and be acted upon by, the other. Each is altered by the other in order to become a constituent (retrievable) of water. -- How, then, are the elements, hydrogen

111

and oxygen, in the mixed body, water? Not actually. This is clear. Potentially, then? This seems the correct thing to say; for what other alternative is there? But, exactly what does this mean? Shall we say, as it seems Aquinas would (if he had taken water to be a mixed body), that what this means is that it is their active and passive qualities which remain, but as altered into water's appropriate mean qualities by their water-constituting interaction? And shall we take this to mean, as it seems Aquinas would, that the substantial form of water is both brought into existence and (having been brought into existence) acts through these mean qualities, until such time as some external agent (or agents) "re-alters" water's mean qualities, i.e., nullifies the prior water-constituting interaction between oxygen and hydrogen, releasing thereby their extreme elemental qualities, and thereby in turn bringing about their re-generation as actual, and separately existing and acting, physical entities?

In a true mixing, thus, the elements do not survive with their respective substantial forms. What survives is their active and passive qualities, appropriately changed (constricted, contracted, restrained; imprisoned, so to say) by alteration into a set of mean qualities. These mean qualities serve as 1) the disposition by which the mixed body is brought into existence, 2) as that by which the mixed body acts, and 3) as that by the removal of which the elements are released (as though from prison) to exist again as actual and separate and free physical realities.

In a mixing to sense only, on the other hand, the ingredients survive with their respective substantial forms. Such a mixing is just a collection or gathering of juxtaposed (not mixed, since they have not altered one another by some appropriate interaction) things, each of which is so small that neither they nor their juxtaposition is perceptible to sense. To sense, but to sense only, such a mixing may, in some cases, appear to be a true mixing.

112

A second answer
The elements remain with their substantial forms, but their substantial forms themselves have been changed into some sort of mean

> 7. Quidam autem, volentes utrasque rationes evitare, in maius inconveniens inciderunt.

> But others, wanting to avoid both these arguments, fell into a greater inconsistency.

There are others, notes Aquinas in 7., who see the weight of the arguments which he presents in 5. and 6., and make an attempt to get around them. But their attempt is a failure. For it generates other and greater difficulties. These difficulties stem in part from the claim in 8. that, though the substantial forms of the elements remain in a mixed body, they do not remain therein in their fullness, and so can take on degrees of more and less; and in part from the further claim in 9. that the substantial forms of the elements (because they are so close to prime matter, and hence most imperfect) are a kind of mean between substantial forms and accidental forms; and so, again, can take on degrees of more and less.

> 8. Ut enim mixtionem elementorum ab eorum corruptione distinguerent, dixerunt formas quidem substantiales elementorum remanere in mixto aliqualiter. Sed ne cogerentur dicere esse mixtionem ad sensum, et non secundum veritatem, posuerunt quod formae elementorum non remanent in mixto secundum suum complementum, sed in quoddam medium reducuntur. Dicunt enim quod formae elementorum suscipiunt magis et minus, et habent contrarietatem ad invicem.

113

For, in order to distinguish a mixing of elements from a corruption of them, they said that the substantial forms of the elements do indeed remain in the mixed body -- in some way. But, lest they be forced to say that there is a mixing only to sense, rather than a true one, they claimed that the forms of the elements do not remain in the mixed body in their fullness. Rather they are reduced to some sort of mean. For they say that the forms of the elements take on degrees of more and less, and that they are contrary to one another.

9.   Sed quia hoc repugnat communi opinioni, et dictis Philosophi dicentis in *Praedicamentis* quod substantiae nihil est contrarium, et quod non suscipit magis et minus;[2] ulterius procedunt, et dicunt quod formae elementorum sunt imperfectissimae, utpote materiae primae propinquiores. Unde sunt mediae inter formas substantiales et accidentales. Et sic, inquantum accedunt ad naturam formarum accidentalium, magis et minus suscipere possunt.

But this is openly against the common opinion, and against what the Philosopher holds in the *Categories,* where he says that nothing is contrary to substance, and that substance does not take on degrees of more and less. This is why they go further, and say that the forms of the elements are most imperfect, being so close to prime matter. Whence they are somehow midway, a kind of mean, between substantial forms and accidental forms. And so, insofar as they approach the nature of accidental forms, they can take on degrees of more and less.

These thinkers, too, points out Aquinas in **8.**, like those whose views were taken to task in **5.** and **6.**, hold that the substantial forms of the elements do indeed survive in the mixed body -- in some way.   And for the same reason, i.e., in order to be able to claim that mixed bodies come into existence by a mixing of elements, not by a corruption of them.   But unlike those other thinkers, who hold that the active and passive qualities of the elements take

---

2   Aristotle, *Categories,* ch. 5, 3 b 24- 33; 3 b 34 - 4 a 9.

on degrees of more and less, these thinkers maintain that it is the substantial forms themselves of the elements that take on degrees of more and less. And they do this in order to avoid having to say that the mixing is a mixing only to sense. The mixing, they say, is a true mixing, because the substantial forms of the elements survive, though not in their fullness. These forms have been reduced by alteration to a kind of mean, since they can take on degrees of more and less. And this mean is the form appropriate to the mixed body which has come into existence.

But these thinkers go further, points out Aquinas in **9.**, and argue (contrary to the common opinion and to the view of Aristotle, in the *Categories*, that a substance has no contraries, nor does it take on degrees of more and less) that the substantial forms of the elements are of a most imperfect sort, since they are so close to prime matter, so close that nothing can be closer. From which they conclude that these substantial forms are in some sense midway, a kind of mean, between substantial forms generally and accidental forms. They are less perfect than other substantial forms, and so can take on degrees of more and less, and have contraries. But they are more perfect than accidental forms, and so can account for the existence of substances.

Arguments of Aquinas against the second answer

10. Haec autem positio multipliciter est improbabilis.

This position, however, is in many ways unacceptable.

In **10.**, Aquinas makes the claim that this position is in many ways improbable ("...multipliciter... improbabilis..."), which one might take on first reading in the sense of "quite unlikely to be true." But, once one has seen the arguments of Aquinas, it becomes clear that "improbabilis" would be better taken to mean: unacceptable and to be rejected, which would appeal to the clear link with the verb "improbare," which means: to disapprove of, to blame, find fault with, reject; to find wrong or dishonest or wicked.

11. Primo quidem quia esse aliquid medium inter substantiam et accidens est omnino impossibile. Esset enim medium inter affirmationem et negationem. Proprium enim accidentis est in subiecto esse, substantiae vero in subiecto non esse. Formae autem substantiales sunt quidem in materia, non autem in subiecto. Nam subiectum est hoc aliquid; forma autem substantialis est quae facit subiectum hoc aliquid, non autem praesupponit illud.

First of all, indeed, because it is entirely impossible that there be something midway, a mean, between substance and accident. For, if that were so, there would be something midway, a mean, between affirmation and negation; since it is proper to an accident to be in a subject, but to a substance not to be in a subject. Though substantial forms are indeed in matter, they are not in a subject; for a subject is some actual individual, and a substantial form is what makes a subject some actual individual. It does not presuppose that actual individual.

12. Item, ridiculum est dicere medium esse inter ea quae non sunt unius generis; quia medium et extrema oportet eiusdem generis esse, ut probatur in decimo *Metaphysicae*.[3] Nihil ergo potest esse medium inter substantiam et accidens.

Also, it is ridiculous to say that there is something midway, a mean, between things which are not of one genus; for the mean and the extremes must be of the same genus, as is proved in book ten of the *Metaphysics*. There can be nothing, therefore, which is a mean between substance and accident.

---

[3] Aristotle, *Metaph.*, Bk. X, ch. 7, 1057 a 20; Aquinas, *In X Metaph.*, lect. 9.

13. Deinde, impossibile est formas substantiales elementorum suscipere magis et minus. Omnis enim forma suscipiens magis et minus est divisibilis per accidens, inquantum scilicet subiectum potest eam participare vel magis vel minus. Secundum id autem quod est divisibile per accidens vel per se, contingit esse motum continuum, ut patet in sexto *Physicorum*.[4] Est enim loci mutatio, et augmentum et decrementum secundum quantitatem et locum, quae sunt per se divisibilia; alteratio autem secundum qualitates quae suscipiunt magis et minus, ut calidum et album. Si igitur formae elementorum suscipiunt magis et minus, tam generatio quam corruptio elementorum erit motus continuus. Quod est impossibile. Nam motus continuus non est nisi in tribus generibus, scilicet in quantitate et qualitate et ubi, ut probatur in quinto *Physicorum*.[5]

Next, it is impossible for the substantial forms of the elements to take on degrees of more and less. For every form which takes on degrees of more and less is divisible *per accidens* (i.e., because of something other than itself), insofar as its subject can participate in that form either more or less. Now, motion is continuous insofar as it is divisible, whether *per accidens* (i.e., because of something other than itself) or *per se* (i.e., because of itself), as is clear in book six of the *Physics*. Change of place, and increase and decrease in size, occur according to place and quantity respectively, which are divisible *per se*. But, alteration is divisible according to qualities which take on degrees of more and less, like hot and white. If, therefore, the forms of the elements take on degrees of more and less, the generation as well as the corruption of the elements will be a continuous motion. But this is impossible. For, continuous motion is found in three genera only, namely in quantity and quality and where, as is proved in book five of the *Physics*.

14. Amplius, omnis differentia secundum formam substantialem variat speciem. Quod autem suscipit magis et minus, differt ab eo quod est minus, et quodammodo est ei contrarium, ut magis album et minus album. Si igitur forma

---

4 Aristotle, *Physics*, Bk. VI, ch. 1, 231 b 15; ch. 2, 233 b 15; Aquinas, *In VI Phys.*, lect. 4.
5 Aristotle, *Physics*, Bk. V, ch. 1, 255 b 9; ch. 2, 226 a 23 - b 8; Aquinas, *In V Phys.*, lect. 1; lects. 3-4.

substantialis ignis suscipiat magis et minus, magis facta vel minus facta speciem variabit, et non erit eadem forma, sed alia. Et hinc est quod dicit Philosophus in octavo *Metaphysicae*,[6] quod sicut in numeris variatur species per additionem et subtractionem, ita in substantiis.

Further, every difference in substantial form varies the species. Now, what takes on degrees of more and less, differs from what is less, and is in some way contrary to it, like the more white and the less white. If, therefore, the substantial form of fire takes on degrees of more and less, then whether made more or made less, it will vary the species, and it will not be the same form, but another. And this is why the Philosopher says in book eight of the *Metaphysics* that, just as in the case of numbers the species is varied by addition and subtraction, so too is it varied in the case of substances.

It is altogether impossible, argues Aquinas in **11.,** that there be something midway, a mean, between substance and accident. For, in that case, there would be a mean between affirmation and negation, since it belongs to an accident to exist in a subject, and to a substance **not** to exist in a subject. -- A thing either is, or is not; there is no inbetween. If there were, then there would be something which, so to say, neither is nor is not. -- There cannot be something which is, but is neither a substance nor an accident; nor can something be a substance up to a point, and simultaneously an accident up to a point. If something exists, it is either a substance or an accident. It cannot be, and not be either. -- Unacceptable, and so to be rejected.

Aquinas moves on to clarify the immediately preceding argument by reminding the reader that whereas substantial forms are in matter, they are nonetheless not in a subect, i.e., not in an actually existing subject. For an actually existing subject is a substance, i.e., a *hoc aliquid*, i.e., some actual individual thing. An accident presupposes the existence of a subject. A

---

[6] Aristotle, *Metaph.,* Bk. VIII, ch. 3, 1043 b 36 - 1044 a 2; Aquinas, *In VIII Metaph.,* lect. 3.

substantial form, on the other hand, does not; by way of significant difference, a substantial form is precisely what accounts for the existence of the subject.

Besides, argues Aquinas in **12.**, the mean and the extremes must belong to the same genus, as is proved in book ten of the *Metaphysics*. If there were a mean between substance and accident, it would follow that substances and accidents and substantial forms, all three, would be substances; or that all three would be accidents, or that all three would be substantial forms. All unacceptable, and so to be rejected.

Furthermore, Aquinas argues in **13.**, it is impossible for the substantial forms of the elements to take on degrees of more and less. For, if they did, then both the generation and the corruption of the elements would be a motion which is a continuous one. And this is impossible, because the generation and the corruption of the elements are motions in the genus of substance. -- To explain. Motion is continuous, as Aquinas notes, if it is divisible, whether divisible *per se* or *per accidens,* as is clear in book six of the *Physics*. Now, change in place, and increase and decrease in size (i.e., growth and its opposite, diminution) are motions which are divisible *per se,* since place and quantity, both, are divisible *per se.* Alteration, on the other hand, is a motion which is divisible *per accidens,* i.e., because of qualities which take on degrees of more and less, like hot and white. So that, if the substantial forms of the elements were to change so as to take on degrees of more and less, the change would be a substantial change, and at the same time a motion which is divisible *per accidens.* And so, the substantial forms of the elements would be undergoing a motion which is continuous, and which is in the genus of substance. But, this is impossible, because motion is continuous in three genera only, i.e., in quantity and quality and where, as is proved in book five of the *Physics.*

Moreover, adds Aquinas in **14.**, every difference in substantial form varies, or changes, the species. It is clear that what takes on degrees of more and less is different from what is less, and is in some way contrary to it. For example, a thing, A, which becomes even *more* white than something else, B, which was already less white than A; or a thing, A, which becomes *less* white than something else, B, which was previously less white than A -- in both cases, A differs from B, and is in some way contrary to B. So that, if the substantial form of fire -- using fire as an example -- takes on degrees of more and less, then, whether it becomes more "fire-y" than it was, or less "fire-y", in either case it will not be the same form, but another. That is, the more "fire-y" fire will not be fire, or, not fire of the same species. The less "fire-y" fire, too, will not be fire, or, not fire of the same species. For, in either case, there would have been a substantial change. And this is what Aristotle had in mind when he wrote, in book eight of the *Metaphysics,* that just as numbers differ in species because of degrees of more, i.e., addition (of units), and degrees of less, i.e., subtraction (of units); so, too, do substances differ in species, but by the addition and subtraction of *differences* (rather than units).

The answer of Aquinas
The elements remain with their powers and with retrievability, but not with their substantial forms

> 15. Oportet ergo alium modum invenire, quo et veritas salvetur mixtionis, et tamen elementa non totaliter corrumpantur, sed aliqualiter in mixto permaneant.
>
> Another way must be found, therefore, which both safeguards a true mixing, and insures, as well, that the elements are not totally corrupted, but remain in some way in the mixed body.

In **15.**, Aquinas begins to give what he takes to be the proper answer to the question: how are elements in a mixed body?, an answer which will both 1) safeguard that the mixing is a true one, rather than a mixing to sense only, and 2) make certain that the elements have become, and remain, ingredients of the mixed body, and so have not been totally corrupted. A true mixing requires that the elements have interacted and have changed one another in some way, but the change cannot be so radical as to have been their total corruption. Still, the elements must have been corrupted -- at least in some way; otherwise the mixed body could not have been generated. Nonetheless, the elements must remain -- at least in some way; otherwise the elements cannot be ingredients of the mixed body. And so, the generation of a mixed body out of elements requires that these elements be both corrupted and not corrupted -- corrupted in one respect (how? is the question); not corrupted in another respect (how? is again the question).

16. Considerandum est igitur quod qualitates activae et passivae elementorum sunt ad invicem contrariae, et suscipiunt magis et minus. Ex contrariis autem qualitatibus suscipientibus magis et minus constitui potest media qualitas, quae utriusque sapiat extremi naturam, sicut pallidum inter album et nigrum, et tepidum inter calidum et frigidum. Sic igitur, remissis excellentiis qualitatum elementarium, constituitur ex eis quaedam qualitas media, quae est propria qualitas corporis mixti, differens tamen in diversis secundum diversam mixtionis proportionem. Et haec quidem qualitas est propria dispositio ad formam corporis mixti, sicut qualitas simplex ad formam corporis simplicis. Sicut igitur extrema inveniuntur in medio, quod participat utriusque naturam, sic qualitates simplicium corporum inveniuntur in propria qualitate corporis mixti.

It must be taken into consideration that the active and passive qualities of the elements are contrary to one another, and take on degrees of more and less. Now, a mean quality which partakes of the nature of each extreme, can be constituted out of contrary qualities which take on degrees of more and less, as pale between white and black, and warm between hot and cold. Thus, therefore, when the excelling intensities of the elementary qualities are diminished, a certain mean quality is constituted out of them, a quality which is the proper quality of a mixed body, a quality which differs however in diverse mixed bodies in accord with diverse proportions of mixing. And this mean quality is the proper disposition to the form of a mixed body, just

121

as the simple quality is to the form of a simple body. Just as the extremes, therefore, are found in a mean which shares the nature of each of them; so too are the qualities of simple bodies found in the proper quality of a mixed body.

17. Qualitas autem corporis simplicis est quidem aliud a forma substantiali ipsius. Agit tamen in virtute formae substantialis. Alioquin calor calefaceret tantum, non autem per eius actionem forma substantialis educeretur in actum, cum nihil agat extra suam speciem. Sic igitur virtutes formarum substantialium simplicium corporum salvantur in corporibus mixtis.

Though the quality of a simple body is indeed other than its substantial form, it acts nonetheless in the power of the substantial form. Otherwise, all that heat would do is make things hot, and a substantial form would not be brought to a state of actuality by its action, since nothing acts beyond the limits of its species. It is in this way, therefore, that the powers of the substantial forms of simple bodies are preserved in mixed bodies.

18. Sunt igitur formae elementorum in corporibus mixtis, non quidem actu, sed virtute. Et hoc est quod dicit Philosophus in primo *De Generatione:* [7] "Non igitur manent actu -- elementa scilicet, in mixto -- ut corpus et album, nec corrumpuntur nec ambo nec alterum. Salvatur enim virtus eorum."

The forms of the elements, therefore, are in mixed bodies; not indeed actually, but virtually (by their power). And this is what the Philosopher says in book one of *On Generation:* "Elements, therefore, do not remain in a mixed body actually, like a body and its whiteness. Nor are they corrupted, neither both nor either. For, what is preserved is their power."

---

[7] Aristotle, *De Gen. et Corrupt.*, Bk. I, ch. 10, 327 b 29-31; see the commentary, *In I De Gen. et Corrupt.*, lect. 24, in fine. St. Thomas' commentary on Aristotle's *De Gen. et Corrupt.* is unfinished, terminating with Bk. I, lect. 17; the rest was written by Thomas Sutton and others (see below, p. 172, footnote 11).

In **16.**, Aquinas begins by pointing out that it is the *active and passive qualities* of the elements, and *not* their substantial forms, which are contrary to one another, and take on degrees of more and less. And one can add to this that the elements change, and are changed by, one another, precisely by means of, and with respect to, their active and passive qualities. Thus, when the most (i.e., the excelling intensity, or the "excellentia," to use the word Aquinas uses, e.g., the hottest, the coldest, the driest, the wettest, i.e., these qualities at their most intense, at their most "excelling") which is the proper degree of some elemental quality meets head on with the most which is the proper degree of some other elemental quality, there results an interaction which tempers or diminishes both mosts (the mosts are the extremes), the result being some sort of more or less, some sort of inbetween, some sort of mean quality. Now, this mean quality is the proper or distinguishing quality of some mixed body, different mixed bodies having appropriately different mean qualities, some closer to one extreme, some closer to the other extreme. And it is through this *mean* quality, as through the required proper disposition, that alteration, as the way to the *generation* of a mixed body, brings the mixed body into existence out of the required elements, mixed according to an appropriate proportion; just as it is through the *extreme* quality, as through the required proper disposition, that alteration, this time as the way to the *corruption* of a mixed body, retrieves, and thereby brings back into existence, the elements which had been the required ingredients of the now-corrupted mixed body.

Aquinas concludes his reflection in **16.** by noting that the qualities of the simple bodies, i.e., of the elements, are found in the proper quality of a mixed body in a way which is similar to the way in which extremes are found in a mean which participates in the nature of each of them. To exemplify this with water and hydrogen and oxygen (taking water as a mixed body, and hydrogen and oxygen as its elements), one can say that the active and passive qualities of water are a mean of some sort, which participates, in some way, in the extremes which are the active and passive qualities of hydrogen and oxygen. And it is not at all necessary for this mean quality to be anything at all like either of the extreme qualities; it may indeed turn out to be a surprise of some sort, even a complete surprise (oxygen supports burning, whereas water quenches -- surprise? -- burning). Only experience will tell.

In **17.**, Aquinas comments briefly on the relation between the qualities of the elements and their substantial forms. He begins by emphasizing the fact that the quality of a simple body, or element, is other than its substantial form. Then he makes his main point, namely that the quality of an element acts, nonetheless, under the influence (guidance) -- *in virtute* -- of its substantial form. Or, to put it a bit differently, the element acts as it does, because of the qualities which it has; and it has the qualities which it has, because of the substantial form which it has. The substantial form of an element, once brought into existence, is not only continuously productive (and receptive) of the proper or distinguishing quality of that element, but performs its proper acts through that quality. Otherwise, the heat of fire -- to use Aquinas' example at this point -- would do nothing but make things hot, and the substantial form of fire would not be brought to a state of actuality through fire's heating action on a combustible material. For nothing can produce what is beyond its kind. Fire produces fire, its own kind, through its proper quality or power, i.e., heat; but as under the influence (guidance) -- *in virtute* -- of its substantial form. -- Neither, one can add, would the substantial form of water (taking water to be a mixed body) be brought to a state of actuality via the interaction between the proper qualities of hydrogen and oxygen, unless this interaction took place under the joint influence (guidance) -- *in virtute* -- of their substantial forms (i.e., the substantial forms of hydrogen and oxygen), as well as of the substantial forms of other things (to be discovered by careful investigation) which might be required to bring about the substantial change in which water is generated.

Aquinas concludes **17.** with the comment that it is *in this way* that the powers *(virtutes)*, or qualities, of the substantial forms of the simple bodies survive in mixed bodies. In what way? one wants to ask, since Aquinas does not make this explicit at this point. It seems that he is making a reference to what he had said at the end of **16.,** namely that the qualities of simple bodies are found in the proper quality of a mixed body in a way which is much like the way in which extremes are found in a mean which participates to some extent in the nature of each of them. Accepting this, one can say that the powers *(virtutes)*, or qualities, of the substantial forms of the elements survive in mixed bodies; but not the substantial forms themselves. And so, the elements have been corrupted with respect to their substantial forms; but they have not been corrupted with respect to their qualities. These elemental qualities survive in the mixed body as tempered mean qualities. When hydrogen and oxygen become water -- as we understand this today -- what **is there,** is neither hydrogen nor oxygen, but water. That is, hydrogen and oxygen are not there actually, though they are there potentially -- and in two senses of "potentially": 1) virtually (by their power), and 2) retrievably. Water, nonetheless, does what water does, through its appropriate mean qualities, which are nothing but the now-tempered qualities of what were earlier, i.e., before the water came into existence, the "excelling" qualities of hydrogen and of oxygen, as separately existing entities. It is the now-tempered (formerly excelling) qualities which actually survive, and actually remain, in the mixed body; but now under the influence (guidance) -- *in virtute* -- of the substantial form of that mixed body.

In **18.,** Aquinas gives a concluding summary statement of how elements are in a mixed body. They survive, and are there, not by reason of their substantial forms, but by reason of their powers, i.e., qualities. He puts it this way: "...the forms of the elements, therefore, are in mixed bodies, not indeed actually, but virtually (by their power)... ." None of the elements is completely corrupted; neither is any of them completely preserved. As Aristotle puts it: "...what is preserved is their power." And -- one might add -- their power, precisely because preserved, is retrievable. And so are their substantial forms retrievable, and precisely via their power, functioning as the appropriate disposition.

Thus, the substantial forms of the elements are not actually present in mixed bodies. Each mixed body has its own, and one, substantial form. And it is this substantial form which manifests *its* proper activities through its proper qualities, which had been the extreme, or excelling, qualities (now brought, or tempered, to a mean) of the formerly separately existing elements. The mixed body, like any corporeal substance, can have actually *but one* substantial form, its own. Potentially, however, i.e., both virtually (in their power) and retrievably, it has as many substantial forms, in number and in kind, as the elements which are required as its ingredients.

PART THREE

ELEMENTS IN THE COMPOSITION
OF PHYSICAL SUBSTANCES

Elements in the Composition
of Physical Substances

According to St. Thomas Aquinas, all physical substances, **including** the elements, are composed out of prime matter and substantial form; and all physical substances, **excluding** the elements, are composed out of elements in addition to being composed out of prime matter and substantial form.

What follows is an attempt to do at least the following: 1) to clarify Aquinas' account of the role(s) which the elements play in the composition of physical substances, with help from what he has to say here and there throughout his many works, and in various contexts, and 2) to determine whether his account of their role(s) can be accepted, i.e., to argue for or against the various claims and arguments of his account, as each may require.

1. If a physical substance is composed out of elements, must it also be composed out of prime matter and substantial form?

It is the view of Aquinas that there are two kinds of composition in physical substances which come to be and cease to be in substantial change: 1) composition out of **prime matter and substantial form**, and 2) composition out of **elements.** What exactly, one wants to ask, is the relation between these two sorts of composition? More specifically, can a physical substance be composed out of elements, without also being composed out of prime matter and substantial form? And, the other way around, can a physical substance be composed out of prime matter and substantial form, without also being composed out of elements?

129

With respect to the immediately preceding question, it seems that **it can,** i.e., it seems that a physical substance **can be** composed out of prime matter and substantial form, without also being composed out of elements. Consider an element itself -- whatever it might be, whether a quark, or something (yet to be discovered) which is a bodily ingredient of a quark, or something else again (still to be discovered) which is a bodily ingredient of that bodily ingredient, and so on. An element itself is not, cannot be, composed out of elements, i.e., out of prior bodily ingredients; for an element itself is the most primitive, the most simple, of all bodily ingredients. But, being a substance which can come to be and cease to be in substantial change, an element must be composed out of prime matter and substantial form. Indeed, an element is the **only** physical substance which is composed **only** out of prime matter and substantial form. Unlike a mixed body -- i.e., a physical thing which is composed **out of elements,** as well as out of prime matter and substantial form, e.g., wood, water, flesh, bones, sticks, stones; and, one might add, molecules, atoms, protons, neutrons, indeed all hadrons -- an element itself cannot be resolved **by alteration** into bodies which are more simple than itself. There are no bodies which are more simple than an element. Only prime matter and substantial form -- and these are not bodies -- are more simple than an element. All other bodies -- and these are mixed bodies -- are composed **both** out of elements (i.e., they can be resolved **by alteration** into bodies which are more simple than they are, and ultimately into elements) **and** out of prime matter and substantial form (because they can come to be and cease to be in substantial change).

With respect to the other question, that is: Can a physical substance be composed out of elements, without also being composed out of prime matter and substantial form?, it seems that it cannot. For, if it could, then certain changes which are in fact substantial changes -- like the change in which sperm and ovum become a human being, or the change in which food becomes part of a human body -- could not be substantial changes (rather,

130

only accidental changes).   Or, to put this in another way, certain things which are in fact substances -- e.g., mixed bodies like men and dogs and horses -- could not be substances (rather, only accidental collections, or aggregates, of elements).   That is, they would differ from one another not substantially, but only accidentally.   The elements out of which they are composed would be genuine substances, but they themselves (i.e., the entities so composed) would differ from one another only by reason of the **number** and the **kind** of their ingredient elements, and by reason of the **way** in which these ingredient elements were put together.   They would differ from one another, by way of comparison, in the way in which **this house** differs from **that house,** e.g., by reason of the **number** (e.g., **1800** for this one, **2000** for that one) and the **kind** (e.g., **pine** for this one, **oak** for that one) of the pieces of wood out of which each has been made, and by reason of the **way** (e.g., **plan A** for this one, **plan B** for that one) in which these pieces of wood have been put together.   And these differences are, all of them, only accidental (predicamental) differences.

2. If a physical substance is composed out of elements as well as out of prime matter and substantial form, are the elements ingredients of its *essence*?

It is the view of Aquinas that prime matter and substantial form are ingredients of the **essence** of any physical substance which comes to be in substantial change, whether it be a simple body, i.e., an element, or a complex body, i.e., something which is composed out of elements. How, one wants to ask, are the elements of a complex body related to that complex body? Are they, like its prime matter and its substantial form, also ingredients of its **essence**?   Or, are they related to that essence in some other way?   As properties perhaps?

Someone might argue that, in the view of Aquinas, the elements of a complex body are ingredients of its **essence**.   For he notes in *C.G.*, III, cap. 22, and elsewhere, that prime matter is in potency to forms in a certain order: first of all, to the forms of the elements; and then, through those, in potency to the forms of mixed bodies; through the forms of mixed bodies, in turn, in potency to the forms (souls) of living bodies; then through those, in potency to the forms (souls) of animal bodies; and lastly, through those, in turn, in potency to the forms (souls) of human bodies. This clearly implies, one might argue, that the elements which are found in the composition of a physical substance are ingredients of its **essence**, whether this substance is as lowly as the mixed body iron, or as lofty as the living body which is a human being. For prime matter can have no form at all if it does not have, in some way, the form of an element(s) -- either actually and only, as in the case of the elements themselves; or virtually and retrievably, along with another which it has actually (but only because of a certain dispositional and instrumental dependence on certain virtually and retrievably present elemental forms), as in the case of all complex bodies. Clearly, one might conclude, if prime matter cannot have a certain substantial form, say the soul of a human being, without the virtual, retrievable, dispositional, and instrumental presence in it of certain required elements, say quarks (in protons, which are in atoms, which are in molecules of certain sorts), then the **essence** of the substance made out of prime matter and such a substantial form **must include** the required elements as well.

This conclusion -- i.e., that the **essence** of such a substance, a complex body, **must include** the required elements as well as prime matter and a certain sort of substantial form -- seems correct (at least at first look); and for the reason given, i.e., because without the intervening dispositional presence of the required elements, prime matter could not have acquired such a form; and the complex body could not have come to be **what it is**. But, for a proper understanding of this, one must emphasize the following. Whereas the **essence** of such a substance **includes** prime matter and such a substantial form **actually** (otherwise the substance could not be **what it is**); it includes the required elements only **potentially**, i.e., **virtually**, or **in their power**, both because 1) a substance can have **actually** only **one** substantial form, its own, and 2) because such a substance, a complex body, needs the powers of the elements as the means or instruments through which it performs its proper

132

activities. Prime matter and substantial form are **actual** ingredients of the essence, i.e., each is present with respect to **what it is**. The required elements are **virtual** ingredients of the essence, i.e., each is present not with respect to what it is, but with respect to **what it can do**, i.e., with respect to **its powers**.

A further look at this conclusion, however, might bring one to want to say the following. Since the required elements are present in the mixed body **not** with respect to **what each is,** but with respect to **what each can do,** i.e., with respect to its **powers,** it might be better to say, perhaps closer to the truth to say, that the elements are among the accidents (predicamental) of the mixed body. For that is exactly what the powers of a substance are, i.e., predicamental accidents. The substantial form of a mixed body, once brought into existence, is not only the cause (efficient, in the sense of sustaining or continuing, and receptive as well) of its powers, but performs its proper activities through those powers. And so, one might want to say, the idea: **virtual ingredient of an essence**, might be better expressed as: **actual accident (predicamental) of that essence**. Moreover, one might want to continue, since the powers of an essence are found **wherever** that essence is found (and since this is so because their continued existence is caused -- efficiently and receptively -- by the substantial form of that essence), the elements which survive as components of a newly generated mixed body are, precisely as surviving in it, **properties** of that mixed body, i.e., commensurately universal *per se* (predicable) accidents.

But this is **not** in accord with what Aquinas writes in *In Boetii De Trinitate,* q. 5, a. 3, c., where he says explicitly, using man as an example, that the four elements are **ingredients of the essence** of a mixed body. Man, exemplifies Aquinas, is something composed of a soul and a body -- of a soul which is a rational soul, and of a body which is made up of the four elements combined in an appropriate ratio. That is, man's **essence** is made up of soul and body, and that **body** is made up of as much of each of the four elements, properly combined (propria mixtione), as is required to constitute an appropriate subject for his soul. Aquinas writes:

133

Sunt . . . quaedam partes a quibus totius ratio dependet, quando scilicet hoc est esse tali toti ex talibus partibus componi, sicut se habet syllaba ad litteras, et mixtum ad elementa; et tales partes [sunt] partes . . . sine quibus totum intelligi non potest, cum ponantur in eius definitione.

Quaedam vero partes sunt quae accidunt toti inquantum huiusmodi, sicut semicirculus se habet ad circulum. Accidit enim circulo quod sumantur per divisionem duae eius partes aequales, vel inaequales, vel etiam plures; non autem accidit triangulo quod in eo designentur tres lineae, quia ex hoc triangulus est triangulus.

Similiter etiam per se competit homini quod inveniatur in eo anima rationalis, et corpus compositum ex quatuor elementis; unde sine his partibus homo intelligi non potest: et sic oportet poni in definitione eius . . .

Sed digitus, pes, manus et huiusmodi, sunt praeter intellectum hominis, unde ex illis ratio essentialis hominis non dependet, unde sine his intelligi potest.

Sive enim habeat pedes, sive non, dummodo ponatur coniunctum ex anima rationali et corpore composito ex quatuor elementis propria mixtione quam requirit talis forma, erit homo. (*In Boetii De Trinitate,* q. 5, a. 3, c.)

There are some parts on which being a whole of a certain kind depends -- when, that is, it belongs to the essence of such and such a whole to be composed of such and such parts; this is how a syllable is related to letters, and a mixed body to elements. Such parts [are] parts . . . without which the whole cannot be understood; and this is why such parts are put into the definition of the whole.

But there are other parts which just happen to, are accidental to, a whole as such; this is how a semicirlcle is related to a circle. For being divided into two equal parts -- or into two unequal parts, or even into several parts -- is something which just happens to a circle. But it does not just happen to a triangle that there are three lines designated in it, because it is by reason of them that a triangle is a triangle.

Similarly, it belongs to man as such that there be found in him a rational soul and a body composed of the four elements. And this is why man cannot be understood without these parts. And so, they must be put into the definition of man . . .

But a finger, a foot, a hand and such like, are outside what it is to be a man. Whence man's essential nature does not depend on them, and so can be understood without them.

For whether a man has feet, or not, so long as he is held to be a conjunction of 1) rational soul, and 2) body composed of the four elements, properly mixed, as required by such a form, he will be a man.

There are two kinds of parts, notes Aquinas in effect. There are essential parts, and there are accidental parts. Essential parts are parts on which a whole depends for being the whole that it is, parts without which it could not be the whole that it is. Letters, for example, are essential parts of a syllable. A syllable could not be a syllable without having letters as its parts. And elements are essential parts of a mixed body. A mixed body could not be a mixed body without having elements as its parts.

Accidental parts are parts on which a whole does **not** depend for being the whole that it is. A circle, for example, can be said to have two semicircles as parts, a semicircle being exactly one half of a circle. But having two semicircles as parts does not make a circle what it is, i.e., a circle. It just happens that a circle can be described as made out of two equal parts, i.e., out of two semicircles. But a circle can just as well be described as made out of two unequal parts; indeed, out of any number of parts, whether equal or not. What a circle is, i.e., the essence of a circle, is this: a closed plane curve every point of which is equidistant from a fixed point within the curve called its center. What a circle is, is **not** something made out of two semicircles. A circle can be divided into parts of various sorts, equal and unequal. But it is not something made up out of these parts. A circle is not made out of semicircles in the way in which a syllable is made out of letters, or a mixed body out of elements. A triangle, by way of contrast, **is** made out of three straight lines (put together in a certain way), in a way which is like the way in which a syllable is made out of letters (put together in a ceratin way), or like the way in which a mixed body is made out of elements (put together in a certain way).

Having talked about the circle, the triangle, the syllable, and the mixed body, in relation to essential parts and accidental parts, Aquinas turns next to talk about man in relation to these two sorts of parts. It belongs to man as man (. . . per se competit homini. . .), notes Aquinas, to be made out of a rational soul and a body composed out of the four elements put together in an appropriate way (propria mixtione). Man cannot be understood without these parts, i.e., without soul and body; and man's body cannot be understood without the four elements appropriately combined. This is why it is necessary to include these parts in man's definition.   A finger, however, or a foot, a hand, an elbow, a knee, and the like -- these are outside what it is to be a man. Whence, the essence of the whole which man is does not depend on them, and what a man is can be understood without them. Whether or not a man has feet or hands, or other like parts -- so long as he is held to be made up out of a rational soul and a mixed body, i.e., a body composed of the four elements put together in the proportion required by the rational soul --   a man will be a man.

This is completely in accord with **what follows from** Aquinas' view that prime matter is in potency to forms in a certain order, i.e., first of all, to the forms of the elements, then through these to the forms of mixed bodies, etc., i.e., from the view that prime matter cannot have a certain substantial form, say the soul of a human being, without the virtual, retrievable, dispositional and instrumental presence in it of certain elements, appropriately put together. For what follows is this: the **essence** of the substance made out of prime matter and such a substantial form **must include** within itself the required elements as well.

3. Is an element in any way an agent cause, in addition to being a special sort of material cause?

Si in aliquo genere aliquod primum invenitur quod sit causa aliorum, eiusdem considerationis est commune genus et id quod est primum in genere illo: quia illud primum est causa totius generis, oportet autem eum qui considerat genus aliquod, causas totius generis considerare. Et inde est quod Philosophus in *Metaphysica* simul determinat de ente in communi et de ente primo, quod est a materia separatum. Sunt autem in genere generabilium et corruptibilum quaedam prima principia, scilicet elementa, quae sunt causa generationis et corruptionis et alterationis in omnibus aliis corporibus. Et inde est quod Aristoteles in hoc libro qui est tertia pars scientiae naturalis, determinat non solum de generatione et corruptione in communi et aliis motibus consequentibus, sed etiam de generatione et corruptione elementorum. (*Prooemium In De Generatione et Corruptione,* n. 2).

If in a given genus of things something first is found which is the cause of the others, the common genus and that which is first in that genus belong to the same consideration. This is so because that first thing is the cause of the whole genus, and the one who considers a given genus should consider the *causes* of the whole genus as well. This is why the Philosopher, in the *Metaphysics*, decides questions about the first being which is separated from matter, along with deciding questions about being in common. Now, in the genus of generable and corruptible things, there are certain first principles, namely the elements, which are the cause of generation, corruption, and alteration in all other bodies. This explains why Aristotle in this book [i.e., in the *De Generatione et Corruptione*], which is the third part of natural science, decides not only questions about generation and corruption in common, and other consequent motions, but questions about the generation and corruption of the elements as well.

The point of a philosophical investigation, as Aquinas sees it, is to come to a knowledge of the causes -- all the causes -- of the things being investigated, and at some designated level of universality. If one is investigating **all** things, in terms of what they have in common, i.e., if one is investigating **ens in communi,** one should strive for a knowledge of all the causes of what they have in common, including a knowledge of the First Being which is separated from matter, i.e., of their First Efficient Cause, God, ". . . de ente primo, quod est a materia separatum." Similarly, if one is investigating **all** generable and corruptible bodies, in terms of what they have in common, one should strive for a knowledge of all the causes of what they have in common, including a knowledge of the elements. For, as Aquinas points out, the elements are causes of generation, corruption, and alteration **in all other generable and corruptible bodies.** One should strive therefore for a knowledge of, strive to decide questions about, the exact causal role(s) which the elements have in relation to all other generable and corruptible bodies.

What can one derive from the comparison which Aquinas makes of the elements to God? Just as God is the first cause of all other beings, i.e., of **ens in communi,** notes Aquinas, so too the elements are first causes of all other generable and corruptible bodies. Elsewhere, and in many places, Aquinas notes that the elements are **intrinsic components** of all other generable and corruptible bodies, and that they have the role of **material** causes. Since he is comparing the elements to God, and not God to the elements, one can safely say that Aquinas is not suggesting that God is an intrinsic and material component of all other things. He is suggesting, rather, that the elements have **another** role, a role **in addition to** that of a material cause -- the role of an **efficient** cause. He is suggesting that an element is matter **and agent**, at the same time -- matter in relation to the **composition** of all other generable and corruptible bodies, and agent in some other relation(s).   What does it mean to say -- one wants to ask -- as we say nowadays, that potassium is good for one's health?   Doesn't potassium, as a remaining material component of our bodies, i.e., as an element (in some sense), **do** something, exercise some sort of **agent causality**,   in addition to being a **material component**?   Or, better (since potassium, along with all the chemical elements in the periodic table, is not a true element, i.e., not an element in the sense defined above, beginning on p. 48),   don't the   two u-quarks and the one d-quark, as remaining material components of a proton, i.e., as true elements, **do** something, exercise some sort of **agent causality**, in addition to being **material components**? Don't they at least "whirl about each other in their proton prison"?, as someone has said. And what, if anything, does their whirling about each other do for the proton of which they are the components? For the atom of which that proton is a component?   For the molecule of which that atom is a component?   For the human being of which that molecule is a component?

To answer these questions in a **completely** acceptable way (this would be a **scientific** answer), one would have to pursue studies in at least these three disciplines: 1) in particle physics,   2) in chemistry,   and   3) in biology. Moreover, most of these questions would have to be asked in a more careful, and more pointed, way. Other questions, no doubt, would have to be asked. The first question seems pointed enough (though perhaps not careful enough), as it stands: what, if anything, does the whirling of the quarks about each other **do** for the proton of which they are the components? This would be a question for particle physics. There would be other questions, e.g.: what exactly do protons **do** within an atom? and what does this **do** for the atom of which the protons are components?   Some questions (there would surely be others) for chemistry: what exactly do atoms **do** within a molecule? and what does this **do** for the molecule of which the atoms are components? Some questions (and there would doubtless be others) for biology: what exactly do molecules **do** within a tissue? and what does this **do** for the tissue of which the molecules are components?; what exactly do tissues **do** within

139

an organ? and what does this **do** for the organ of which the tissues are components?; what exactly do organs **do** within a living body, e.g., the human body? and what does this **do** for the living body of which the organs are components?

To answer these questions in an **incipiently** acceptable way (this would be a **philosophical** answer), one would have to keep in mind what is meant by the **virtual, retrievable, dispositional and instrumental presence** of the lower in the higher, i.e., of certain required elements (the simplest and lowliest of bodily components, like quarks and electrons), and of other required bodily components as well (complex and higher ones, like the chemical elements of the periodic table, and the molecules made out of these) in progressively more and more complex bodily things, all the way up to, and including, of course, the most complex bodily thing which we know, i.e., man. That is, one would have to keep in mind Aquinas' view 1) that prime matter is in potency to forms in a certain order (above, pp. 131-132), and see this in relation to his view 2) that whereas a mixed body, like any corporeal substance, can have **actually** only one substantial form, its own; **potentially**, nonetheless, it **can** have -- indeed **must** have -- at least as many substantial forms, in number and in kind, as the elements which are required as its ingredients, i.e., without which it could neither **be** nor **act** (above, p. 126).

To say that a mixed body **could not be** without a certain number of certain kinds of elements (and atoms and molecules) is to say that without their intervening **dispositional presence**, prime matter **could not have acquired** a given sort of substantial form (nor continue to possess it), and so the mixed body could not have come to be, nor continue to be, **what it is**. To say that the mixed body **could not act** without a certain number of certain kinds of elements (and atoms and molecules) is to say that it depends on their **instrumental presence**, i.e., that it needs the **powers** of the elements (and of the atoms and the molecules) as the means, the instruments, the **instrumental agent** causes, through which it performs its proper activities.

140

Thus, elements (along with certain sorts of atoms and molecules) are not only **material** causes of a special sort, they are also **agent** causes of a special sort, i.e., **instrumental agent** causes.

Aquinas makes this point, though **only** about substantial forms which are **souls** (since souls are his concern in the context), when he writes in the *De Homine:*

> **Tota . . . natura corporalis subiacet animae, et comparatur ad ipsam sicut materia et instrumentum.** *(S.T., I, q. 78, a. 1. c.)*

> **The whole of corporeal nature is an underlying subject to the soul, and is related to it as** *matter and instrument.*

All corporeal things, observes Aquinas -- i.e., everything bodily, down to and including the ultimate bodily components which are the elements -- are related to **souls** of all types, whether intellectual or sensitive or vegetative, as that which can be their matter (subject) and their instrument, i.e., as that in which they can exist (their **matter**) and through which (their **instrument**) they can perform their proper activities, i.e., life activities like self-nourishment, growth, reproduction, sensation.   What Aquinas says here about the substantial forms of all **living things**, i.e., about souls (souls, recall, are his concern in this context), is also the case, as he sees it, with respect to the substantial forms of all **non-living things** as well. That is, all **lower** non-living things, down to and including the elements, are related to the substantial forms of all **higher** non-living things, as that which can be their matter (subject) and their instrument, i.e., as that in which these substantial forms can exist (their matter) and through which (their instrument) they can perform their proper activities.

An instrument, it might be helpful to note at this point, can be either a **separated** instrument or a **conjoined** instrument, as Aquinas points out in his commentary on Aristotle's *On the Soul* (*In II De Anima*, lect. 9, n. 348). A separated instrument is one whose form is a form different from that of the principal agent. For example, the pen with which I write is a separated instrument, inasmuch as its form is different from my form, i.e., from my substantial form, or soul. A conjoined instrument, on the other hand, is an instrument whose form **is** the form of the principal agent. A conjoined instrument might be a bodily part, like a hand; or a bodily organ, like the heart; a molecule, like carbon dioxide; an atom, like oxygen; or an element, like a quark or an electron. All of these are, in various ways, parts or components of **mixed bodies** (a mixed body is any body which is composed of elements, whether living or non-living), however lowly (e.g., quarks are components of the lowly proton), or however exalted (e.g., quarks, protons, atoms, molecules, hands, etc. are components of man); and their form **is** the form of the mixed body. Thus, my hand, and my pen, are instruments by which my soul writes, and without which my soul could **not** write. Like all instruments, both my hand and my pen contribute something which arises out of the nature and power of each. My hand (directed by my soul) holds and moves the pen with certain hand-appropriate motions by which letters and words are formed; my pen contributes the ink. Without my hand, and without my pen, my soul could not write, though my soul is the principal agent. Without my soul, neither my hand nor my pen could write; for neither my hand nor my pen is the principal agent. An instrumental agent is a moved mover of sorts, a moved mover with two functions: 1) an instrumental function, i.e., it performs as directed by the power of, and to the end of, the principal agent, and 2) a proper function, i.e., it performs by something of itself. Thus, my soul moves my hand to move the pen. My soul uses my hand to do what a hand can do; and my hand uses the pen to do what a pen can do. But both the hand and the pen, as used by the soul, are used to do what the soul wants to do, i.e., to write.

Now, quarks are related to the form of a proton as matter and **conjoined** instrument. That is, the proton uses its component quarks to do what quarks, as put together into a proton, can do -- in order to do what a proton, as proton, does. And since the component quarks are a conjoined instrument, their form is the form of the proton. Protons, in turn (and therefore also quarks, inasmuch as they are components of the proton), are related to the form of an atom as matter and **conjoined** instrument. That is, an atom uses its component protons and quarks to do what protons and quarks, as put together into an atom, can do -- in order to do what an atom, as atom, does. And since the component protons are a conjoined instrument, their form is the form of the atom. Molecules, in turn (and therefore also quarks and protons and atoms, inasmuch as they are components of the molecule), are related to the forms of progressively higher bodily things, up to and including man, as matter and **conjoined** instrument. And man, for example, uses his component bodily organs (e.g., heart and lungs), molecules (e.g., carbon dioxide), atoms (e.g., oxygen), and elements (e.g., quarks and electrons) to do what they, as put together into man, can do -- in order to do what man, as man, does. And since these components are, all of them, conjoined instruments, their form is the form of man. -- It should be clear, therefore, that elements (along with atoms and molecules and bodily organs, etc.) are each, in their own way, not only material causes of a special sort, but also agent causes of a special sort, i.e., **conjoined instrumental** agent causes.

143

4. Is a mixed body, i.e., a physical thing made out of certain elements combined in a certain ratio, the same as a natural organed[8] body, i.e., the appropriate subject of soul?

> Materia prima est in potentia primo ad formam elementi. Sub forma vero elementi est in potentia ad formam mixti; propter quod elementa sunt materia mixti. Sub forma autem mixti considerata est in potentia ad animam vegetabilem; nam talis corporis [i.e., corporis mixti] anima actus est. Itemque anima vegetabilis est in potentia ad sensitivam; sensitiva vero ad intellectivam. . . . . . Sunt ergo elementa propter corpora mixta; haec vero propter viventia; in quibus plantae sunt propter animalia, animalia vero propter hominem. (*C.G.*, III, cap. 22)

> Prime matter is in potency first of all to the form of an element. Then, as existing under the form of an element, it is in potency to the form of a mixed body. This is why elements are the matter of a mixed body. Moreover, considered under the form of a mixed body, it is in potency to the vegetable soul. It is of such a body, thus, that the soul is the act. Similarly, the vegetable soul is in potency to the sensitive soul, and the sensitive to the intellectual. . . . . . The elements therefore exist for the sake of mixed bodies, and mixed bodies for the sake of living things, among which plants exist for the sake of animals, and animals for the sake of man.

> Anima est actus corporis physici habentis vitam in potentia, . . . [et] tale est omne corpus organicum. Et dicitur corpus organicum, quod habet diversitatem organorum. Diversitas

---

8   To translate "organicum" as "organed" is to invent a word which seems to convey the sense of "organicum" better than the commonly used word "organized." For "organized," as said of a body, can be taken to mean: having an **orderly** structure and/or function; or, put together into a whole of **ordered and interdependent** parts; whereas "organicum" means precisely: having bodily organs, in the way in which "uniformed" means: having (wearing) a uniform, or "armed" means: having (bearing) arms, e.g., a gun. A bodily organ is an instrument (organon) by means of which the living thing performs its life activities; but unlike a gun, it is, of course, a **conjoined** instrument (see above, pp. 141-142, beginning at "An instrument, it might be helpful to note at this point, can be either a **separated** or a **conjoined** instrument, . . . ".

autem organorum necessaria est in corpore suscipiente vitam propter diversas operationes animae.   (*In II De Anima*, lect. 1, n. 230)

The soul is the act of a physical body having life in potency, . . . [and] such is every body which is organed.   Those bodies are said to be organed which have a diversity of organs. And a diversity of organs is necessary in a body which takes on life, because of the diverse operations of the soul.

Si aliqua definitio communis debeat assignari, quae convenit omni animae, erit haec: *Anima est actus primus corporis physici organici*. Non autem oportet addere: *potentia vitam habentis*. Loco enim huius ponitur *organicum*, ut ex dictis patet. (*In II De Anima*, lect. 1, n. 233)

If a common definition of the soul is to be given, one which applies to every soul, it will be this: *Soul is the first act of a physical body which is organed*. And it is not necessary to add: *having life in potency*. For in place of that, one adds: *organed*, as is clear from the things that have been said.

What Aquinas writes in the passages just above raises some questions about the nature of the body of which the soul is said to be the act or actuality. 1) Is it a mixed body? For Aquinas does say: ". . . nam talis corporis [sc. mixti] anima actus est." 2) Or is it a physical body having life potentially, i.e., having a diversity of organs ordered to a diversity of life activities?   For Aquinas also says: "Anima est actus corporis physici habentis vitam in potentia, [i.e., actus corporis physici **organici**, quod est corpus habens]. . . diversitatem organorum . . . propter diversas operationes animae."   3) Is a mixed body **the same as** a physical body with a diversity of organs ordered to performing a diversity of life activities?   4) Or does being a mixed body **imply** being a physical body with such organs?   5) Or, the other way around, does being a physical body with such organs **imply** being a mixed body?   6) If being a physical body with such organs implies being a mixed body, what is the role of the component elements with respect to the life activities performed by the living thing? 7) Does such a body need to be composed of **certain sorts** of elements, in addition to having **certain sorts** of organs, in order to enable the living thing to perform its appropriate life activities?

What Aquinas writes in the passage just below provides the beginnings of some sort of answer to these questions. In the context in which these lines appear, he is concerned to make clear why it is that one can speak of **three** types of soul, of **four** modes of living, and of **five** powers of soul. The criterion for distinguishing the three types of soul is the way in which life activities **rise above** the activities of merely bodily or corporeal things, i.e., of matter in its non-living states. The criterion, secondly, for distinguishing the four modes of living is the way in which life activities **are found together** in various grades of living thing. And lastly, the criterion for distinguishing the five genera of powers of soul is the **scope or range of the object** to which the activities of soul are ordered. Of special interest in the context in which these lines appear are Aquinas' remarks with respect to the three types of soul:

> Diversae animae distinguuntur secundum quod diversimode operatio animae supergreditur operationem naturae corporalis: tota enim natura corporalis subiacet animae, et comparatur ad ipsam sicut materia et instrumentum.
>
> Est ergo quaedam operatio animae, quae intantum excedit naturam corpoream, quod neque etiam exercetur per organum corporale. Et talis est operatio *animae rationalis*.
>
> Est autem alia operatio animae infra istam, quae quidem fit per organum corporale, non tamen per aliquam corpoream qualitatem. Et talis est operatio *animae sensibilis:* quia etsi calidum et frigidum, et humidum et siccum, et aliae huiusmodi qualitates corporeae requirantur ad operationem sensus; non tamen ita quod mediante virtute talium qualitatum operatio animae sensibilis procedat; sed requiruntur solum ad debitam dispositionem organi.

Infima autem operationum animae est, quae fit per organum corporeum, et virtute corporeae qualitatis. Supergreditur tamen operationem naturae corporeae: quia motiones corporum sunt ab exteriori principio, huiusmodi autem operationes sunt a principio intrinseco; hoc enim commune est omnibus operationibus animae; omne enim animatum aliquo modo movet seipsum. Et talis est operatio *animae vegetabilis:* digestio enim, et ea quae consequuntur, fit instrumentaliter per actionem caloris, ut dicitur in *II de Anima...* (S.T., I, q. 78, a. 1, c.)

Diverse souls are distinguished in accord with the diverse ways in which the operation of the soul rises above the operation of corporeal nature. For the whole of corporeal nature is an underlying subject to the soul, and is related to it as matter and instrument.

Now, there is a certain operation of soul which rises above corporeal nature to such an extent that it is in no way even performed by a bodily organ. And such is the operation of the rational soul.

There is another operation of the soul, below the one just noted, which is indeed performed by a corporeal organ, but not through some corporeal quality. And such is the operation of the sensible soul. For even though hot and cold, and wet and dry, and other such corporeal qualities are required for the operation of the senses, they are not required in such a way that the operation of the sensible soul proceeds by means of the power of such qualities. They are required, rather, only for the proper disposition of the organ.

The lowest of the activities of soul is the one which is performed by a corporeal organ, and by means of the power of a corporeal quality. But even this operation rises above the operation of corporeal nature, because the motions of bodies derive form some exterior principle, whereas such operations arise from an intrinsic principle. And this is common to all operations of soul, for every thing which has a soul in some way moves itself. And such is the operation of the vegetable soul; digestion, for example, and the things which follow, is performed instrumentally through the action of heat, as is said in Bk. II of *On the Soul.*

In Aquinas' remarks concerning the operations of the vegetating soul, and those of the sensing soul, one finds some sort of reply to the last, the seventh, of the questions raised above on pp. 144-145, i.e., to the question: Does such a body [i.e., corpus physicum organicum] need to be composed of certain sorts of elements, in addition to having certain sorts of organs, in order to enable the living thing to perform its appropriate life activites? Certain sorts of bodily organs are required, quite obviously (on the basis of minimal **scientific** sense observation), for the performance of vegetative activities, e.g., stomach, intestines, liver. Similarly (but on the basis of **ordinary, everyday** sense observation and introspection), certain bodily organs are required for the performance of sensory activities, e.g., eye, ear, tongue . But, in addition to the instrumental causality of bodily organs of certain sorts, such activities require, quite clearly, the presence and accompanying instrumental causality of certain sorts of elements (and compounds as well). Digestion, exemplifies Aquinas, takes place through the accompanying instrumental causality of the powers of the quality heat, which requires that the element fire be a component of the body of the living thing. Nowadays we would say (on the basis of some minimal **scientific** investigation) that digestion takes place through the accompanying instrumental causality of the powers of various **compounds,** like saliva in the mouth, hydrochloric acid in the stomach, and bile in the duodenum.

Speaking generally of the basic vegetative activites, i.e., self-nourishment, growth and reproduction, we would say, nowadays, that they take place through the accompanying instrumental causality of the powers of various **minerals,** like chromium, iron, magnesium, calcium, manganese, copper, potassium, selenium, zinc; of various **vitamins,** like choline, folic acid, niacin, ascorbic acid, d-alpha tocopherol; of various **enzymes,** like bromelain, lactase, amylase, protease, lipase; of various and countless **phytochemicals**; and of hosts of other as yet unknown, as yet undiscovered, **instrumental materials**; all of these being instances of the **"materia et instrumentum"** of which Aquinas speaks in the *S.T.*, I, q. 78, a. 1, c. -- updated, of course, to reflect the thinking of our times.

Speaking generally of the activities of the sensing soul, we might say nowadays, following Aquinas (though some might object -- see the immediately following paragraph), that they are performed by the relevant bodily organs, though **not** by means of the powers of any minerals, or vitamins, or enzymes, or phytochemicals; but that, nonetheless, certain sorts of minerals, vitamins, etc., are required to keep the relevant bodily organs in good and healthy working order. For example, the minerals and phytochemicals contained in Gyu Hwa Tea, which is a blend of the herbs *Flos chrysanthemi* and *Semen cassiae torae*, are claimed by the Chinese to keep the focusing muscles of the eye in peak working order, resulting in heightened focusing ability, and thereby sharpened vision.

But, someone might object that sensory activity, like vegetative activity, **is performed** by means of the powers of various elements and/or compounds; and that it is **not** true that these elements and compounds are required **just** to keep the relevant bodily organs in good working order. For, doesn't vision in faint light take place by means of the photosensitivity of the rhodopsin in the retinal rods? And doesn't color vision take place by means of the chromatosensitivity of the retinal cones?

In response to this objection, it should be noted that sensory activity takes place by virtue of a **special sort of sensible** form, as Aquinas argues quite plausibly in many places, e.g., by virtue of a special sort of **visible** form, which the bodily organ is capable of receiving from an appropriate object, **both** by virtue of its being the particular sort of bodily organ which it is, e.g., an eye,

149

and by virtue of the activities of certain elements and/or compounds which are among its constituents, e.g., the chemical and electrical activities initiated by the impact of faint light on the photosensitive rhodopsin in the retinal rods. This sensible form is quite unlike an ordinary sensible form, in that it is received into the seeing organ, i.e., the eye -- the eyeball plus optic nerve plus proper cortical area -- in such a way that the eye remains the eye that it was. That is, the eye can take on the visible features of a tree, say, without having to take on the physical matter of a tree. In the physical world, it is tree-matter which takes on the visible features of a tree. In the activity of seeing, it is eye-matter (i.e., eyeball plus optic nerve plus proper cortical area) which takes on the visible features of a tree. And these eye-received tree-features (this is the **special sort of sensible** form) become the means by which seeing a tree takes place.

Thus, whereas digestion takes place by virtue of the action of certain bodily organs, like stomach and intestines, **and also**, as Aquinas would say, by virtue some bodily quality, like heat, i.e., by the action of the power of the element fire; seeing takes place by virtue of the relevant bodily organ, **and also** by the visible form for the reception of which it has been properly disposed by virtue of some bodily quality, like the photosensitivity of rhodopsin. Rhodopsin of proper quality and in proper quantity, among other things, is required for an eye to be in good and healthy working order, i.e., "for the proper disposition of the organ," as Aquinas would put it. The chemical and electrical activities initiated by rhodopsin, when affected by faint light, do not have the same role in the activity of seeing that the action of HCl has in the activity of digesting. For, whereas rhodopsin enables the eye to receive the visible form, and the visible form is that by virtue of which the eye does its seeing; the action of HCl is precisely that (at least one of the relevant things) by virtue of which the stomach does its digesting. Which is to say that vegetative activity takes place by virtue of the relevant bodily organ(s) **in concert with** the power of certain **bodily** elements and/or compounds; whereas sensory activity takes place by virtue of the relevant bodily organs (properly disposed for the reception of sensible forms by virtue of the powers of certain bodily elements and/or compounds) **in concert with** the relevant received sensible form. And the sensible form is not an ordinary sort of sensible form. It is rather a special sort of sensible form, a form which can be received into a matter which is not an ordinary sort of physical matter, i.e., into a bodily organ of sensation. That is, for example, as noted above, the visible features of tree-matter can be received into eye-matter.

This, then, seems to be an acceptable answer to the seventh question raised above on p. 146, namely the question: Does a natural or physical organed body need to be composed of certain sorts of elements, in addition to having certain sorts of bodily organs, in order to enable the living thing to perform its appropriate life activities?, namely this answer: **Yes.** But, for the performance of **vegetative** activities, it needs these composing elements (and/or compounds) **as material instrumental causes.** For the performance of **sensory** activities, however, it needs these composing elements (and/or compounds) **for the proper disposition of the sensory organ.** Properly disposed, the sensory organ becomes capable of receiving a **special sort of sensible** form. And this form takes on the role of an instrumental cause.

This answer to the seventh question is also an answer to the sixth question, i.e., to the question about "the **role** of the component elements [and compounds] with respect to the life activities performed by the living thing."

Is the body, of which the soul is said to be the actuality, a mixed body (question one)? The answer is clearly: **Yes.** But, not just a mixed body. It is observed to be a mixed body, indeed, but **with bodily organs** for performing life activities. Moreover, it would be difficult to see how a living thing could perform its life activities without certain relevant bodily organs.

Is the body, of which the soul is said to be the actuality, an organed body (question two)? The answer is clearly: **Yes.** But, one must add that organed bodies are observed to be mixed bodies as well. Indeed, it would be difficult to see how an organed body could perform life activities by means of its organs alone, without help from certain component elements and/or compounds. Which provides an answer to question five: **Yes;** being an organed body does imply being a mixed body.

The answer to question three is quite clear: **No;** a mixed body is not the same as a natural organed body. For, there are mixed bodies which are **not** organed bodies, e.g., gold, silver; salt, pepper, sugar; water, oil.

And this supplies the answer to question four: **No;** being a mixed body does **not** imply being an organed body.

5. **Elements in the definition of a mixed body**
   (**The elements as** *definientia*)

The things said so far in PART THREE lead quite naturally to considerations about the role of elements in the definition of a mixed body. A definition, as Aquinas understands it, is a statement which identifies and describes the causes -- **all** the causes, whenever possible -- of a thing's becoming, of its being, and of its activities. That is, a definition is an attempt to answer the question: What, both extrinsic and intrinsic to a thing, accounts for these facts: 1) that the thing has come into existence (its becoming), 2) that it is now in existence (its being), 3) that it does what it does (its activities)? An identification and description of **all** relevant causes, **both** those which are **intrinsic** to the thing, i.e., matter, form, **elements,** compounds, organs (if the thing has organs), **and** those which are **extrinsic** to the thing, i.e., agents and ends, provide a **complete** answer to this question, a **complete** definition of the thing. A definition in terms of what is **intrinsic** (only) -- matter, form, **elements,** organs (if there are organs) -- expresses **what a thing is,** i.e., its **essence,** and thereby also explains **why it does what it does.** A definition in terms of what is **extrinsic** (only), on the other hand, identifies and describes either **what produced the thing, and what accounts for its continued existence,** i.e., its agent(s), or **what the thing is for,** i.e., its end(s). Clearly, agents and ends are not ingredients of the essence of a thing. And this is why such definitions do **not** express **what a thing is**.

Now, as Aquinas sees it, a definition in terms of what is **intrinsic** to a thing identifies and describes the thing's **matter** and its **form**. For example, when man is defined as something composed of sensitive body and rational soul, "sensitive body" designates the matter and "rational soul" designates the form. But a definition in terms of what is intrinsic can also, as Aquinas sees it, identify and describe the thing's **proximate genus** and its **specific difference**. For example, when man is defined as a rational animal, "animal" designates the proximate genus and "rational" designates the specific difference. Moreover, as Aquinas sees it, the genus of the genus-difference definition derives from, is taken from, matter; the specific difference from form; and the genus-difference definition, as a whole, from the matter-form definition, as a whole. For example, man's genus, animal, is taken from man's matter, the sensitive body; man's specific difference, rational, from man's form, the rational soul; and man's genus-difference definition, rational animal, from man's matter-form definition, something composed of sensitive body and rational soul. Since "is taken from" means simply **furnishes the content of the concept of**, one can say either that man is an animal (using the genus with "is") or that man **has** (as a component part) a sensitive body (using the matter with "has"); and one has said the same thing. **To be** an animal means **to have** (as a component part) a sensitive body. Similarly, one can say either that man **is** rational (using the specific difference with "is") or that man **has** (as a component part) a thinking soul (using the form with "has"); and one has said the same thing. **To be** rational means **to have** (as a component part) a thinking soul. Similarly, again, one can say either that man **is** a rational animal (using the genus and the specific difference with "is") or that man **has** (is composed of) a sensitive body and a thinking soul (using the matter and the form with "has"); and one has said the same thing. **To be** a rational animal means **to have** (to be composed of) a sensitive body and a thinking soul.

Furthermore, as Aquinas would most certainly say, an identification and description of each of the **elements** and compounds and organs (if it has any organs) of a thing would provide a more detailed account of the thing's **matter**, and thereby of the genus which is taken from matter. There is more than a very strong hint at this in what Aquinas writes in *In Boetii De Trinitate*, in a passage considered briefly above (pp. 136-137), while reflecting on the question whether elements are **ingredients** of the **essence** of a thing which is composed of them:

> . . . per se competit homini quod inveniatur in eo anima rationalis, et corpus compositum ex quatuor elementis; unde sine his partibus homo intelligi non potest: et sic oportet poni in definitione eius . . .

> Sed digitus, pes, manus et huiusmodi, sunt praeter intellectum hominis, unde ex illis ratio essentialis hominis non dependet, unde sine his intelligi potest.

> Sive enim habeat pedes, sive non, dummodo ponatur coniunctum ex anima rationali et corpore composito ex quatuor elementis propria mixtione quam requirit talis forma, erit homo. *(In Boetii De Trinitate,* q.5, a.3, c.)

> . . . it belongs to man as such that there be found in him a rational soul and a body composed of the four elements. And this is why man cannot be understood without these parts. And so, they must be put into the definition of man . . .

> But a finger, a foot, a hand, and such like, are outside what it is to be a man. Whence man's essential nature does not depend on them, and so can be understood without them.

> For whether a man has feet, or not, so long as he is held to be a conjunction of 1) rational soul, and 2) body composed of the four elements, properly mixed, as required by such a form, he will be a man.

It is clear that man cannot **be,** nor therefore can man **be understood,** except as composed of a rational soul and a sensitive body. And man's sensitive body, as Aquinas sees it, cannot **be,** nor therefore can it **be understood,** except as composed of the **four elements** (today, we would say, composed of certain quarks and leptons) put together in the way required by man's rational soul. And this is why, as Aquinas sees it, the **rational soul** and the **sensitive body** and the **four elements** (today, certain quarks and leptons) must be put into the definition of man, the elements (today, quarks and leptons) being included in order to provide details with respect to the nature of man's body. A finger, however, or a hand or an elbow, a toe or a foot or a knee -- these, and other parts like them, are outside what it is to be a man. Experience teaches us that a man can exist without them. And this is why such parts do not have to be put into man's definition. But there are other parts, like the brain, the heart, the lungs, the liver, the intestines, without which -- experience teaches us -- man cannot exist. These, therefore, are clearly parts of what it is to be a man, and so must be included in man's definition. And although Aquinas makes no mention of bodily parts like these in the passage quoted just above, he would most certainly recognize parts like these as bodily organs which must be included in an account of man's body.

6. Ingredients in the definition of an element
(The elements as *definienda*)

The matter of a mixed body, according to Aquinas, cannot **be,** nor can it **be understood,** except as composed of the **four elements** (today, we would say, except as composed of certain quarks and leptons), put together in the way required by the form of that mixed body. But what about the elements themselves (or today, the quarks and leptons themselves)? What are **their** intrinsic components; what are the ingredients of **their** essences; how are **they** to be defined? What is that **within** them which accounts for the fact 1) that they have come into existence (their becoming), 2) that they are now in existence (their being), and 3) that they do what they do (their activities)? The question here is **not** about the meaning of the word "element," the meaning considered above, and in some detail (pp. 46-52). Nor is it about the word "element" in the very general sense in which **any cause at all which enters the composition of a thing** can be said to be an element, a sense which Aquinas notes as he comments on Aristotle's *On the Heavens*, the sense in which matter and form can be said to be the universal elements of all things which come to be in change, even though they themselves (i.e., matter and form) are **not bodies**.[9] Nor is it about the nature of matter and form themselves. The question is rather about the **elements themselves**, about those elements which **are bodies**, i.e., about earth, water, air and fire, both in general and in particular. In general. Are these bodily elements composed of matter and form? If so, does the matter of each have something in common with the matter of the others? Does the form of each have something in common with the form of the others? If so, then they have both a common genus and a common specific difference. In particular. How is the element **earth** to be defined? What sort of matter does earth have? This will supply its genus. What sort of form does earth have? This will supply its specific difference. Similarly with respect to water and air and fire. For us today, how is a quark to be defined? How is a lepton to be defined? Further, how is each of the various types of quark to be defined? For example, the u-quark, and the d-quark? And how, the various types of lepton? For example, the electron, and the electron-neutrino? Would a matter-form definition (and its derivative, a genus-difference definition) be acceptable, appropriate, possible? If not, what sort of definition would be acceptable, appropriate, possible?

---

[9]   . . . non enim quaelibet causa potest dici elementum, sed solum quae intrat rei compositionem. Unde universalia elementa sunt materia et forma, ut patet in *I Physic.*, quae tamen **non** sunt corpora. Hic autem intendit Philosophus de elementis quae sunt **corpora** . . . (*In III De Caelo*, lectio 8, in medio).

The following comments of Aquinas (on pp. 157-158) can be used to provide the beginnings of some sort of **general** account of the essences of the four elements.

> ... omne quod est melius, Deo attribuendum est. Sed, apud nos, composita sunt meliora simplicibus, sicut corpora mixta elementis, et elementa suis partibus. Ergo non est dicendum quod Deus sit omnino simplex. (*S.T.,* I, q.3, a.7, obj. 2)

> ... everything which is better is to be attributed to God. But, here in this world, composed things are better than simple things, like mixed bodies which are better than the elements, and the elements which are better than their parts. Therefore, it is not to be said that God is utterly simple.

Just above, in a possible objection to God's utter simplicity, Aquinas explicitly states that the elements are **composed out of parts,** just as mixed bodies are composed out of the elements. But he says nothing about the nature of these parts.

> ... elementorum corpora sunt simplicia, et non est in eis compositio nisi materiae et formae ... (*C.G.,* III, cap. 23)

> ... the bodies of the elements are simple, and there is no composition in them except out of matter and form ...

Here, however, Aquinas explicitly states that the elements are **simple.** And what is simple, one wants to note, cannot be composed of parts. Nonetheless, Aquinas immediately adds that there **is** a composition in the elements, i.e., a composition out of **matter and form,** but **only** out of matter and form; thereby **both** identifying the nature of the parts out of which the elements are composed, **and** limiting the composition to just one kind. He must mean that the elements are simple **precisely as bodies,** i.e., that they are **not** composed out of parts which are **bodily** parts (... elementorum **corpora** sunt simplicia...). The elements, thus, are both composed and simple; composed with respect to matter and form, simple with respect to bodily components.

But this is puzzling. For how can something which is a body -- the elements are bodies -- have no bodily components?

> ... non enim quaelibet causa potest dici elementum, sed solum quae intrat rei compositionem. Unde universalia elementa sunt materia et forma, ut patet in *I Physicorum*, quae tamen non sunt corpora. Hic autem intendit Philosophus de elementis quae sunt corpora ... (*In III De Caelo*, lectio 8, n.   )

> ... not just any cause can be called an element, but only those which enter the composition of a thing. Whence the universal elements [of physical things] are matter and form, as is clear from Bk. I of the *Physics;* but matter and form are not bodies. Here, however, the Philosopher intends to treat of those elements which *are* bodies ...

Just above, in terms of the meaning of the word "element" pointed out earlier (p. 156), Aquinas sheds some light on what it means to say that each of the four elements is both composed and simple. This meaning of "element" is a very general meaning, i.e., **any cause, whether a body or not, which in any way enters the composition of a thing** can be called an element. In this sense of "element," matter and form, as intrinsic causes, are universally the elements of all substances which can come to be in change, though they themelves (i.e., matter and form) are **not** bodies. And so, one can argue, since each of the four elements is a substance which can come to be in change, each is composed out of matter and form; even though no one of them comes to be, nor is composed, out of prior bodily things. There **are no** prior bodily things. The four elements are, each of them, the **ultimate bodily things** out of which all other sorts of bodily things come to be. That is, there are no bodily things prior to the elements, out of which the elements themselves could come to be, in such a way that these prior bodily things could survive in the elements in a way which would be like the way in which the elements themselves survive in the mixed bodies which come to be out of them. When an element comes to be, it can come to be only out of another element. And what survives in it from the one out of which it came to be, can be only **prime matter**. Which means that the form by which it differs fom the element out of which it came to be, must be a **substantial** form.

How, then, is it that each of the four elements is a **bodily** thing, something three-dimensional? How, since each is composed out of prime matter and substantial form, and **only** out of prime matter and substantial form; and neither of these components is a body?

Though it is true, for Aquinas, that neither prime matter nor substantial form is a body, i.e., that neither is something of itself three dimensional, and that prime matter and substantial form are the only ingredients in the **essence** of an element (indeed, in the **essence** of **any** substance which can come to be in change); it is also true, for Aquinas, that these dimensions are a **property** of any such substance. That is, by means of its substantial form in one of its several grades (or functions), i.e., **in its grade of corporeity**, any such substance is **continuously** productive of its three dimensions, much like the sun is **continuously** productive of light; and by means of its prime matter, in its (i.e., prime matter's) role as ultimate subject, any such substance is continuously receptive of those three dimensions. So that, although its three dimensions are **not** ingredients of its **essence**, such a substance **does have** three dimensions -- as a **property** which is **caused by the ingredients** of its essence -- produced (continuously), as by an agent cause, by its substantial form; and received (continuously), as by a subject, by its prime matter.

It may be helpful, at this point, to consider briefly the following comments of Aquinas (on pp. 159-164), as a kind of continuation of his **general** account of the essences of the four elements. He is concerned to point out the distinctive contributions of prime matter and of substantial form to the **individuation** of physical substances, but what he points out is quite clearly relevant to our present concern.

The contribution of prime matter:

> ... materia ... est subjectum primum.   ... Primum autem
> subjectum est quod in alio recipi non potest ...   ... materia ...
> est principium individuationis ut est primum subjectum ...
> (*De Natura Materiae et Dimensionibus Interminatis,* cap. 1; vol.
> 27, 489 b - 490 a)

> ... matter ... is the first subject.   ... Now, a first subject is a
> subject which cannot be received into another. . .   ... And
> matter. . . is the principle of individuation precisely as it is the
> first subject ...

To say that prime matter is the **first** subject is to say that there is nothing,
no subject, prior to prime matter into which prime matter itself could be
received; that prime matter is the **ultimate** subject, the **irreceivable** subject.
It is also to say that prime matter is that into which all physical forms are
received, both substantial and accidental; substantial forms (including of
course the forms of each of the four elements), immediately into prime
matter; accidental forms (including of course three dimensional quantity),
into the physical substance itself, but by virtue of the receptivity of prime
matter.   This is what is of relevance to our present concern.

With respect to individuation, now, the irreceivability of prime matter
is what accounts for the fact that a physical substance cannot be received into
another as into a subject, i.e., for the fact that it is a **substance**, an **ultimate**
existing **subject** (one of the basic features of **an individual**), thereby
differentiating it from substantial forms and from accidental forms as well,
neither of which is an individual in the sense of an ultimate existing subject.
Each exists **in another** as in a subject, and is individuated (with respect to its
being irreceivable into yet another) by that other; the substantial form, by the
irreceivability of the prime matter in which it exists; accidental forms, by
the irreceivability of the substance itself (composed of prime matter and
substantial form) in which they exist.

160

. . . impossibile est quamcumque partitionem ante formam substantialem in ea [sc. in materia prima] ponere, cum inductio formae sit generatio compositi, cujus solum est habere partes per se. Materia [prima] autem et forma [substantialis] non habent partes per se, sed tantum per accidens. Unde non dividitur nisi per accidens, ad divisionem scilicet totius. Ex quo manifestum est quod priusquam compositum constitueretur, nulla partibilitas fuit ex parte materiae, cum hoc non competit sibi nisi per accidens. (*De Natura Materiae et Dimensionibus Interminatis*, cap. 2, vol. 27, 493 b)

. . . it is impossible that there be any partition at all in it [i.e., in prime matter] before the substantial form, since the coming in of the substantial form is the generation of the composite, to which alone it belongs properly (per se) to have parts. Whence it [i.e., matter] is not divided except through the division of something else (per accidens), i.e., at the division of the whole. From which it is clear that before the composite was constituted, there was no way at all that matter could be divided into parts, since that does not belong to matter except through something else (per accidens).

Three-dimensional quantity, notes Aquinas, belongs properly (per se) to the composite of prime matter and substantial form, i.e., to the ultimate existing subject; and to prime matter (to the substantial form, too) only because it is an ingredient in the essence of the ultimate existing subject. Prime matter is nothing but pure receptive potentiality for substantial form; and substantial form is simply what actualizes that potentiality. Neither one nor the other, therefore, is **as such** three dimensional. Each is three dimensional in virtue of the three dimensionality of the substance. This is what is of relevance to our present concern.

With respect to individuation, now, the three dimensionality of prime matter, which it has in virtue of the three dimensionality of the substance of the essence of which it is an ingredient, is that in virtue of which prime matter can be divided into various parts, into each of which it can receive a diverse substantial form, thus accounting for the fact of **many individuals**

161

within a same species.

The contribution of substantial form:

> ... actualitas formae accidentalis causatur ab actualitate subjecti; ita quod subjectum, inquantum est in potentia, est susceptivum formae accidentalis; inquantum autem est in actu, est eius productivum. Et hoc dico de proprio et per se accidente; nam respectu accidentis extranei, subjectum est susceptivum tantum; productivum vero talis accidentis est agens extrinsecum. (S.T., I, q. 77, a.1, c.)

> ... the actuality of an accidental form is caused by (derived from) the actuality of the subject, in such a way that the subject, to the extent that it is in potency, is receptive of the accidental form; and to the extent that it is in act, it is productive of that accidental form. And I say this about a proper and per se accident. For with respect to an extraneous accident, the subject is receptive only; and what is productive of it is an extrinsic agent.

Here, Aquinas points out that it is the physical substance itself, by virtue of the components of its essence, which accounts for the fact that it has all the per se accidents which it has, including its three dimensional quantity. By virtue of its prime matter, the physical substance is **receptive of** its per se accidents, including its three dimensions; and by virtue of its substantial form, which is that by which it is in act, the physical substance is **productive** of them. There are, of course, certain accidents with respect to which a physical substance is receptive **only**, and this by virtue of the receptivity of the prime matter in it, e.g., the **shape** which the marble of a given statue happens to have. The **productive** cause of this shape, i.e., the sculptor, is quite clearly something extrinsic to, something not included in, the essence of the marble. This is what is of relevance to our present concern.

With respect to individuation, now, the substantial form is that which (as formal cause) accounts for 1) the fact that a newly generated physical substance both begins to be, and continues to be, an **actual existing individual**, and (as productive cause) accounts for 2) the fact that prime matter is three-dimensionally extended, and so capable of being divided into various parts, each of which can become an **individual quantitatively divided from others**.

> . . . forma perfectior virtute continet quidquid est inferiorum formarum. Et ideo una et eadem existens, perficit materiam secundum diversos perfectionis gradus. Una enim et eadem forma est per essentiam, per quam homo est ens actu, et per quam est corpus, et per quam est vivum, et per quam est animal, et per quam est homo. Manifestum est autem quod unumquodque genus consequuntur propria accidentia. Sicut ergo materia intelligitur perfecta secundum esse ante intellectum corporeitatis, et sic de aliis; ita praeintelliguntur accidentia quae sunt propria entis, ante corporeitatem. *(S.T., I, q. 76, a. 6, ad 1).*

> . . . a more perfect form contains in its power (virtute) whatever belongs to inferior forms. Thus, one and the same form perfects matter with respect to diverse grades of perfection. For it is essentially one and the same form through which man is a being in act, and through which he is a body, and through which he is a living thing, and through which he is an animal, and through which he is a man. Moreover, it is clear that certain proper accidents are consequent upon each genus. Therefore, just as matter is understood as perfected by existence before being understood as perfected by corporeity, and similarly with respect to other grades; so too the accidents which are proper to being are understood before corporeity itself is understood.

> . . . cum anima sit forma substantialis, quia constituit hominem in determinata specie substantiae, non est aliqua alia forma substantialis media inter animam et materiam primam; sed homo ab ipsa anima rationali perficitur secundum diverssos gradus perfectionum, ut sit scilicet corpus, et animatum corpus, et animal raionale. *(Q. D., De Anima, a. 9, c.)*

163

. . . since the soul is a substantial form, because it constitutes man in a determinate species of substance, there is no other substantial form between the soul and prime matter. Rather, it is by the rational soul itself that man is perfected with respect to diverse grades of perfection, so as to be a body, and an animated body, and a rational animal.

. . . per formam substantialem, quae est anima humana, habet hoc individuum non solum quod sit homo, sed quod sit animal, et quod sit vivum, et quod sit corpus, et substantia, et ens.. (*Q.D., De Spiritualibus Creaturis,* a. 3, c.)

. . . through the substantial form, which is the human soul, this individual is not only a man, but also an animal, and a living thing, and a body, and a substance, and a being.

In the three quotations just above, Aquinas is making the point that the **one** substantial form of an individual bodily substance, whether element or mixed body, is that which confers upon it all its **essential** characteristics, along with all its **properties**, i.e., its per se accidental characteristics. Thomas, for example, is a man. It is his one substantial form which confers upon him the essential characteristics proper to a man, of which there are several. To be a man is to be a body, to be a living thing, to be a sensing thing, to be rational. And it is Thomas' one substantial form, by informing prime matter, which makes him a body, living, sensing, rational. It is also through that same substantial form that Thomas is a being, i.e., an actually existing substance. His substantial form, thus, has a number of grades (or functions): the grade of being, the grade of corporeity, the grade of animation, etc. Consequent upon the substantial form in each of its grades, as effects following naturally from their cause (sometimes **formal** cause, sometimes **productive or agent** cause) are the properties or per se accidents of that grade. For example, following upon the substantial form in its grade of animation are the three vegetative powers, i.e., the power of nutrition, of growth, and of reproduction.

Following upon the substantial form in its grade of sensitivity are the sensory powers, both internal and external. The property, or per se accident, consequent upon the substantial form in its grade of corporeity is three dimensional quantity.

The same is to be said about an element. This particle of fire (the smallest possible particle of fire), for example, has its various characteristics from its one substantial form, both those which belong to its essence, and those which follow on its essence as properties or per se accidents. To be a particle of fire is to be a being, i.e., an ultimate existing subject, to be a body, and to be fire. The substantial form of fire has at least these three grades (or functions): 1) that of being (i.e., of substantiality), by which fire is an ultimate existing subject (essential), and from which follow (as from a formal cause) being true, being good, being beautiful, etc. (the properties or per se accidents of being); 2) that of corporeity, by which fire is a body (essential), and from which follow (as from a productive or agent cause) three dimensions (the property or per se accident of corporeity); and 3) that of being the species or kind of element which it is, by which it is fire (essential), and from which follows (as from a productive or agent cause) being hot (one of the properties or per se accidents of fire).

It may be helpful, at this point, to describe the birth of an element in the following way, a way which is quite in accord with how Aquinas might describe it. Suppose that one of the four elements (the smallest possible particle of that element) is coming to be out of another of the four elements (the smallest possible particle of this other element). Now the corruption (the going out of existence) of the one particle is identically the generation (the coming into existence) of the other particle. What survives in the newly generated particle, from the just corrupted particle, is prime matter, pure receptive potentiality for all physical forms, both substantial and accidental. And the effect of the agent causality of the appropriate change-inducing causes (whatever these might be) is the conferring of the substantial form of the newly generated particle on the prime matter which was formerly actualized by the substantial form of the just corrupted particle. As soon as that new substantial form is introduced into prime matter, and just so long as it remains in prime matter, its continuous agent causality confers three dimensions on prime matter. To be sure, the prime matter which was formerly actualized by the substantial form of the now corrupted particle was then, too, in possession of three dimensions, by reason of the continuous agent causality of that prior substantial form. So that there was never a moment in which prime matter was without three dimensions, since there was never a moment in which prime matter was without a substantial form. **Of itself**, however, prime matter is without dimensions, i.e., it is in this respect like a mathematical point. Any substantial form, too, **of itself**, is without dimensions, i.e., **like** a mathematical point. But each, i.e., prime matter and substantial form, is also quite unlike a mathematical point. A mathematical point is not only dimensionless, but also incapable of any sort of physical causality. A substantial form, by way of contrast, though dimensionless, **is capable of** physical causality, and of various sorts, including an agent causality with respect to quantity, i.e., if has the power to spread prime matter out three-dimensionally, and to keep it that way (a kind of "**small**" **Big Bang,** -- **small**, since it occurs within, and is limited to, the confines of any given physical substance, whether an element or a mixed body). Prime matter, too, though dimensionless, is capable of physical causality. But its causality is of a different sort, i.e., of a **receptive** sort. It has a receptive capacity, a **continuously** receptive capacity, not only with respect to the three dimensions productively emitted by the substantial form which is informing it (the substantial form in its grade or function of corporeity), but with respect to any and every other feature (both substantial and accidental) which that substantial form has it in its power to confer on prime matter. Thus, the substantial form of the newly generated particle confers (as a formal cause) on the prime matter, which has survived in it from the now corrupted prior particle, **not only** corporeity (which is among the features of the substantial essence of the newly generated particle) and (as a productive cause) the three dimensions which are consequent on corporeity (these dimensions are predicamental accidents, and so not of the substantial essence of the newly generated particle), **but** all the other features (both those which belong to its substantial essence, and those which are among its productively emitted predicamental accidents) which pertain to the newly generated particle, e.g., a certain limit on its dimensions, being hot, or being cold, or wet, or dry.

The preceding   (pp. 157-167) can be taken to be Aquinas' **general account** of the essences of the four elements. The following (pp. 167-183) can be taken to be his **particular account** of the essence of **each** of them.

It will be good to begin with an account of the essence of fire. For, while reflecting on the appropriateness of Boethius' definition of **"persona,"** i.e., **rationalis naturae individua substantia**, Aquinas, to illustrate a point, not only suggests a definition of fire, but a definition which, it seems, can be used as a pattern to define the other three elements as well.   He writes:

> . . . quia substantiales differentiae non sunt nobis notae, vel etiam nominatae non sunt, oportet interdum uti differentiis accidentalibus loco substantialium, puta si quis diceret: *ignis est corpus simplex, calidum et siccum;*   accidentia enim propria sunt effectus formarum substantialium, et manifestant eas. (*S.T.*, I, q. 29, a.1, ad 3)

> . . . because substantial differences are not known to us, or even because they haven't been named, it is necessary sometimes to use accidental differences in the place of substantial ones, for

instance if one were to say: *fire is a simple body, hot and dry.*
For proper accidents are effects of substantial forms, and
manifest them.

Fire, suggests Aquinas, can be defined as **a simple body, hot and dry.** To
explain. Bodies are either **simple,** i.e., elements, or **complex (mixed),** i.e.,
made out of elements.   A mixed body is composed out of prime matter and
substantial form, and out of simple bodies, i.e., elements, as well.   And these
elements are put together **not** by a **simple aggregation,** in the way in which a
heap is made out of stones; **nor** by a **composition** which **both** puts them
together in a given order, in the way in which a **house** is put together out of
wood and stones, **and** holds them together by using certain sorts of joining
materials like nails and glue and mortar; but by a **mixing (per mixtionem)** in
which the elements affect and alter one another so as to remain in the mixed
body in a special way (i.e., virtually, or with their powers, and retrievably),
though not actually (i.e., not with their substantial forms).[10]

A simple body, by way of contrast, is composed out of prime matter
and substantial form indeed, but **not** also out of simple bodies.   It has
no composing **bodily** ingredients.   There are no prior bodily things out of
which simple bodies could be composed.   Simple bodies, i.e., elements, are the
ultimate bodily constituents of all other bodily things.   The expression
"simple body," it is clear, functions as a genus in this definition of fire.   That
is, **all** elements have this **in common** that they are simple bodies.

The expression "hot and dry," by way of contrast, it is clear, functions as a
specific difference.   Hot and dry are proper accidents of fire, caused by, and
manifesting, the substantial form of fire.

---

[10] . . . quod plura corpora veniant ad constitutionem unius, hoc non potest esse nisi tribus modis:
vel per simplicem aggregationem, sicut ex lapidibus fit acervus;
vel per compositionem, quae est cum ordine partium determinato, et ligamento, sicut ex
lignis et lapidibus fit domus;
vel **per mixtionem,** sicut ex elementis efficitur mixtum.
. . . in tertio . . . modo oportet esse alterationem componentium, quia mixtio est miscibilium
alteratorum unio, ut in *I De gener.* dicitur . . . (*In II Sent.,* d. 17, q. 3, a. 1, sol.).

168

But, **being hot** belongs to fire in a primary or immediate way, i.e., precisely because fire is **fire,** whereas **being dry** belongs to fire in a secondary or derived way, i.e., precisely because fire is **hot.** Or, fire is hot, because it is fire; and it is dry, because it is hot; as if to say, explains Aquinas, that by the intensity of its heat, it has consumed (or destroyed or dissipated or vanquished or evaporated) wetness. Fire is so hot, it has to be dry. **Pure** fire is as hot as hot can be, and therefore also as dry as dry can be.

Although two of the four elemental qualities, explains Aquinas, belong to each of the elements -- fire is hot and dry, air hot and wet, water cold and wet, earth cold and dry -- one of these four qualities belongs principally to each of the four elements as properly its own, the other belonging to each in some secondary way. Aquinas puts it as follows:

> Quamvis quatuor qualitatum elementalium duae conveniunt singulis (nam ignis est calidus et siccus, aer calidus et humidus, aqua frigida et humida, terra frigida et sicca), in singulis tamen elementis singulae harum qualitatum principaliter inveniuntur quasi proprie ipsis:

> nam ignis proprium est calidum, quia enim ignis est nobilissimum inter elementa et propinquissimum caelesti corpori, convenit ei proprie et secundum se calidum, quod est maxime activum, siccum vero competit ei propter excessum caliditatis, quasi iam humiditate consumpta;

> aeri vero competit quidem calidum secundario, ex affinitate ad ignem, secundum se autem competit ei humidum, quod est nobilius inter qualitates passivas, quasi calore resolvente humiditatem et non consumente, propter maiorem distantiam a prima cause caloris, quae est corpus caeleste;

> aquae vero proprie et secundum se competit ei frigidum, quod est secunda qualitas activa, quasi privative se habens ad calidum, competit autem ei humidum secundario secundum propinquitatem ad aerem;

terrae vero competit quidem frigidum secundario, quasi ex propinquitate aquae, siccum autem competit ei proprie et per se, quasi propter longissimam distantiam a fonte caloris non resoluta terra in humiditatem, sed in ultima grossitie permanente . . . (*In De Sensu et Sensato,* Tract. I, De Sensu Exteriori, cap. 9, circa princ.)

Of the four elemental qualities, two are found together in each of the elements; fire is hot and dry, air hot and wet, water cold and wet, earth cold and dry. Nonetheless, just one of these qualities is found principally in each of the elements as though properly its own.

Being hot is proper to fire. For, since fire is the most noble of the elements, and closest to the heavenly bodies; being hot, which is in the highest degree active, belongs to fire properly and because of itself. Being dry, however, belongs to fire because of the intensity of its heat, as though wetness had already been consumed.

To air, being hot belongs secondarily, because of its closeness to fire. Being wet, however, which is the more noble of the passive qualities, belongs to air because of itself, as though by its heat driving away, but not consuming, wetness because of its greater distance from the first causes of heat, which are the heavenly bodies.

To water, properly and because of itself, belongs being cold, which is the second active quality, since it is privatively related to being hot. And being wet belongs to water secondarily, because of its closeness to air.

To earth, being cold belongs secondarily, as though because of its closeness to water. Being dry, however, belongs to earth properly and because of itself, as though earth had not been resolved into humidity because of its great distance from the source of heat, but had remained in utmost density.

Fire is the most noble of the elements, explains Aquinas, i.e., among the elements it is the closest to, most like, the heavenly bodies, which are the first causes of heat.   And this is why -- though fire is both hot and dry -- being hot, which is as active as active can be, belongs to fire immediately, i.e., as an accident which is properly its own because of itself; whereas being dry is an accident which belongs to it mediately or derivatively, i.e., because of its first being hot. Thus, it is hot because it is fire; and it is dry because it is hot. -- And so, fire can be defined as a **simple body** (the genus, which affirms composition out of prime matter and substantial form, and denies composition out of simpler bodies), **hot immediately and dry derivatively** (the specific difference, expressed in terms of proper accidents, which are caused by, and manifest, the substantial form).

This definition of fire can be used as a pattern to define **air,** as noted above, and the two other elements as well.   **Air** can be defined as **a simple body, wet and hot.**   Being hot, explains Aquinas, is an accident which belongs to air only secondarily, i.e., because of its closeness, its likeness, to fire; whereas being wet -- the **more** noble passive quality (the **less** noble passive quality is being dry) -- is an accident which belongs to air because of itself, as though, by the heat which is in it, driving away but not totally vanquishing wetness, because it is further away from, less like, the heavenly bodies than fire is. Thus, it is wet because it is weaker than, i.e., less hot than, fire; and hot because it is close to, in a way like, fire. -- And so, air can be defined as a **simple body** (the genus, which affirms composition out of prime matter and substantial form, and denies composition out of simpler bodies), **wet primarily and hot secondarily** (the specific difference, expressed in terms of proper accidents, which are caused by, and manifest, the substantial form).

Patterning the definition of **water** after that of fire, one can say that **water is a simple body, cold and wet.**   Being cold -- the **second** active quality, inasmuch as it is privatively related to being hot (the **first** active quality) -- is an accident which belongs to water properly and because of itself. Being wet, however, is an accident which belongs to water because it is close to air. It is nonetheless, less like the heavenly bodies than air is. Thus, it is cold because it is water; and it is wet because it is close to air. -- And so, water can be defined as a **simple body** (the genus, which affirms composition out of prime matter and substantial form, and denies composition out of simpler bodies), **cold primarily and wet secondarily** (the specific difference, expressed in terms of proper accidents which are caused by, and manifest, the substanital form).

The definition of **earth,** too, can be patterned after that of fire. **Earth** can be defined as **a simple body, dry and cold.** Being cold is an accident which belongs to earth only secondarily, because of its closeness to water. But being dry -- the **less** noble passive quality, because (can one say?) it is privatively[11] related to being wet (being wet is the **more** noble passive quality) -- is an accident which belongs to earth properly and because of itself. Earth is dry, as though not yet released into humidity, because it is so far away from (of the elements, the least like) both fire and the heavenly bodies. Thus, it is dry because it is earth, and as such so far away from, so unlike, fire; it is cold because it is close to water. -- And so, earth can be defined as **a simple body** (the genus, which affirms composition out of prime matter and substantial from, and denies composition out of simpler bodies), **dry primarily and cold secondarily** (the specific difference, expressed in terms of proper accidents, which are caused by, and manifest, the substantial form).

---

[11]   . . . siccitas . . . non est aliud quam humiditatis privatio . . . (*In II De Gen. et Corrupt.,* lect. 3, in fine).   --   Fr. Weisheipl points out that St. Thomas' "commentary on **De generatione** is unfinished, terminating with Book I, lect. 17, the remainder being written by Thomas Sutton and others. William of Tocco himself saw Thomas writing this commentary on **De generatione,** and testified that he believed this to have been Thomas's 'last work in philosophy.' " (Weisheipl, James A., O.P.   *Friar Thomas D'Aquino: His Life, Thought, and Works* (with corrigenda and addenda).   The Catholic University of America Press: Washington, D.C.. 1983; p. 317). -- My comments on *In II De generatione,* therefore, reflect "Thomas Sutton and others;" but what they have to say is not, as far as I can see, inconsistent with anything which Aquinas would hold.

To summarize, and perhaps to clarify as well. Fire, as Aquinas sees it, is hot because it is fire, and dry because it is hot. And it is hot, because it is more like the heavenly bodies than any other element. The heavenly bodies are just above fire, and in contact with it. Being hot is fire's unique property, the property which differentiates fire from the other elements. -- Air is wet because it is air. It is hot because it is like fire, indeed more like fire than either water or earth are. Fire is just above air, and in contact with it. And this is why air is hot. But being wet is air's unique property, the property by which air differs from the other elements. -- Water is cold because it is water, and wet because it is like air, indeed more like air than earth is. Air is just above water, and in contact with it. And this is why water is wet. But being cold is water's unique property, the property which differentiates water from the other elements. -- Earth is dry because it is earth, and cold because it is like water. Earth is in no way like air or fire, not even in its dryness. Water is just above earth, and in contact with it. And this is why earth is cold. But being dry is earth's unique property, the property by which earth differs from the other elements.

Now, the dryness of earth is different from the dryness of fire. Fire is dry because, as the most noble of the elements, it is as hot as hot can be, and as such, i.e., **propter excessum caliditatis,** consumes, or dissipates, any wetness which might have invaded it from the air which is just beneath it, and in contact with it -- . . . **siccum . . . competit ei [sc. igni] propter excessum caliditatis, quasi iam humiditate [aeris] consumpta.** Fire is dry (has no wetness in it), because its heat drives that wetness out, or, better put, does not allow it to enter fire at all; the heat of fire consumes wetness.[12] Earth, by way of difference, is dry because it is the least noble of the elements, the

---

[12] Duae . . . sunt causae siccitatis: una est frigus condensans et comprimens humidum, et per consequens removens; siccitas enim non est aliud quam humiditatis privatio. Alia causa est caliditas humiditatem consumens. (*In II De Gen. et Corrupt.*, lect. 3, in fine).

furthest away from the first source of heat, i.e., the heavenly bodies, and because of this in no way fluid (fire and air and water are "fluid", i.e., they flow, each in is own way), but rather as dense, as compact, as solid, and therefore, as non-flowing, as can be -- . . . **siccum competit ei [sc. terrae] quasi propter longissimam distantiam a fonte caloris [sc. a caelesti corpore] non resoluta terra in humiditatem, sed in ultima grossitie [i.e., denseness, solidness, compactness] permanente.** Moreover, because earth is as dense, as compact, as solid as can be, there is no room, there are no empty spaces, within it, to permit the wetness of air or of water to invade it. Earth is as dense, as compact, as solid as the atoms of Democritus. Lastly, earth is dry because its coldness condenses, compresses, and thereby removes, whatever air or water and accompanying wetness might have attempted to invade it (if this were possible; and it seems that it is not, because of the absolute density of earth).

One might ask why, according to Aquinas following Aristotle, **only** the contraries **hot-cold** and **wet-dry** figure in an account of the elements, and not others like heavy-light, hard-soft, supple-brittle, rough-smooth, coarse-grained/fine-grained. All of these are clearly contraries which are related to touch and physical contact, but not all are capable of acting upon, and of being acted upon by, one another. And this is most clearly required of the elements. The elements must be capable of affecting one another, and of being affected by one another and by the heavenly bodies, since they **both** come together to constitute mixed bodies **and** are changed into one another. It is clear that if a heavy body is put into contact with a lighter body, the lighter body does not thereby become heavier, nor the heavier one lighter. But it is clearly the case that if a hot body (e.g., a hot hot-water bottle) is placed in contact with a cooler body (e.g., my hand), the cooler body becomes thereby hotter, and the hotter thereby cooler. Similarly, if a wet body (e.g., a turkish towel) is placed in contact with a dry, or drier, one (e.g., another towel) the dry or drier one becomes thereby wetter, and the wetter one thereby drier. Neither does a hard body put into contact with a softer one become thereby softer. Nor does the softer body become thereby harder; and similarly with respect to the other contraries mentioned above.

If the definition of each of the four elements includes, appropriately, a specific difference which is expressed in terms of proper accidents (proper accidents are caused by, and manifest, the substantial form), each of these accidents, too, should be defined in some appropriate way, in order to make the definitions of each of the elements more complete. **Being hot,** the principal or dominating[13] property of **fire,** is an **active** quality which gathers together (congregat) things which are like one another, things which have a like nature (homogenea), and thereby separates (segregat) things which are unlike one another, things which are different in nature (heterogenea);[14] for example, it purifies metals. **Being cold**, the primary or dominating property of **water,** is also an **active** quality. But, unlike being hot, it gathers together anything and everything (congregat **omnia**), both things which are of the same nature and things which are of different natures.[15] For example, freezing gathers together not only portions of water, but all sorts of debris, in the ice which is its effect. **Being wet,** the primary or dominating property of air, is a **passive** quality. To be wet is to have no set limit or boundary of its own, but to be easily limited or bounded by the limits or boundaries of other

---

[13] . . . elementa, cum sint quatuor, et quodlibet habeat duas qualitates, non tamen habet eas aequaliter, sed . . . in unquoque **dominatur** una: sicut in terra magis dominatur siccitas quam frigiditas, in aqua magis frigiditas quam humiditas, in aere magis humiditas quam caliditas, in igne vero magis dominatur caliditas quam siccitas.   Non est autem intelligendum, ut quidam dicunt, quod terra, licet sit magis sicca quam frigida, propter hoc sit siccior igne . . .   (*In II De Gen. et Corrupt.,* lect. 3, in fine). -- Though being dry is the dominating property of earth, earth is not drier than fire.   Earth in simply more dry than it is cold.   Similarly, though being cold is the dominating property of water, water is not colder than earth.   Water is simply more cold than it is wet.   Again, though being wet is the dominating property of air, air is not wetter than water.   Air is simply more wet than it is hot.

[14] . . . calidum . . . est quod congregat homogenea sibi . . ., . . . [et] licet . . . calidum segregat, sicut dicunt quidam ignem facere, tamen illud segregare est congregare, quia congregans homogenea, segregat heterogenea per accidens . . .   (*In II De Gen. et Corrupt.,* lect. 2, in medio).

[15] . . . quod . . . frigidum sit activum patet . . . per hoc, quia congregat omnia, tam quae sunt ejusdem naturae, quam illa quae sunt diversae . . . (*Ibid.*).

things[16] (to accept a given shape is a way of being affected, of being passive). For example, air (and water, too) accepts the shape of the inside of the bottle into which it has been blown (poured). **Being dry,** the primary or dominating property of earth, is also a **passive** quality. To be dry is to be such that whereas it has a boundary of its own, it is only with difficulty, sometimes with great difficulty, that it can be bounded by the limits or boundaries of other things.[17] For example, a brick has to be cut and chiseled in order to be made to fit exactly into a hole in a wall.

Moreover, though **being dry,** according to Aquinas, is the primary or dominating property of **earth** (this means simply that earth is drier than it is cold)[18], it is not the case, as Aquinas sees it, that earth is drier than fire, to which being dry belongs only secondarily. For, there are two causes of dryness, as noted above (p. 173, footnote 12): one is coldness, condensing and compressing wetness, thereby removing it; the second cause is heat, consuming wetness. Now, the heat of fire is more potent with respect to consuming wetness than the coldness of earth is with respect to condensing and compressing it. And this is why fire is drier than earth, Indeed, because fire is the hottest of the hot,[19] it is also the driest of the dry. But it is hot primarily, and dry secondarily, i.e., precisely because it is hot.

Similarly, though **being wet,** according to Aquinas, is the primary or dominating property of **air** (this means simply that air is wetter than it is hot), it is not the case, as Aquinas sees it, that air is wetter than water, to which being wet belongs only secondarily. Water is wetter than air, as is

---

[16]   . . . humidum . . . est indeterminatum proprio termino, bene terminabile termino alieno . . . (*Ibid.*).

[17]   . . . siccum autem terminatur termino proprio, difficulter autem terminabile termino alieno . . . (*Ibid.*).

[18]   How exactly, one might ask, is this to be understood? Perhaps as follows. If one measures both dryness and coldness on a scale of one (the least) to ten (the most), "drier than cold" might mean, for example, that dryness measures at 9, and coldness at 3.

[19]   . . . [ignis] est calidissimum omnium calidorum . . . (*In II De Gen. et Corrupt.*, lect. 3, in fine).

clear to sense observation.[20]   And of itself, one can say, water is the wettest of the wet. Similarly again, though **being cold,** according to Aquinas, is the primary or dominating property of **water** (this means simply that water is colder than it is wet), it is not the case, as Aquinas sees it, that water is colder than earth, to which being cold belongs only secondarily. For earth is further away from the first cause of heat, i.e., the heavenly bodies, than any other element; and so is the coldest of all the elements,[21] and so the coldest of the cold -- **frigidissima omnium frigidorum,** one might say.

If Aquinas, following Aristotle, is correct in the claim that **only** the contrary qualities **hot-cold** and **wet-dry** are relevant in distinguishing the four elements from one another, since, as he argues, only these qualities enable the elements to affect, and to be affected by, one another (see above p. 172); it seems nonetheless, on the basis of one's ordinary sense-observational experience[22] of fire, air, water, and earth, that Aquinas is not quite correct as regards what the primary or dominating quality of each element is. The primary or dominating quality of fire seems to be **being hot** (as for Aquinas);

---

[20] . . . [aqua est] humida magis quam calida. Non tamen magis quam aqua . . .   . . . aqua est magis humida quam aer; sensu enim sensibilia judicamus: manifestum est autem omnibus habentibus sensum tactus quod aqua humidior est quam aer . . .   (*In II De Gen. et Corrupt.,* lect. 3, in fine).

[21] . . . [aqua] est . . . minus frigida quam terra, quod sic patet. Frigiditas enim causatur ex distantia ab orbe, sicut caliditas ex propinquitate. Cum ergo inter cetera elementa terra magis distet a caelo, necessario sequitur quod terra **frigidissima sit inter omnia elementa** . . . (*In II De Gen. et Corrupt.,* lect. 3, in fine).

[22] [. . . quod elementa transmutantur ad invicem, hoc] **videmus ad sensum.** [Videmus enim] quod eadem materia, quae nunc est sub frigiditate aquae, aliquando est sub caliditate aeris; et quod erat sub caliditate aeris, aliquando est sub caliditate ignis . . .   (*In II De Gen. et Corrupt.,* lect. 1, in fine).   . . . hoc . . . **ad sensum videmus,** [quod] ipsa [elementa] sunt ad invicem generata, . . . cum . . . **videamus** quod alteratio secundum passiones tactus [sc. secundum caliditatem, humiditatem, siccitatem et frigiditatem] est inter ea . . . (*In II De Gen. et Corrupt.,* lect. 4, circa princ.)   It is quite clear, as indicated in these two brief quotes, that **sense observational experience** is what determines what is to be said about the nature of each of the four elements. But how can one decide by sense observation whether the primary or dominating quality of air is **being dry** (as I would want to say) or **being wet** (as **Aquinas** says), whether that of water is **being wet** (as I would want to say) or **being cold** (as **Aquinas** says), and whether that of earth is **being cold** (as I would want to say) or **being dry** (as **Aquinas** says)?

of air, **being dry** (rather than **being wet,** as for Aquinas); of water, **being wet** (rather than **being cold,** as for Aquinas); of earth, **being cold** (rather than **being dry,** as for Aquinas). Moreover, still on the basis of one's ordinary sense-observational experience, it seems that each of the elements has **more than** just one secondary quality (there is **just one,** for Aquinas), in some sense of "secondary."

To make this clear, it will be helpful to consider each of the elements in a **pure** state. **Pure fire** -- fire which is just fire and nothing else, i.e., fire with nothing in it of air or of water or of earth, in any conceivable way of being in it -- is of itself, and primarily, hot; it is dry secondarily (in the sense of derivatively), i.e., precisely because it is hot. It is wet, in some secondary sense of wet, only wherever and whenever and to the extent that it has been (if it can be) invaded by evaporated water.   It is clear that fire can never be cold, without thereby ceasing to be fire.   Fire, in its pure state, is as hot as hot can be, and so, as dry as dry can be, since fire consumes wetness.   But fire is not as wet as wet can be; perhaps never wet in any way at all.

Pure air -- air which is just air and nothing else, i.e., air with nothing in it of fire or of water or of earth, in any conceivable way of being in it -- is of itself, and primarily, dry. In some secondary sense, it is hot (wherever and whenever it is in contact with fire), and wet (wherever and whenever and to the extent that it has been invaded by evaporated water), and cold (wherever and whenever it is in contact with earth). Pure air is as dry as dry can be, (of itself and primarily, as opposed to derivatively, in the way in which fire is as dry as dry can be); but not as hot as hot can be, nor as wet as wet can be, nor as cold as cold can be.

Pure water -- water which is just water and nothing else, i.e., water with nothing in it of fire or of air or of earth, in any conceivable way of being in it -- is of itself, and primarily, wet. In some secondary sense, it is hot (wherever and whenever it is in contact with fire), and cold (wherever and whenever it is in contact with earth). It is clear that water can never be dry, without thereby ceasing to be water.   Water, in its pure state, is as wet as wet can be; but not as cold as cold can be, nor as hot as hot can be.

Pure earth -- earth which is just earth and nothing else, i.e., earth with nothing in it of fire or of air or of water, in any conceivable way of being in it -- is of itself, and primarily, cold.   In some secondary sense, it is hot (wherever and whenever it is in contact with fire), dry (wherever and whenever it is in contact with a breeze, i.e., air in motion, or with fire), and wet (wherever and whenever and to the extent that it has been invaded, if it can be, by liquid water).   Pure earth is as cold as cold can be, but not as hot as hot can be, nor as wet as wet can be, nor as dry as dry can be.

But, someone might ask, is there a difficulty here? That is, if earth is of itself, and primarily, **cold,** how can it ever be hot, even in some secondary sense, without ceasing thereby to be earth? Or, just how hot can earth become without ceasing to be earth? Shall we say that earth remains earth until it has become as hot as hot can be, i.e., so hot that nothing can be hotter, at which point it has become **fire**? It is clear to ordinary sense observation that earth can be made warm, or even quite hot, without thereby ceasing to be earth.[23] Was it correct, then, to have said that pure earth is of itself, and primarily, cold? Or, should one ask: How exactly is the word "earth" to be understood here, when it is being used to designate one of the four **elements**? It cannot be taken to mean what one ordinarily means by the word "soil," as in "the **soil** in which plants grow," for soil in that sense can become very hot indeed without ceasing thereby to be soil.   What exactly does the theory of the four elements take the element earth to be?

And that question gives rise to the same question about each of the other elements.   Thus, exactly what, according to the theory of the four elements,

---

[23]   This raises the question whether the **earth** of ordinary sense-observational experience is the same as the **earth** of the theory of the four elements, i.e., whether it is the same as the **element** earth.

is **the element** fire? And **the element** air? And **the element** water? -- These four questions give rise, in turn, to the following ones. 1) What exactly is heat (calidity), the primary or dominating property of the element fire? And what is there about the elements air and water and earth which allows calidity to penetrate, to invade, to possess (are these the right words?) them, thereby changing them in different ways? 2) What exactly is dryness (siccity, aridity), the primary or dominating property of the element air? And what is there about the elements fire and water and earth which allows siccity to penetrate, to invade, to possess (are these the right words?) them, thereby changing them in different ways? 3) What exactly is wetness (humidity), the primary or dominating property of the element water? And what is there about the elements fire and air and earth which allows humidity to penetrate, to invade, to possess (are these the right words?) them, thereby changing them in different ways? 4) What exactly is coldness (frigidity), the primary or dominating property of the element earth?[24] And what is there about the elements fire and air and water which allows frigidity to penetrate, to invade, to possess (are these the right words?) them, thereby changing them in different ways?

How, now, are these questions to be answered? It will be helpful to begin with an answer to the **general** question: What is an element? and then, in terms of that, to move on to the **particular** questions: What exactly, according to the theory of the four elements, is the element fire? The element air? The element water? The element earth?

As regards the **general** question: What is an element?, this seems an acceptable answer. An element is a simple body, i.e., something composed out of prime matter and a substantial form (but **not** out of any prior bodies, since there are none), which (substantial form), as efficient cause, not only

---

[24] See above pp. 177-178, where it was noted that, according to one's ordinary sense-observational experience, the primary or dominating quality of air seems to be **being dry** (rather than **being wet**), of water, **being wet** (rather than **being cold**), and of earth, **being cold** (rather than **being dry**).

extends the element three-dimensionally, but also causes it to have certain proper accidents by which it can both **affect,** and **be affectd by,** the other elements,[25] so as to undergo the **substantial changes** in which it is transformed into other elements, and the **alterations** by which it becomes an ingredient in the make-up of mixed bodies.

The **particular** questions, now -- beginning with the element fire. What exactly, according to the theory of the four elements, is the **element** fire?[26] That is, what exactly are the proper accidents of fire? The answer seems to be the following. The element fire is hot, it is dry, it emits light, it is translucent, even transparent (diaphanous) in a way, it is light in weight, it has an upward rising motion. Now which of these proper accidents is (are) relevant to the **substantial changes** and to the **alterations** mentioned in the preceding paragraph? It is obvious to sense observation that being hot is relevant, and being dry, too; as Aquinas rightly claims. But, what about emitting light?[27] And translucency? Transparency? Being light in weight? Having an upward rising motion? What sense observations can be made to establish their relevancy, if they are relevant?

What exactly, in the theory of the four elements, is the **element** air? That is, what exactly are its proper accidents? Air is dry, it is transparent (diaphanous), it is light in weight, it has an upward rising motion, it has the

---

25   And **by the heavenly bodies** as well.   . . . nec terrae siccitas, nec caliditas aeris videntur ad generationem ignis posse sufficere: ignis enim multo calidior est quam aer, et siccior quam terra . . .   . . . licet illa caliditas [sc. aeris] non sufficiat, juvatur tamen et intenditur **per virtutem corporis caelestis, et luce Solis, et per virtutem aliarum stellarum** . . . (*In II De Gen. et Corrupt.,* lect. 4, in fine).
26   It is becoming increasingly clearer, at this point, that **fire,** i.e., the fire of ordinary sense-observational experience, is not the same thing as the **element** fire, i.e., the fire of the theory of the four elements. This seems also to be the case with the other three elements. That is, the air and the water and the earth **of ordinary sense-observational experience** seem **not** to be the same as the **elements** air and water and earth.
27   . . . per ipsam [sc. **lucem**] movet caelum materiam generabilium et corruptibilium ad **omnem** formam . . . (*In II De Gen. et Corrupt.,* lect. 2, in princ.).   Can this claim, i.e., the claim that **light** has a causal impact with respect to the generation and the corruption of **all** physical things, be substantiated by sense observation(s)? By what sorts of sense observations?

181

capability to become wet (moist, humid), it has the **capability** to become warm (even hot), it has the **capability** to become cool (even cold). Which of these proper accidents is (are) relevant to the **substantial changes** and to the **alterations** mentioned above? It is clear to sense observation that **being dry** is relevant, as Aquinas rightly notes. But what about the others, especially the **capabilities**? And what sense observations can be made to establish that they are relevant, if they are?

What exactly, according to the theory of the four elements, is the **element** water? That is, exactly what are its proper accidents? Water is wet, it is transparent (diaphanous), it is heavy, it has a downward falling motion, it has the **capability** to become warm (indeed hot), the **capability** to become cool (indeed cold), the **capability** to be either a liquid, or a solid (as in ice and snow), or a gas (as in steam). Which of these proper accidents is (are) relevant to the **substantial changes** and to the **alterations** mentioned above? It is clear to sense observation that **being wet** is relevant, as Aquinas correctly observes. But what about the others, especially the **capabilities**? And what sense observations can be made to substantiate their relevancy, if they are relevant?

Lastly, what exactly, in the theory of the four elements, is the **element** earth? That is, exactly what are its proper accidents? Earth is cold, it is dry, it is opaque, it is heavier than water, it has a downward falling motion, it has the **capability** to become warm (indeed hot), the **capability** to become wet (moist). Perhaps others. Which of these proper accidents is (are) relevant to the **substantial changes** and to the **alterations** mentioned above? **Being cold** and **being dry** are relevant, as Aquinas correctly notes, and sense observation confirms. But what about the others, especially the **capabilities**? And by what sense observations can their relevancy be shown, if they are relevant?

It would be very difficult indeed -- more important, it would be without purpose -- to try to get a settled answer to these questions about each of the four ancient elements; for we know today that these four cannot possibly be **the** elements of physical things, inasmuch as they are themselves composed out of prior bodily constituents (which does not befit an element), and inasmuch as it is quite clear today that **the** elements are, as a matter of established scientific fact, quarks and leptons of various sorts.   Nonetheless, these reflections on the ancient four have a lesson to impart, a valuable and important lesson.   The lesson is this: in any attempt to identify and to describe **the** elements of things in the physical world (whether one claims that they are fire and air and water and earth, as people claimed in days gone by; or that they are quarks and leptons of various sorts, as people claim today) -- one must identify and describe them by using, in some way, **the method of sense observation**.   Moreover, to be sure that the elements have been identified and described in an appropriate and acceptable way, so that everybody, if possible, would find the account a convincing one, one would have to sophisticate (to enhance, to fortify) the required sense observations with a **creative** use of controlled experiments, observational instruments, and measuring instruments -- as people do today when, for example, they use Tevatron, the world's most powerful "atom smasher," i.e., particle accelerator, at Fermi National Accelerator Laboratory (Fermilab), in Batavia, Illinois.

7. The elements and creation

> . . . illa quae non possunt produci in esse nisi per creationem, a Deo immediate sunt.   Manifestum est autem quod corpora caelestia non possunt produci in esse nisi per creationem.   Non enim potest dici quod ex materia aliqua praeiacenti sunt facta, quia sic essent generabilia et corruptibilia, et contrarietati

subiecta, quod eis non competit, ut motus eorum declarat. Moventur enim circulariter; motus autem circularis non habet contrarium. Relinquitur igitur quod corpora caelestia sint immediate in esse a Deo producta.

Similiter etiam elementa secundum se tota non sunt ex aliqua materia praeiacenti, quia illud quod praeexisteret, haberet aliquam formam, et sic oporteret quod aliquod corpus aliud ab elementis esset prius eis in ordine causae materialis, si materia praeexistens elementis haberet *formam aliam.* Oporteret tamen quod unum eorum esset aliis prius in eodem ordine, si materia praecedens *formam elementi* haberet. Oportet igitur etiam ipsa elementa immediate esse a Deo producta. (*Compendium Theologiae,* c. 95).

. . . things which cannot be brought into being except through creation, are immediately from God. It is clear that heavenly bodies cannot be brought into being except through creation. For, it cannot be said that they were made from some preexisting matter, because if that were the case they would be generable and corruptible, and subject to contrariety, neither of which belongs to them, as their motion makes clear. For they are moved in a circular way, and circular motion has no contrary. It remains therefore that heavenly bodies are brought into being immediately by God.

Similarly the elements, too, taken together in their totality, do not come into being from some preexisting matter, because that which preexisted, would have had some form. And so, some body different from the elements would have had to have been prior to them in the order of material cause, if the matter which existed before the elements had had *another form.* Moreover, one of them would have had to have been prior to the others in the same order [i.e., in the order of material cause], if the preexisting matter had had the *form of an element.* The elements too, therefore, must be brought into being immediately by God.

The heavenly bodies, argues Aquinas, cannot be brought into being except by creation, and so, immediately by the power of God, and not from

184

some pre-existing matter. If they had been brought into being out of a pre-existing matter, then they would have been generable and corruptible. And in the view of Aquinas (which we now know to be incorrect), they are neither generable nor corruptible. They would have been subject, too, in the view of Aquinas, to the contrariety of the four elements, for anything which is not an element and which is brought into being out of a pre-existing matter, must be composed out of the elements, and so subject to the effects of their contrary qualities, i.e., to the effects of being hot or cold, and of being wet or dry. But, the heavenly bodies, according to Aquinas, are not composed out of these elements, and so not subject to their contrarieties.[28] And this is evident, notes Aquinas, from their circular motion, which has no contrary. Aquinas concludes, therefore, that the heavenly bodies are brought into being immediately by the creative power of God, and not from a pre-existing matter.

Similarly, neither can the **elements** be brought into being from some pre-existing matter. For, explains Aquinas, if that were the case, then the pre-existing matter would have had some form, either that of an element, or of something other than an element. Now, it is impossible that there be **bodily things** *other than* **elements,** which are prior to the elements. And it is just as impossible that there be **bodily things which** *are* **elements,** which are prior to the elements. For, an element is a bodily thing prior to which (as material cause) there can be no **bodily thing** at all, of whatever kind. The elements, therefore, concludes Aquinas, must be brought into being immediately by the creative power of God, and not from some pre-existing matter.

But what, then, is to be made of the claim of Aquinas that although both the heavenly bodies and the elements are simple bodies, i.e., not composed of

---

28   We know today, of course, that the heavenly bodies, i.e., the sun, the moon, the planets, the stars, and such like, are composed out of the **same** elements out of which **all mixed bodies** are composed; not out of the four of Aquinas, to be sure, but out of the **same** elements nonetheless -- i.e., quarks and leptons of various kinds -- and are subject, therefore, to the effects of **their** differing and contrary qualities.

prior bodies, they are nonetheless composed out of matter and form? Doesn't it follow from that, that both the heavenly bodies and the elements are generable and corruptible? Isn't anything composed out of matter and form generable and corruptible? -- Aquinas would respond that the matter of the heavenly bodies and that of the elements is not the same sort of matter.[29] The matter which is an ingredient of the nature of the elements is **prime** matter, whereas that of the nature of the heavenly bodies is not. And that is why the elements are generable and corruptible, whereas the heavenly bodies are not.

Moreover, someone might object, since Aquinas holds that the elements, unlike the heavenly bodies, are generable and corruptible, he should not have concluded that the elements can be brought into being only by the creative power of God. Indeed, Aquinas explicitly maintains in many places that the elements can be generated out of one another. For example:

> . . . si . . . unum [elementum] omnino alteri praedominatur, tunc transmutantur adinvicem, et non fit mixtio, sed corruptio debilioris, et generatio sive augmentum praedominantis . . . (*In II De Gen. et Corrupt.*, lect 8, in medio).

> . . . if . . . one [element] totally overpowers another, then they are changed into one another, and a mixing is not brought about, but rather a corruption of the weaker one, and a generation or an increase of the overpowering one . . .

---

29 . . . materia corporis caelestis, secundum se considerata, non est in potentia nisi ad formam quam habet. . . . . . illa forma sic perficit illam materiam, quod nullo modo in ea remanet potentia **ad esse**, sed **ad ubi** tantum, . . . Et sic non est eadem materia corporis caelestis et elementorum, nisi secundum analogiam, secundum quod conveniunt in ratione potentiae. . . (*S.T.*, I, q. 66, a. 2, c., in fine). -- . . . materia corporis caelestis est alia a materia elementi, quia non est in potentia ad formam elementi. . . (*S.T.*, I, q. 66, a. 2, ad 4). -- . . . caelum, cum sit secundum suam naturam incorruptibile, habet materiam quae **non** potest subesse aliam formam . . . (*S.T.*, I, q. 68, a. 1, c. in medio). -- It is to be noted that matter "quae **potest** subesse aliam formam" is prime matter. The matter of the heavenly bodies, according to Aquinas, cannot exist under another form; it has **no** potentiality with respect **to being (nullo modo** in ea remanet potentia **ad esse**), but only with respect to place (sed **ad ubi tantum**).

. . . primo ostendit [Philosophus] quod elementa ad invicem transmutantur, tali ratione. Generatio est ex contrariis, et in contraria; omnia elementa habent contrarietatem ad invicem, quia eorum differentiae sunt contrariae. Ostensum est ergo quod elementa adinvicem generantur. Majorem propositionem ostendit inducendo in singulis elementis, dicens quod quaedam elementa secundum ambas differentias contrariantur, sicut ignis et aqua. Ignis enim est calidus et siccus, aqua vero frigida et humida. Calidum autem et frigidum sunt contraria, et similiter humidum et siccum. Quaedam autem contrariantur solum secundum alteram qualitatem, sicut aer et aqua, quia aer est calidus, et aqua est frigida, sed in humiditate conveniunt. Simile est de terra et igne, et de terra et aqua. Sic ergo concludit quod universaliter manifestum est quod quodlibet elementum ex quolibet generetur. (*In II Gen. et Corrupt.*, lect. 4, circa princ.).

. . . first [the Philosopher] shows that the elements are changed into one another, with the following reason. Generation is *from* contraries, and *into* contraries. All the elements have contrarieties with respect to one another, because they have differences which are contraries. The elements, therefore, are generated from and into one another. He shows the major proposition to be true by arguing inductively from each of the elements. Some elements, he points out, are contrary to one another according to both differences, like fire and water. For fire is hot and dry, whereas water is cold and wet. Now, hot and cold are contraries, and so are wet and dry. Other elements are contrary to one another according to one quality only, like air and water. Air is hot, and water is cold, but they agree in being wet. This is likewise the case as regards earth and fire; as regards earth and water, too. Thus, he concludes, it is universally true that any element is generated from just any other element.

. . . licet omnia elementa in hoc conveniant quod quodlibet ex quolibet generatur, differunt in hoc quod quaedam ipsorum facilius et citius, et quaedam tardius et difficilius ad invicem transmutantur. Quaecumque enim habent symbolum, idest convenientiam, in aliqua qualitate, citius et facilius transmutanur ad invicem; illa vero, quae in nulla qualitate conveniunt, tardius et difficilius. Et ratio hujus est quia, cum ea quae habent symbolum transmutantur, non est necesse transmutari nisi tantum alteram qualitatem; quando vero ea quae transmutantur ad invicem in nulla qualitate coveniunt, utramque qualitatem necesse est transmutari; facilius autem est unum transmutari quam plura. (*In II De Gen. et Corrupt.*, lect. 4, circa medium).

. . . although all the elements have this in common that any one of them can be generated from and into any other one of them, they differ in that some of them undergo these generations more easily and more quickly, whereas others more slowly and with more difficulty. Those which have a quality in common are changed into one another more quickly and more easily; whereas those which do not have a quality in common, more slowly and with more difficulty. And the reason for this is that, in the case of those which have a quality in common, it is necessary that only one quality be changed; whereas in the case of those which have no quality in common, it is necessary that both qualities be changed. And, of course, it is easier for one quality to be changed than it is for more than one to be changed.

Although the elements are generable and corruptible, indeed such that they can be generated out of one another, this in no way affects Aquinas' claim (in the *Comp.Theol.*, c. 95; see above pp. 182-183) that the elements must be brought into being immediately by the power of God. For the careful reader will notice Aquinas' careful introductory comment, namely: . . . elementa **secundum se tota** . . ., i.e., the elements **taken together in their totality** . . .. Aquinas is writing about God's creating the heavens and the earth, about what happens ". . . in prima . . . corporalis creaturae productione . . .," i.e., "in the first production of corporeal creatures," as he puts it in the *Summa of Theology*. [30] God's power is such that He could have created **all** corporeal things (the elements, the heavenly bodies, and mixed bodies as

---

[30] . . . in prima . . . corporalis creaturae productione non consideratur aliqua transmutatio de potentia in actum. Et ideo formae corporales quas in prima productione corpora habuerunt, sunt immediate a Deo productae, cui soli ad nutum obedit materia, tanquam propriae causae . . . (*S.T.*, I, q. 65, a. 4, c., in fine). It is clear from the context that the **corporeal created things** (. . . corporales creaturae . . .) mentioned here are generable and corruptible things, i.e., **terrestrial** bodily things, and **not** heavenly bodies.

well) in the same beginning instant. But He could **not,** in that beginning instant, have created something (or some things) such that the elements and the heavenly bodies could have come on the scene **later on** as deriving from these **first** created things as out of a pre-existing matter. For anything which is brought into being out of a pre-existing matter must be composed out of the elements (whether one takes these elements to be the four of which Aquinas speaks, or to be the quarks and leptons of which people speak today). And neither the elements (this is correct) nor the heavenly bodies (this is correct according to Aquinas, but not according to people today) can be composed out of (prior) elements. There can be no bodily things prior to the elements. The elements, whatever one takes them to be, are the **absolutely first** bodily things.

Someone might ask the question whether God could have, in the beginning instant, created **just one** of the elements, and then have had the other elements, followed by mixed bodies in an ordered progression from lower kinds to higher kinds on up to man, come on the scene **at a later time,** and as derived from that **one element** as from an original pre-existing matter. There would, of course, be the need for some corporeal agent cause(s) to act on that one element, and this might give rise to some difficulties. Could one part of fire, for example -- if fire had been that one original element -- exercise its activity, and so function as a corporeal agent, with respect to another part(s) of fire, which would function as matter, so as to produce air and water and earth out of the part(s) being acted on, and then, out of all four of the elements, once produced, produce mixed bodies as well? Could one part of **any one** of the elements, whichever one had been the **one original** element, function as a corporeal agent with respect to another part(s) of that same element (which would function as matter) so as to produce the three other elements, and then, out of all four of the elements, once produced, produce mixed bodies as well?

Fire is hot and dry. Can fire, one part(s) acting on another part(s), produce air and water and earth? Can the hot and dry (fire), acting on the hot and dry

189

(fire), produce the wet and hot (air)? Whence would the wet arise? Can the hot and dry (fire), acting on the hot and dry (fire), produce the cold and wet (water)? Whence would the cold arise? And whence the wet? Can the hot and dry (fire), acting on the hot and dry (fire), produce the dry and cold (earth)? Whence would the cold arise? -- It seems, thus, that there could **not** have been **just one** element created in that beginning instant.

Could **two** of the elements, then, have been created in that beginning instant? Say, fire and water, since between them they have all four of the primary qualities, i.e., hot and dry (in fire), cold and wet (in water)?

fire: hot and dry
water: cold and wet

Further, could the heat of fire overpower the coldness of water, which is already wet, so as to eliminate that coldness altogether, and thereby produce air (the wet and hot)? Which would overpower (and eliminate) which? Would the heat of fire overpower (and eliminate) the coldness of water, thereby producing air? Or, would the coldness of water overpower (and eliminate) the heat of fire, which is already dry, thereby producing earth (the dry and cold)? Would something **in addition to fire and water** be needed to determine which would overpower (and eliminate) which? And what would this something additional be? -- Further, could the dryness of fire overpower the wetness of water, which is already cold, so as to eliminate that wetness altogether, and thereby produce earth (the dry and cold)? Again, which would overpower (and eliminate) which?

Or, could air and earth (rather than fire and water) have been created as the original two, since they, too, have between them all four of the primary qualities, i.e., wet and hot (in air), dry and cold (in earth)? And which two would have been better as the original two, fire and water, or air and earth? And why?

190

air: wet and hot

earth: dry and cold

Which quality of which of the two elements, air and earth, would overpower (and eliminate) which quality of the other element? Would anything in addition to these two elements be needed to determine which would overpower (and eliminate) which? And what would this something additional be? Would it be some sort of primitive, rudimentary, super-dense, super-hot particle(s) which could bang out to become a star(s), perhaps the sun of our solar system? The question: Is something additional needed, and what? is raised in the commentary on *II De Gen. et Corrupt.*, where one reads:

> ... dubitatur de hoc quod hic dicit Philosophus, quod corrupta **frigiditate terrae et humiditate aeris fiet ignis. Hoc enim non videtur possibile esse, quia nec terrae siccitas nec caliditas aeris videntur ad generationem ignis posse sufficere. Ignis enim multo calidior est quam aer, et siccior quam terra ... ... licet illa caliditas [sc. caliditas aeris] non sufficiat, juvatur tamen et intenditur per virtutem corporis caelestis, et luce solis, et per virtute aliarum stellarum ...** (*In II De Gen. et Corrupt.*, lect. 4, in fine).

> ... there is a difficulty with respect to what the Philosopher says here, that fire comes to be at the corruption of the coldness of earth and the wetness of air. It seems impossible for this to happen, because neither the dryness of earth nor the heat of air can suffice for the generation of fire. For fire is much hotter than air, and much drier than earth ... ... although the heat of air does not suffice, it is helped and intensified by the power of the body of the heavens, by the light of the sun, and by the power of other stars ...

How can the heat of fire be generated by (from?) the heat of air, since fire is so much hotter than air? Indeed, fire is as hot as hot can be. Similarly, how

191

can the dryness of fire be generated by (from?) the dryness of earth, since fire is so much drier than earth? Indeed, fire is as dry as dry can be (and precisely because it is as hot as hot can be). Something in addition to air and earth is required, suggests the commentary, namely the agent causality of some heavenly body, like the sun, and/or some star(s). Their agent causality will intensify the heat of air, and thereby intensify the dryness of earth, so as to suffice for the generation of fire.

Furthermore, what exactly would be needed (and it seems that it would be something in addition to the two original elements, whichever they had been, whether fire and water, or air and earth) to give rise to the first and lowest of **mixed** bodies? To the first and lowest of **living** mixed bodies? To the first and lowest of **animal** mixed bodies? To the highest of mixed bodies, that of **man**? -- These are questions, one can quite readily see, which touch, **though in a very medieval way,** on whether, and how, the Big Bang can be used to understand the origin, expansion, and evolution of the universe as a whole, and whether and how some form of Darwinism can be used to understand the origin and evolution of life on the planet earth.

8. Opus creationis, opus distinctionis, et opus ornatus

In [creaturae corporalis] . . . productione tria opera Scriptura commemorat, scilicet opus creationis, cum dicitur, *In principio creavit Deus caelum et terram,* etc. (*Gen.,* 1, 1); opus distinctionis, cum dicitur, *Divisit lucem a tenebris, et aquas quae sunt supra firmamentum ab aquis quae sunt sub firmamento* (*Gen.,* v, 4, 7); et opus ornatus, cum dicitur, *Fiant luminaria in firmamento,* etc. (*Gen.,* v, 14). (*S.T.,* I, q. 65, prooemium).

Scripture mentions three works in the production [of corporeal creatures], namely the work of creation, when it is said, *In the beginning God created heaven and earth,* etc.; the work of distinction, when it is said, *He divided the light from the darkness, and the waters which are above the firmament from the waters which are below the firmament;* and the work of adornment, when it is said, *Let there be light-giving bodies in the firmament. . .*

. . . in recapitulatione divinorum operum, Scriptura sic dicit, *Igitur perfecti sunt caeli et terra, et omnis ornatus eorum (Gen., 2, 1).* In quibus verbis triplex opus intelligi potest, scilicet *opus creationis,* per quod caelum et terra producta leguntur, sed informata. Et *opus distinctionis,* per quod caelum et terra sunt perfecta, sive per formas substantiales attributas materiae omnino informi, ut Augustinus vult; sive quantum ad convenientem decorem et ordinem, ut alii Sancti dicunt. Et his duobus operibus additur *ornatus.* Et differt ornatus a perfectione. Nam perfectio caeli et terrae ad ea pertinere videtur quae caelo et terrae sunt intrinseca; ornatus vero ad ea quae sunt a caelo et terra distincta. Sicut homo perficitur per proprias partes et formas. ornatur autem per vestimenta, vel aliquid huiusmodi. Distinctio autem aliquorum maxime manifestatur per motum localem, quo ab invicem separantur. Et ideo ad opus ornatus pertinet productio illarum rerum quae habent motum in caelo et in terra.

Sicut autem supra dictum est, de tribus fit mentio in creatione, scilicet de caelo et aqua et terra. Et haec tria etiam formantur per opus distinctionis tribus diebus: primo die, caelum; secundo die distinguuntur aquae; tertio die fit distinctio in terra, maris et aridae. Et similiter in opere ornatus, primo die, qui est quartus, producuntur luminaria, quae moventur in caelo, ad ornatum ipsius. Secundo die, qui est quintus, aves et pisces, ad ornatum medii elementi, quia habent motum in aere et aqua, quae pro uno accipiuntur. Tertio die, qui est sextus, producuntur animalia quae habent motum in terra, ad ornatum ipsius.

Sed sciendum est quod in productione luminarium non discordat Augustinus ab aliis Sanctis. Dicit enim luminaria esse facta in actu, non in virtute tantum; non enim habet firmamentum virtutem productivam luminarium, sicut habet terra virtutem productivam plantarum. Unde Scriptura non dicit, *Producat firmamentum luminaria,* sicut dicit, *Germinet terra herbam virentem.* (S.T., I, q. 70, a. 1, c.).

. . . briefly summarizing the [creating] works of God, Scripture says, *The heavens and the earth, therefore, were brought to a kind of completion, and all their adornment as well.* A threefold work can be understood in these words. There is the work of *creation,* about which one reads that heaven and earth were produced, but not yet brought to full form. There is also the work of *distinction,* by which heaven and earth were moved toward some sort of completion, either by the substantial forms given to a completely formless matter, as Augustine wants it; or with respect to a certain fitting beauty and order, as other holy authors say. And to these two works, there is added the work of *adornment.* The work of adornment differs from the work of being moved toward a kind of completion. Now, being moved toward completion seems to pertain to those things which are *intrinsic* to heaven and earth; whereas adornment, to those which are *distinct from* heaven and earth. Man, for example, is brought to a kind of completion by his proper parts and forms; but is adorned by clothing, or something else of that sort. Now, the distinction of things from one another is made most manifest by their moving from place to place, thereby separating themselves from one another. And so, it pertains to the work of adornment to produce those things which move about in heaven and on earth.

As said above, three things were mentioned in the *work of creation,* namely heaven and water and earth. And these same three things were given some form during the three days of the *work of distinction.* On the first day, heaven was given some form. On the second day, the waters were distinguished. On the third day, a distinction was made on earth, of sea from dry land. And similarly, in the *work of adornment.* On the first day of adornment, which is the fourth from the beginning, the light-giving bodies which are in motion in heaven for its adornment, were produced. On the second day, which is the fifth, birds and fishes were produced to adorn the middle element, because they move about in air and water, which are taken here as one thing. On the third day, which is the sixth, we see produced, for the adornment of the earth, the animals which move about upon it.

It should be noted at this point that Augustine does not disagree with other holy authors as regards the production of the light-giving bodies. For he says that these light-giving bodies were made *actually,* and not only in the power of other things. The firmament does not have the power to produce the light-giving bodies in the way in which earth has the power to produce plants. And so, Scripture does not say, *Let the firmament produce the light-giving bodies,* as it says, *Let earth sprout forth green plants.*

In the beginning -- in the beginning instant of the existence of the physical universe, **just after** the **first now** of time -- everything in that universe was in some way all together, in the minutest possible particle of matter; and so, that universe was then as small as small can be, as small as it could possibly be. To explain. Within their cause, i.e., within God, "before" they were produced (if one can speak of such a **before**), all the physical things that came to be, were gathered together as though within a mathematical point, since God is a spirit, and as such something without dimensions. There in God, these things took up no space at all. There was no space for them to take up. They were there, within His infinite power to call them into existence, but not as within some preexisting matter, nor as with dimensions, nor therefore as taking up any space. There was then only God, nothing but God. There was then neither matter, nor dimensions, nor space -- there was then nothing **outside of** God as distinct from Him -- for God had not yet created. Nor was there any matter, or dimensions, or space **within God** as part of His nature, for God is a spirit. As soon as God spoke His creating word, **Fiant (Let them be),** the power of this word hurled these things -- i.e., the three, heaven and water and earth (. . . de tribus fit mentio in creatione, scilicet de caelo et aqua et terra . . .) -- out from within Him, hurled them out into their own existence, with a motion of increasing speed, and into a space (the empyrean heaven?)[31] which came to be with them, and with that same increasing speed. Now, nothing material can be in motion with the speed of light. And so, some might want to say, the speed of the motion with which these material things came forth from the essence of God, in Whom they had tarried, motionless and dimensionless, for an eternity, was less than that of light, even though it was very great, since there was nothing "outside" God, if one can speak of such an **outside,** which could possibly impede this speed. But, others might want to point out, the speed of their emerging motion could not have been very great, since they, previously motionless and dimensionless, emerged into existence with a motion which **had to begin,** and with dimensions which **had to be taken on.** Motion takes time. Taking on dimensions takes time. And so, in the beginning instant of its existence, the material universe must have been as small as small can be, and in motion with an emerging motion as slow as a motion can be. It takes time for a motion which is beginning, to take on acceleration. Similarly, it takes time for a thing which is taking on dimensions, to take them on. -- And so, in the beginning -- in that beginning instant of the existence of the physical universe, **just after** the first now of time, which (now of time) is not time itself, but that from which time begins [32] -- all bodily things were **in some way** all together (**exactly how** is to be discovered and described) in a particle of

---

[31]   There are some, Aquinas notes, who identify the heaven which was created on the first day along with water and earth, as the **empyrean** heaven: ... communiter dicitur quatuor esse **primo** creata, scilicet naturam angelicam, **caelum empyreum,** materiam corporalem informem, et tempus... (*S.T.,* I, q. 66, a. 4, c., in princ.; see also *S.T.,* I, q. 46, a.3, c., in fine). Since the empyrean heaven is the highest, the outermost, heaven and as such containing the whole physical universe (containing, therefore, all the lower heavens, and all the heavenly bodies which inhabit them, including our Earth which is at the center of the spherical whole) within the space it provides (. . . locus intelligitur in caelo empyreo **omnia continente** ... ; *S.T.,* I, q. 66, a. 4, ad 5), one can conclude that the empyrean heaven began to exist **just after** the **first now** of time, as containing all (. . . omnia continente . . .), however small that heaven was when it first began to be; and indeed, it must have been as small as small can be, when it first began to be. One can also conclude, since the heaven was created on the first day along with water and earth, that the fifth body, or fifth essence, if there had been such a thing, was created along with the four terrestrial elements.

[32] . . . nihil fit nisi secundum quod est. Nihil autem est temporis nisi **nunc.** Unde non potest fieri [tempus] nisi secundum aliquod **nunc,** non quia in ipso primo **nunc** sit tempus, sed quia ab ipso incipit tempus. (*S.T.,* I, q. 46, a. 3, ad 3).

matter so small that it could not possibly have been any smaller, and with the emerging motion of each of these things so slow that it could not possibly have been any slower, if they were to exist in their own natures (outside God), as things distinct from and created by God. In some way, the first three were there, i.e., heaven and water and earth; in some way, the firmament was there, and the waters which came to be both above it and below it; in some way, the sea was there, and the dry land; in some way, the light-giving bodies which were to adorn heaven, were there; in some way, the birds and the fishes which were to adorn the air and water, were there; in some way, the animals, and man too,[33] which were to adorn earth, were there.

How, then? In the elements, in some way? In the elements as in their producing agent causes, at least in some **partial** way?[34] In the elements as in their pre-existing material components as well? Aquinas writes:

> . . . ad opus creationis pertinet producere ipsam elementorum substantiam; ad opus autem distinctionis et ornatus pertinet formare aliqua ex praeexistentibus elementis . . . (S.T., I, q. 68, a. 1, c., in medio).

> . . . it belongs to the work of creation to produce the substance of the elements, whereas it belongs to the work of distinction and of adornment to form certain other things out of the already existing elements . . .

> . . . oportet dicere quod materia prima [non] fuit creata omnino sine forma . . . (S.T., I, q. 66, a. 1, c., in medio).

> . . . it must be said that prime matter was [not] created completely without form . . .

---

33   Man was there, but **only** with respect to the body, **not** the soul. Man's soul is not, cannot be, educed from the potency of matter, since it has an operation which **is performed** without any dependence on man's body. See below, pp. 228-241, section 11, **The elements and the eduction of substantial forms from the potency of matter,** especialy pp. 236-238.

34   The other partial agent causes would be, no doubt, the (some) heavenly bodies, like the sun and/or the (some) stars.

... formae elementorum sunt quae primo adveniunt materiae
[primae]... (*S.T.,* I, q. 68, a. 1, c., in medio).

... the forms of the elements are the first forms which come to
[prime] matter...

... materia prima est in potentia primo ad formam elementi.
Sub forma vero elementi est in potentia ad formam mixti ...
Sub forma autem mixti considerata est in potentia ad animam
vegetabilem ... Itemque anima vegetabilis est in potentia ad
sensitivam; sensitiva vero ad intellectivam ... Sunt ergo
elementa propter corpora mixta; haec vero propter viventia; in
quibus plantae sunt propter animalia, animalia vero propter
hominem. (*C.G.,* III, cap. 22).

... prime matter is in potency first of all to the form of an
element. Then, as existing under the form of an element, it is
in potency to the form of a mixed body . . . Moreover,
considered under the form of a mixed body, it is in potency to
the vegetable soul . . . Similarly, the vegetable soul is in
potency to the sensitive soul, and the sensitive to the intellectual
. . . The elements therefore exist for the sake of mixed bodies,
and mixed bodies for the sake of living things, among which
plants exist for the sake of animals, and animals for the sake of
man.

Since prime matter cannot be created completely without form, and so
must have been created with forms of some sort; and since the forms of the
elements are the first forms which come to prime matter; it follows that
prime matter was created with the forms of the elements. The elements,
therefore, were produced on the first day (as part[35] of the **opus creationis**);

---

[35] The other parts of the **opus creationis** were the empyrean heaven, the angels, and time:
... communiter dicitur quatuor esse **primo** creata, scilicet naturam angelicam, caelum

and mixed bodies, i.e., things made up out of the elements, came into existence later on (as pertaining to the **opus distinctionis** and to the **opus ornatus**).

9. The elements and the heavenly bodies

It will be helpful at this point to look a bit at what Aquinas has to say about the nature of the **heavens,** and of the **heavenly bodies** which inhabit them. For they exercise a certain wide-ranging agent causality on the four terrestrial elements, i.e., fire, air, water, and earth. The elements depend on the heavens and the heavenly bodies not only for their existence as elements, but also for their transformations into one another, and for their becoming ingredients of mixed bodies, and in a determinate order from the lower (less perfect) to the higher (more perfect) sorts. This will make clear how the four elements fit into the developmental (in a way, evolutionary) **tria opera** of God's creative production of corporeal creatures, i.e., into the **opus creationis,** the **opus distinctionis** and the **opus ornatus,** in which there is a passage from being not yet fully formed to becoming progressively more fully formed.

The nature of the heavens and of the heavenly bodies

Each of the heavens,[36] and each of the heavenly bodies,[37] as Aquinas sees

---

empyreum, materiam corporalem informem, et tempus . . .   (*S.T.,* I, q. 66, a. 4, c., in princ.; see also *S.T.,* I, q. 46, a .3, c., in fine).   The **four** of this commonly held view are not inconsistent with the **three** mentioned in Scripture. The **empyrean of the four** is simply the highest, or outermost, sphere of the **heaven of the three,** and the place in which the angels were created: . . . conveniens fuit quod angeli in supremo corpore crearentur, tanquam toti naturae corporae praesidentes, sive id dicatur caelum empyreum, sive qualitercumque nominetur . . .   (*S.T.,* I, q. 61, a. 4, c.). The **not yet fully formed corporeal matter of the four** (. . . materia corporalis informis . . .) is the **water and earth of the three,** and the **time of the four** is the measure of their (i.e., of the water and the earth) motion.
[36]   From the highest to the lowest, the heavens are: the empyrean heaven, wholly luminous; the aqueous or crystalline heaven, wholly transparent; the starry heaven, in part transparent, in part actually luminous, and divided into eight spheres (or heavens),

199

it, is a fifth body (quintum corpus),[38] or a body of a fifth essence (quinta essentia).[39]   That is, each is composed of a matter and a form so related that the matter is completely actualized by the form which it has. Its matter is in potency to that form alone, and to no other. The matter of each of them, therefore, is a matter quite unlike prime matter, which is the matter of the four terrestrial elements, and of all mixed bodies. Each of the heavens, and each of the heavenly bodies, nonetheless, is exactly like each of the four terrestrial elements in being a **simple** body, i.e., a bodily thing which is not composed out of prior bodily things.   A simple body is composed out of a matter and a form, and out of nothing else. A mixed body, by way of contrast, is composed out of prior bodily things (i.e., out of the elements) as well as out of a matter and a form.

Furthermore, in the view of Aquinas, the heavens and the heavenly bodies which are their inhabitants, are incorruptible.

> . . . aliquid [dicitur] esse corruptibile . . . per hoc quod in seipso aliquod principium corruptionis habet, vel contrarietatem vel saltem potentiam materiae . . . (*S.T.,* I, q. 50, a. 5, ad 3).

---

the highest being the sphere (or heaven) of the fixed stars, followed by the spheres (or heavens) of the seven planets.   --   Ad distinctionem . . . caelorum sciendam, considerandum est quod **caelum** tripliciter dicitur in Scripturis. Quandoque enim dicitur proprie et naturaliter. Et sic dicitur caelum corpus aliquod sublime, et luminosum actu vel potentia, et incorruptibile per naturam. Et secundum hoc, ponuntur tres caeli. Primum totaliter lucidum, quod vocant **empyreum.** Secundum totaliter diaphanum, quod vocant **caelum aqueum** vel **crystallinum.** Tertium partim diaphanum et partim lucidum actu, quod vocant **caelum sidereum;** et dividitur in octo sphaeras, scilicet in sphaeram stellarum fixarum, et septem sphaeras planetarum; quae possunt dici octo caeli. (*S.T.,* I, q. 68, a.4, c.)

[37]   See *In II De Caelo et Mundo,* lect. 15, n. 2, where Aquinas, commenting on how long, and why, it takes the various planets to move through their circular orbits (. . . pertransire circulum suum . . .), mentions each of what were then taken to be the seven planets, which are, from the lowest to the highest: the moon, the sun, Mercury, Venus, Mars, Jupiter, and Saturn -- followed, higher still, by the fixed stars.

[38]   Alii . . . dixerunt caelum non esse de natura quatuor elementorum, sed esse **quintum corpus,** praeter quatuor elementa. Et haec est opinio Aristotelis. (*S.T.,* I, q. 68, a. 1, c.).

[39]   . . . Augustinus sequitur in hoc opinionem Platonis, non ponentis **quintam essentiam** . . . (*S.T.,* I, q. 66, a. 2, ad 1).

> . . . a thing is said to be corruptible . . . because it has *within itself*
> some princple of corruption, either some contrariety or at least
> the potency of matter . . .

Aquinas is here pointing out that the corruptibility of a thing derives from what is *intrinsic* to that thing, and not from something extrinsic to it, like the power of God to reduce it to absolute nothingness by withdrawing from it His conserving causality. A thing is said to be corruptible because it has **within itself** some source of corruption; either some sort of contrariety, like that which derives from being composed out of the four elements, in which are found the contrary pairs hot-cold and wet-dry; or because it is composed out of prime matter and substantial form, prime matter being such that while actualized by one form, it can, given the causality of certain appropriate agent cause(s), become actualized by another form. Neither the heavens nor the heavenly bodies, in the view of Aquinas, have within themselves any sort of contrariety, since they are not composed out of the four elements; nor are they composed out of prime matter and substantial form, though they are composed out of matter and form. The heavens and the heavenly bodies, therefore, are incorruptible.

This becomes clearer in the following.

> . . . materia corporis caelestis . . . non est in potentia nisi ad
> formam quam habet . . .   Unde illa forma sic perficit illam
> materiam, quod nullo modo in ea remanet potentia ad esse, sed
> ad ubi tantum, ut Aristoteles dicit. (*S.T.,* I, q. 66, a.2, c., in fine).

> . . . the matter of a heavenly body . . . is in potency only to the
> form which it has . . .   Whence that form perfects that matter
> in such a way that in no way does there remain in it a potency
> with respect to being, but only with respect to place . . .

201

The matter of each heavenly body, as Aquinas sees it, is such that its potentiality for form is totally actualized by the form which it has. That is, its form so perfects its matter that there remains in the heavenly body no potentiality with respect to **existence,** but only with respect to **place.** Its matter, unlike prime matter, cannot take on any other form. And so, a heavenly body cannot go out of **existence** by corruption, nor can it come into **existence** by generation: . . . nullo modo in ea remanet potentia **ad esse** . . .; though it can go out of this **place** into another one: . . . remanet in ea potentia **ad ubi** tantum . . . The potentiality of the matter of the moon, for example, is such that it is actualized by the substantial form of the moon, but **only** by that form, and **totally** by that form. Similarly, the potentiality of the matter of the sun is such that it is actualized by the substantial form of the sun, but only and totally by that form. Similarly, too, for each of the other five planets, i.e., Mercury, Venus, Mars, Jupiter, and Saturn. So, too, for each of the fixed stars, and for each of the heavens as well.

The heavens have **three** basic charateristics (and what can be said of each of the heavens can be said of each of the heavenly bodies as well, as Aquinas sees it).

> . . . caelum . . . dicitur in Scripturis quandoque . . . proprie et naturaliter. Et sic dicitur caelum corpus aliquod sublime, et luminosum actu vel potentia, et incorruptibile per naturam. . . (S.T., I, q. 68, a. 4, c., in medio).

> . . . the word "heaven" is sometimes used in the Scriptures . . . properly and naturally. And in this way heaven is said to be some body high up, and light-giving either actually or potentially, and incorruptible by nature . . .

These are the three basic characteristics. 1) Each is a **corpus sublime,** i.e., a body which is up high, away from our Earth, or having a high location (. . . **habens situm altum** . . . , as Aquinas puts it in *In II Sent.,* d. 14, a. 4, ad 4). 2) Each is **luminosum,** i.e., light-giving, either actually or potentially; that is,

202

it is capable either of emitting (or reflecting) light, or of being illuminated. 3) Each is **incorruptibile per naturam,** incorruptible by nature, because it is not composed out of the four elements, the contrarieties of which are a source of corruptibility; and because it does not include prime matter as an ingredient of what it is.

Their incorruptibility, as Aquinas sees it following Aristotle, is connected with their circular motion.

> . . . cum . . . corpus caeleste habet naturalem motum diversum a naturali motu elementorum, sequitur quod eius natura sit alia a natura quatuor elementorum. Et sicut motus circularis, qui est proprius corporis caelestis, caret contrarietate, motus autem elementorum sunt invicem contrarii, ut qui est sursum ei qui est deorsum; ita corpus caeleste est absque contrarietate, corpora vero elementaria sunt cum contrarietate. Et quia corruptio et generatio sunt ex contrariis, sequitur quod secundum suam naturam corpus caeleste sit incorruptibile, elementa vero sunt corruptibilia. (*S.T.,* I, q. 66, a. 2, c., circa princ.).[40]

> . . . since . . . a heavenly body has a natural motion which is diverse from the natural motion of the elements, it follows that its nature is other than the nature of the four elements. And just as circular motion, which is proper to a heavenly body, lacks contrariety, whereas the motions of the elements are contrary to one another, upward motion being contrary to downward motion; so too the heavenly body itself is without contrariety, whereas the elements themselves are with contrariety. And since corruption and generation are from contraries, it follows that a heavenly body is according to its nature incorruptible, whereas the elements are by their natures corruptible.

---

40   For an extended and detailed version of this argumentation, see *In I De Caelo et Mundo,* lect. 4, nn. 9-18; also lect. 6. In Aristotle, see *De Caelo,* Bk. I, ch. 2, 269 a 18 - b 17; ch . 3, 270 a 12 - 22.

Without reflecting on what is unacceptable about this argument for the **clearly false claim** that the heavenly bodies are incorruptible, it is interesting to notice that Aquinas himself (in the brief passage immediately below) noticed a very interesting fact, i.e., that Plato and **all** philosophers before Aristotle felt (a sound feeling, indeed, one wants to add) that **all** bodies in the physical universe are of the nature of the four elements, i.e., that any physical body is either one of the four elements or composed out of some combination of them; and that, therefore, **all physical bodies, terrestrial and heavenly,** share in a matter of the same nature.

> . . . Plato . . . et omnes philosophi ante Aristotelem posuerunt omnia corpora esse de natura quatuor elementorum. Unde cum quatuor elementa communicent in una materia, ut mutua generatio et corruptio in eis ostendit; per consequens sequebatur quod omnium corporum [et terrestrium et caelestium] sit materia una. Quod autem quaedam corpora sint incorruptibilia, Plato adscribebat non conditioni materiae, sed voluntati artificis, scilicet Dei, quem introducit corporibus dicentem: *Natura vestra estis dissolubilia, voluntate autem mea indissolubilia, quia voluntas mea maior est nexu vestro.* (S.T., I, q. 66, a. 2, c., in princ).[41]

---

[41]   See also *S.T.*, I, q. 50, a. 5, ad 2:   . . . Plato . . . existimabat [corpora caelestia] esse ex elementis composita, et ideo secundum suam naturam dissolubilia, sed voluntate divina semper conservantur in esse.   --   Elsewhere, having observed that the firmament -- i.e., the "vault or arch of the sky," which is to say, the heaven -- which the Scriptures say was made on the second day, can be understood in two ways, either 1) as the starry heaven, or 2) as the considerably lower arch of the sky which is that part of air in which clouds are condensed; Aquinas carefully points out how Plato and Empedocles differed in their respective views on the nature of the starry heaven, i.e., of the "firmamentum in quo sunt sidera," or "firmamentum illud in quo fixae sunt stellae." Aquinas writes: . . . Quidam . . . dixerunt firmamentum illud [sc. in quo sunt sidera] esse ex elementis compositum. Et haec fuit opinio Empedocles, qui tamen dixit ideo illud corpus indissolubile est, quia in eius compositione lis non erat, sed amicitia tantum.   Alii vero dixerunt firmamentum esse de natura quatuor elementorum, non quasi ex elementis compositum, sed quasi elementum simplex.   Et haec fuit opinio Platonis, qui posuit corpus caeleste esse elementum ignis. (*S.T.*, I, q. 68, a. 1, c., circa princ,).

... Plato ... and all philosophers before Aristotle held that all bodies are of the nature of the four elements. Whence, since the four elements share a common matter, as the mutual generation and corruption among them shows; it follows therefore that there is but one matter for all bodies [both terrestrial and heavenly]. That some bodies are incorruptible, Plato attributed not to the condition of matter, but to the will of the artificer, namely God, Whom he brought in as saying to the heavenly bodies: *By your nature itself you are dissolvable, but by my will undissolvable, because my will is greater than what holds you together*

The causality of the heavens and of the heavenly bodies

... principia activa in istis inferioribus corporibus non inveniuntur nisi qualitates activae elementorum, quae sunt calidum et frigidum et huiusmodi ...   Sed ... huiusmodi *accidentia* se habent sicut materiales dispositiones ad formas *substantiales* naturalium corporum.   Materia autem non sufficit ad agendum.   Et ideo oportet super has materiales dispositiones ponere aliquod principium activum ... quod per sui praesentiam et absentiam causet . . . generationem et corruptionem inferiorum corporum.   Et huiusmodi sunt corpora caelestia.   Et ideo quidquid in istis inferioribus generat, movet ad speciem sicut instrumentum caelestis corporis; secundum quod dicitur in *II Physic.* quod *homo generat hominem, et sol.*   (*S.T.*, I, q. 115, a. 3, ad 2).

... there are no active principles found in bodies here below except the active qualities of the elements, which are hot and cold and the like ...   But *accidents* of this sort are but material dispositions for the *substantial* forms of natural bodies. And matter is not enough to do the work of an agent cause. This is why it is necessary that there be above these material dispositions some active principle ... which by its presence and its absence causes ... the generation and corruption of bodies here below. The heavenly bodies are active principles of this kind. And so, whatever generates here below, causing the motion which produces a [substantial] species, does this as an instrument of a heavenly body. And this is why it is said in Bk. II of the *Physics* that *man, and the sun, generates man.*

The four terrestrial elements and their proper qualities are not enough, of themselves, to explain, as agent causes, the generation and corruption of terrestrial bodies, neither the transformations of the elements into one another, nor the entering of the elements into the composition of mixed bodies. There is need for additional agent causes, and of sufficient power, to do this work, namely the heavens and the heavenly bodies, without whose light[42] terrestrial agents could not function as agents at all. Indeed, these terrestrial agents could not even remain in existence without the conserving causality, through light (and heat), of the heavens and the heavenly bodies. Moreover, they are but **particular** instrumental agents of the heavens and the heavenly bodies, which function as **universal** agents. This is why Aristotle says that though **man generates man**, since in nature like generates like, it is man as instrument of the sun -- **homo generat hominem, et sol.** The sun, as universal cause, generates man, but through man as particular cause. In this same sense, the sun generates dog through dog, and tree through tree. It is only life forms of the **lowest** sort, those -- exemplifies Aquinas (and wrongly) -- which come to be through putrefaction,[43] (perhaps maggots, to suggest an

---

[42]   . . . sicut calor est qualitas activa consequens formam substantialem ignis, ita **lux** est qualitas activa consequens formam substantialem solis, vel cuiuscumque alterius corporis a se lucentis, si aliquod tale est . . .   (*S.T.*, I, q. 67, a. 3, c., in fine).   . . . **lux** caelestium corporum causat formas substantiales in istis inferioribus . . .   (*Ibid.*, obj. 3).   . . . sicut calor agit ad formam ignis quasi instrumentaliter in virtute formae substantialis [ignis], ita **lumen** agit quasi instrumentaliter in virtute corporum caelestium ad producendas formas substantiales [in istis inferioribus] . . .   (*Ibid.*, ad 3).

[43]   . . . ad generationem animalium imperfectorum [sicut patet in animalibus generatis per putrefactionem] sufficit agens universale, quod est virtus caelestis, cui assimilantur [haec animalia] non secundum speciem, sed secundum analogiam quandam . . .   Ad generationem vero animalium perfectorum non sufficit agens universale, sed requiritur agens proprium, quod est **generans univocum** . . .   (*S.T.*, I q. 45, a. 1, obj, 3 and ad 3). -- Observation, we can point out in our day, confirms the fact that the lowly life forms said by those in Aquinas' day to be "generated from putrefaction" have and need a **generans univocum.** Indeed, all life forms, as we know today, have and need a **generans univocum.**   And, one suspects, if Aquinas knew about what **he** took to be the elements, what **we** today know about what **we** take to be the elements, he would also have said that **ignis generat ignem, et sol,** and that **aer generat aerem, et sol,** and similarly for the other elements, water and earth. That is, he would have seen that in any generation, whether of **living** things or **non-living**

example, i.e., the legless larvae of the housefly) which are produced **directly** by the sun, i.e., **without** the intervening **particular** instrumental causality of some terrestrial agent.

Applying the immediately preceding (pp. 205-207) to the three works of the initial six-day production of corporeal creatures, i.e., to the **o p u s creationis**, the **opus distinctionis**, and the **opus ornatus**, one can see in Aquinas' thinking a kind of primitive and implicit version of a physical universe which has banged out of, expanded out of, an initially infinitesimally miniscule one, coupled with a similarly primitive and implicit version of the evolution of life on the planet Earth. A bare outline of this expansion of the universe, and of this evolution of life, was presented above on pp. 195-199. Some details can be added at this point, as a kind of commentary (over pp. 207-227) on the two passages which follow:

> . . . ad *opus creationis* pertinet producere ipsam **elementorum substantiam**; ad *opus distinctionis et ornatus* pertinet formare aliqua ex praeexistentibus elementis . . .   (*S.T.*, I, q. 68, a. 1, c., in medio).

> . . . it belongs to the *work of creation* to produce the substance of the elements, whereas it belongs to the *work of distinction* and *of adornment* to form certain other things out of the already existing elements . . .

> Sicut . . . supra dictum est, de tribus [in Scripturis] fit mentio *in creatione,* scilicet de caelo et aqua et terra.   Et haec tria etiam formantur per opus distinctionis tribus diebus: primo die, caelum; secundo die distinguuntur aquae; terio die fit distinctio in terra, maris et aridae. Et similiter in opere ornatus, primo die, qui est quartus, producuntur luminaria, quae moventur in caelo, ad ornatum ipsius.   Secundo die, qui est quintus, aves et pisces, ad ornatum medii elementi, quia habent motum in aere

---

things, there is required an **agens univocum** of an appropriate sort in addition to an **agens universale.** How else could the final effect come to be of the **particular sort** that it is?

et aqua, quae pro uno accipiuntur. Tertio die, qui est sextus, producuntur animalia quae habent motum in terra, ad ornatum ipsius. (*S.T.*, I, q. 70, a. 1, c.).

As . . . was said above, three things were mentioned [in the Scriptures] in the *work of creation,* namely heaven and water and earth. And these same three things were given some form during the three days of the *work of distinction.* On the first day, heaven was given some form. On the second day, the waters were distinguished. On the third day, a distinction was made on earth, of sea from dry land. And similarly, in the *work of adornment.* On the first day of adornment, which is the fourth from the beginning, the light-giving bodies which are in motion in heaven, for its adornment, were produced. On the second day, which is the fifth, birds and fishes were produced to adorn the middle element, because they move about in air and water, which are taken here as one thing. On the third day, which is the sixth, we see produced, for the adornment of the earth, the animals which move about upon it.

Three things, note the Scriptures, were brought into being as pertaining to the **opus creationis,** namely heaven and water and earth. Water and earth, taken together, are being contrasted with **heaven,** and thus quite obviously include in some way **all terrestrial bodies,** mixed bodies as well as elements. And so, since "it belongs to **the work of creation** to produce the substance of the elements," one can conclude that all mixed bodies were in some way there **in the substance of the four elements,** when these elements first began to exist.

With heaven and the four elements, effects of the **opus creationis,** already in existence on the first day, the **opus distinctionis** was begun, and **on that same first day** -- continuing on the second and third days, and followed by the **opus ornatus** on days four through six. -- "On the first day," writes

Aquinas (above, p. 194), "**heaven** was given some form." This turns out to mean, as Aquinas notes, that heaven was given **light** (lux, lumen), and this light was the sun's light. But, adds Aquinas, this light was not then yet fully formed -- **sed adhuc informis.** That is, the sun **itself,** the **substance** of the sun, was there; and it had some sort of general light-emitting power -- **virtutem illuminativam in communi,** explains Aquinas, but **not yet a fully formed light-emitting power,** not yet of the special and determinate sort required for producing **particular** effects, which it acquired only later on -- **postmodum data est ei.**[44] Aquinas writes:

> . . . illa lux fuit solis, sed adhuc informis, quantum ad hoc quod iam erat substantia solis, et habebat virtutem illuminativam in communi; sed postmodum data est ei specialis et determinata virtus ad particulares effectus. Et secundum hoc, in productione huius lucis, distincta est lux a tenebris . . . (*S.T.,* I, q. 67, a. 4, ad 2).

> . . . that light [i.e., the light given to heaven on the first day] was the light of the sun,[45] but not then fully formed, i.e., the *substance* of the sun was already there, and it had illuminating power of a *common* sort; but it was *only afterwards* that the special and determinate power to produce *particular* effects was given to it. And according to this, in the production of this light, light was distinguished from darkness . . .

---

44   Without stating exactly what these **special and determinate** powers are, and what these **particular** effects are, Aquinas writes: . . . si . . . lux primo die facta intelligitur lux corporalis [for some, like Augustine, suggested that this light might be a **spiritual** light], oportet dicere quod lux primo die fuit producta secundum communem lucis naturam; quarto autem die attributa est luminaribus determinata virtus ad determinatos effectus; secundum quod videmus alios effectus habere radium solis, et alios radium lunae, et sic de aliis . . . (*S.T.,* I, q. 70, a. 1, ad 2). -- But, Aquinas does not say exactly what the effects of the rays of the sun are (**day** light, warmth, sun tan?) as different from the effects of the rays of the moon (**night** light, coolness, a man and a woman falling in love?).

45   This light was, no doubt, in some way the light of other light-giving bodies as well, which, like the sun, were already there. That is, the **substance** of these other light-giving bodies was there, and they had some sort of light-emitting power, but **not** yet for producing **particular** effects.

"On the second day" of the six (which was also the second day of the **opus distinctionis**), writes Aquinas (above, p. 194), **water** was given some form, i.e., "the waters were distinguished;" those which are above the firmament (the firmament is some **intermediate part** of the **whole** heaven) were divided from those which are below the firmament.   There is more than one way to interpret the nature of the firmament, as well as the nature of the waters both above and below the firmament, as Aquinas indicates in some detail in *S.T.*, I, q. 68, aa. 1-3.   And it would be difficult, maybe impossible, to choose one over another.   In any case, the important point is this, that the firmament itself, a **not yet fully formed transparent body**, divides waters from other waters, i.e., **these** not yet fully formed transparent bodies from **those** others, all of which can be designated as "waters" (including air), i.e., divides the higher ones, which could be of one nature, from the the lower ones, which could be of another nature (though both might well be of the same nature), the lower ones being obviously **heavier**, and the higher ones being **lighter**, whatever other characteristics they might have.   Aquinas writes:

Sic igitur sive per firmamentum intelligamus caelum in quo sunt sidera [sc. caelum sidereum] sive spatium aeris nubilosum [sc. pars aeris in qua nubes condensantur], convenienter dicitur quod firmamentum dividit aquas ab aquis, secundum quod per aquam *materia informis* significatur; vel secundum quod *omnia corpora diaphana* sub nomine aquarum intelliguntur. Nam caelum sidereum distinguit corpora inferiora diaphana a superioribus.   Aer vero nubilosus distinguit superiorem aeris partem, in qua generantur pluviae et huiusmodi impressiones, ab inferiori parte aeris, quae aquae connectitur, et sub nomine aquarum intelligitur. (*S.T.*, I, q. 68, a. 3, c., in fine).

Thus, therefore, whether by the firmament we understand the heaven in which there are stars [i.e., the sidereal or starry heaven] or the cloudy part of the air [i.e., that part of the air in which the clouds come to be condensed], it is suitably said that the firmament divides the waters from the waters, according as water is taken to signify matter which is not yet fully formed; or

210

according as all transparent bodies are understood as included under the name of waters. For the starry heaven distinguishes the lower transparent bodies from the higher ones. And the cloud-bearing [part of the] air distinguishes the higher part of the air, in which rain, and other threatening things[46] of that sort, are generated, from the lower part of the air, which touches the waters below, and so is understood as included under the name of waters.

"On the third day," the last of the **opus distinctionis**, writes Aquinas (above, pp. 193-194), the **earth** was given some form, i.e., "a distinction was made on earth, of sea from dry land." Of the two interpretations noted by Aquinas in *S.T.*, I, q. 69, a. 1, namely that of Augustine, and that of other Holy authors, that of the other Holy authors seems more likely. They suggest an interpretation in which **a not fully formed matter** comes first in time, and is then moved toward becoming **more fully formed**. Matter, of course, did **not** lack **all** form, since there already existed the three, namely heaven and water and earth ("water and earth" being taken to signify the four elements). But these three did lack certain appropriate distinctions as well as a certain complement of beauty. Heaven lacked both the beauty of light, and the distinction of day from night. Water (understood to include air as well, as Aquinas suggests; but fire, too, one ought to add)[47] lacked both the beauty of an appropriate orderliness, and the distinction of the upper waters from the lower ones. Lastly, earth too lacked the beauty of an appropriate orderliness,

---

[46] "Other threatening things of that sort" might include **thunder and lightning** as well, lightning being taken by Aquinas to be some form of fire.

[47] Since "water and earth" signify the four elements, and since fire ought to be mentioned and included somewhere, it seems clear that it ought to be included under "water" rather than under "earth," because of fire's natural **upward** motion. That is, since water is understood to include **air**, which has a higher natural place than water, water ought also to be understood to include **fire**, which has a higher place still. It would not make sense to include fire under "earth," since earth has the **lowest** place.   Aquinas puts it like this: . . . ignis et aer, quia non distinguuntur a vulgo, inter partes mundi non sunt expresse nominata a Moyse, sed computantur cum medio, scilicet aqua, maxime quantum ad inferiorem aeris partem.   Quantum vero ad superiorem, computantur cum caelo, ut Augustinus dicit. (*S.T.*, I, q. 74, a. 1, ad 2). -- To put any of the parts of air and fire together with heaven would seem to be unacceptable, if one takes heaven to be a **fifth** body; unless one is considering only **location.**

and the distinction of dry land from the sea. And so, with respect to the third day, Aquinas writes:

> Tertio . . . die formatum est ultimum corpus, scilicet terra, per hoc quod discooperta est aquis; et facta est distinctio in infimo, quae dicitur terrae et maris. Unde satis congrue, sicut informitatem terrae expresserat dicens quod terra erat *invisibilis* vel *inanis*, ita eius formationem exprimit per hoc quod dicit, *Et appareat arida.* [48] (*S.T.,* I, q. 69, a. 1, c., in fine).

> On the third . . . day, the last body, namely earth, was given some form, by the removal of its covering of water. And a distinction was made in that lowest of bodies, i.e., the distinction of dry land and sea. Whence just as the Scriptures had expressed sufficiently suitably the *incomplete formedness* of the earth by saying that the earth was *invisible* and *empty,* so too the Scriptures express sufficiently suitably the earth's *being given further form* by saying, *And let the dry land appear.*

One can suggest at this point that heaven -- by means of the power of the light (and perhaps of the accompanying heat, as well) which was given to it on the first day of the **opus distinctionis** -- brought about in some way, i.e., slowly, developmentally, progressively moving from incomplete formedness toward fuller and fuller completion, the distinction of the second day (that of the waters above the firmament from those below it) and the distinction of the third day (that of the dry land from the sea). To make this suggestion acceptable, one would have to say that the light given to heaven on the first day was not only the light of the sun, but somehow and in some not yet fully

---

[48]   It can be said, perhaps, that it was natural, in the beginning, for water to **cover** the earth **completely,** just as it was for air to **surround** both water and earth **completely.**   But then, in order to have plants and animals on the earth, it became necessary for some of this covering of water to be removed; and this took place, according to some philosophers, by the heating action of the sun evaporating the waters, thereby drying some of the land: . . . potest dici quod naturale esset quod aqua undique esset circa terram, sicut aer undique est circa aquam et terram; sed propter necessitatem finis, ut scilicet animalia et plantae essent super terram, oportuit quod aliqua pars terrae esset discooperta aquis.   Quod quidem aliqui philosophi attribuunt actioni solis, per elevationem vaporum desiccantis terram. (*S.T.,* I, q. 69, a. 1, ad 4).

formed way, the light of other light-emitting bodies, like the planets and the stars, as well -- as already noted above, on p. 208 in footnote 38.[49]

On the fourth day, which is the first day of the **opus ornatus,** points out Aquinas (above, p. 207), "the light-giving bodies which are in motion in heaven for its adornment, were produced." If the heavenly bodies are taken to be of the same nature as terrestrial bodies, as some took them to be; then they were produced by God out of the already existing four elements.   If, however, they are taken to be of a nature different from that of terrestrial bodies, and so by nature incorruptible, as others took them to be; then they must have been produced by God on the first day as to their substance, **but not yet fully formed,** along with the sun; so that on the fourth day all of them were **given further form** by being given a more fully formed, a more determinate, light-emitting power for producing **particular** effects, the sun for these effects, the moon for those effects, and other heavenly bodies for still other effects.   Aquinas writes:

> . . . secundum . . eos qui ponunt caelestia corpora ex natura quatuor elementorum, nulla difficultas accidit, quia potest dici quod sunt formata ex praeiacenti materia . . .   Sed secundum eos qui ponunt corpora caelestia esse alterius naturae ab elementis, et incorruptibilia per naturam, oportet dicere quod substantia luminarium a principio fuit creata; sed prius erat informis, et nunc formatur, non quidem forma substantiali, sed per collationem determinatae virtutis.   -- Ideo tamen non fit mentio a principio de eis, sed solum quarta die, ut Chrysostomus dicit, ut per hoc removeat populum ab idololatria, ostendens luminaria non esse deos, ex quo nec a principio fuerunt.   (*S.T.,* I, q. 71, a. 1, ad 1).

---

[49] This suggestion implies that the light of the sun **alone** would not suffice to bring about the distinctions of the second and third days, and that these distinctions may have taken a very long period of time, so that "day" in "first day" and in "second day" and in "third day" might mean a period of time considerably longer than an ordinary day of twenty four hours.

... according to those ... who hold the heavenly bodies to be of the nature of the four elements, there is no difficulty, because it can be said that they were formed out of already existing matter ... But, according to those who hold the heavenly bodies to be different in kind from the elements, and incorruptible by nature, it must be said that the substance of the light-emitting bodies was created at the beginning, but that at first it was not fully formed, and now was being given further form, not indeed by means of a substantial form, but by the conferring of a determinate power. -- And the reason why there was no mention of them at the beginning, but only on the fourth day, as Chrysostom says, was to remove the people from idolatry, by showing that the light-emitting bodies were not gods, not being in existence from the beginning.

On the fifth day, the second of the **opus ornatus,** writes Aquinas (above, p. 207), "birds and fishes were produced to adorn the middle element, because they move about in air and water, which are here taken as one thing." In responding to an objection to the fittingness of the way in which the **opus ornatus** of the second day is described, Aquinas makes some interesting and instructive comments about the elements. The objection is as follows:

> . . . videtur quod inconvenienter hoc opus [sc. opus ornatus quintae diei] describatur. Illud enim aquae producunt, ad cuius productionem sufficit virtus aquae. Sed virtus aquae non sufficit ad productionem omnium piscium et avium, cum videamus plura eorum generari ex semine. Non ergo convenienter dicitur: *Producant aquae reptile animae viventis, et volatile super terram.* (S.T., I, q. 71, a. un., obj. 1).

> . . . it seems that this work [i.e., the work of adornment of the fifth day] was not fittingly described. For the waters produce that for the production of which the power of the waters suffices. But the power of the waters does not suffice for the production of all fishes and birds, since we see that many of them are generated from seed. Therefore, it is not fittingly said: *Let the waters produce the creeping things having a living soul, and the things with wings to fly over the earth.*

214

Aquinas' response to this objection:

... Avicenna posuit *omnia* animalia [and, therefore, not only fishes and birds] posse generari ex aliquali elementorum commixtione *absque semine,* etiam per viam naturae.

Sed hoc videdur inconveniens, quia natura determinatis mediis procedit ad suos effectus. Unde illa quae *naturaliter* generantur *ex semine* non possunt sine semine generari.

Et ideo dicendum est aliter, quod *in naturali generatione* animalium [including, therefore, fishes and birds], principium *activum* est virtus formativa quae est in semine, in iis quae ex semine generantur; loco cuius virtutis, in iis quae ex putrefactione generantur, est virtus caelestis corporis. *Materiale* autem principium in utrorumque animalium generatione, est aliquod elementum vel elementatum.

In prima autem rerum institutione [by way of contrast to *in naturali generatione,* as in the previous paragraph], fuit principium *activum* Verbum Dei, quod ex materia elementari produxit animalia *vel in actu,* secundum alios Sanctos, *vel virtute,* secundum Augustinum. Non quod aqua aut terra habeat in se virtutem producendi omnia animalia, ut Avicenna posuit, sed quia hoc ipsum quod ex materia elementari, virtute seminis vel stellarum, possunt animalia produci, est ex virtute primitus elementis data. (*S.T.,* I, q. 71, a. un., ad 1).

... Avicenna held that *all* animals [and therefore not only fishes and birds] can be generated from some sort of mixing or other of the elements, and *without seed,* even by nature's own ways.

But this seems to be unacceptable, because nature proceeds to its effects by certain determined means. Whence those things which are naturally generated from seed cannot be generated without seed.

And so, something different must be said, that *in the natural generation* of animals [including therefore fishes and birds], the

215

active principle is the formative power which is in the seed, in the case of those which are generated from seed; whereas in the case of those which are generated from putrefaction, in the place of the power in the seed is the power of a heavenly body. The *material* principle, however, in the generation of either of these kinds of animals is some element, or something made out of the elements [i.e., some mixed body].

But *in the first production of things* [by way of contrast to *in their natural generation*], the *active* principle was the Word of God, which produced animals out of elemental matter either actually, as some Holy authors would have it, or in the power [of other things], as Augustine would have it. Not that water or earth has in itself the [active] power to produce all animals, as Avicenna held; but because this, namely that animals can be produced out of elemental matter, by the [active] power of seed or by that of the stars, derives from the power [both active and material] given to the elements in the very beginning.

What is interesting and instructive about Aquinas' response is the following. The elements play a **dual** role in the natural generation of corporeal things (in naturali generatione; per viam naturae) as well as in their first production by God (in prima rerum institutione). The role of the elements is in part that of a **material** cause and in part that of an **agent** cause.[50] But their agent causality is **of itself** of insufficient power to account for the transformations of the elements into one another, and for their entering as ingredients into the composition of mixed bodies. The insufficiency of their agent causality needs to be aided by, completed by, the active formative power of seed (in the case of those living things, whether plants and animals, which are generated from seed), **in conjunction with** the active power of the light (and heat) of the appropriate heavenly body(-ies); and **at least by**[51] the active power of the light (and heat) of the appropriate heavenly body(-ies), in the

---

[50] See above section 3, pp. 136-142, on the sort of agent cause an element is, in addition to being a special sort of material cause.

[51] See, however, footnote 43, above p. 205, on the need for an **agens univocum** for **any kind** of generation, in addition to an **agens universale**.

case of the generation of all other physical things, i.e., of the elements from one another, and of mixed bodies of all other sorts (i.e., other than living things generated from seed) from the elements, and from lower forms of mixed bodies, as well.

What is **most particularly** interesting and instructive about the response of Aquinas lies in its very last few lines, beginning with: In prima autem rerum institutione . . . For these last few lines speak of the role of the power (both active and material) which was given to the elements by God **in the very beginning (primitus)** . . . hoc ipsum quod ex materia elementari . . . possunt animalia [et plantae, et omnia alia terrestrialia] produci est ex virtute **primitus** elementis data . . . In the first production of things (. . . in prima . . . rerum institutione . . .), the **active** principle was the Word of God, which produced animals, including the fishes and the birds of the fifth day, either **actually,** as some thinkers suggested, or **in the power of other things antecedently brought into being,** as other thinkers suggested. But this does **not** mean that the elements as antecedently produced had **in themselves** all of the active power required to produce the fishes and the birds of the fifth day (and the land animals of the sixth day). It means rather that they, i.e., the things of the fifth and sixth days, were capable of being actively produced **out of the elements** by the formative power of seed and/or by that of the stars, **only because of the powers, both active and material, which were given to the elements themselves at the very beginning** -- . . . hoc ipsum quod ex materia elementari, virtute seminis vel stellarum, possunt animalia produci, est **ex virtute [activa et materiali] primitus elementis data** . . . The elements, from the very beginning, were given a nature, both active and material, such that all terrestrial physical things could be derived from them **as from their primary material constituents.**

On the sixth day, the third of the **opus ornatus,** notes Aquinas (above, pp. 193-194) "we see produced, for the adornment of the earth, the animals which move about upon it." Although some were of the opinion, notes

Aquinas, that land animals were produced **in actu,** i.e., **as actually existing;** others, like Augustine, suggested that they were not produced as actually existing, but rather **potentialilter,** i.e., **as in the power of other things,** antecedently brought into being, to produce them at some later time.

> **Et hic etiam [sc. in opere ornatus sextae diei], secundum Augustinum, animalia terrestria producuntur** *potentialiter;* **secundum vero alios Sanctos,** *in actu.* **(S.T., I, q. 72, a. un., c.).**
>
> **And here too [i.e., in the work of adornment of the sixth day], according to Augustine, the land animals were produced as in the power of other things, whereas according to other Holy authors, they were produced as actually existing.**

Aquinas seems to prefer the suggestion of Augustine, a suggestion, let us be reminded, which was made as regards the work of the fifth day as well, and which comes to this. The four elements, from the very beginning, were given a nature, both active and material, such that all terrestrial things, including the land animals of the sixth day, **could be derived from** the elements as from their primary material constituents -- given, of course, in order to bring about **the actual derivation**, the accompanying **active** formative powers of the elements themselves (admittedly insufficient), as completed by the diverse **active** formative powers of various sorts of heavenly bodies. These combined active formative powers were capable of explaining, as agent causes, the generation and corruption of terrestrial bodies -- not only the transforming of the elements into one another, but the entering of the elements into the composition of mixed bodies, as well. Unlike heaven, or the firmament, which (on the false assumption that it is of a **fifth** essence, and not of the essence of the four elements) does not have within it the power to produce the light-emitting bodies which adorn it;[52] the

---

[52] . . . non enim habet firmamentum [sc. caelum] virtutem productivam luminarium, sicut habet terra [et aqua, et aer, et ignis, i.e., quatuor elementa] productivam plantarum [et avium et piscium et animalium terrestrium] . . .   (S.T., I, q. 70, a. 1, c., in fine). And

four elements do have the power, both active and material, to produce the fishes and the birds and the land animals which adorn the planet Earth, i.e., which adorn the water (the fishes) and the air (the birds) and the dry land (the animals) -- in conjunction, of course, with the **universal** agent causality of the appropriate heavenly bodies, and the **particular** agent causality of the appropriate univocal causes.[53]

10. The seventh day and beyond, like the first day and beyond: unfolding, developing, evolving out of the matter, and by the agent causality, of the elements

Having reflected on what God had made on **each** of the six days, Aquinas devotes a question (q. 73) to considerations pertaining **specifically** to the seventh day, and another one (q. 74) to questions pertaining to all seven days **in common**.

From q. 73, the following:

> . . . nihil postmodum a Deo factum [sc. post septimum diem] est totaliter novum, quin aliqualiter in operibus sex dierum praecesserit. Quaedam enim praeextiterunt *materialiter*, sicut quod Deus de costa Adae formavit mulierem. Quaedam vero praeextiterunt in operibus sex dierum, non solum materialiter, sed etiam causaliter; sicut individua quae nunc generantur, praecesserunt in primis individuis suarum specierum. Species

---

that is why Augustine holds, notes Aquinas, that the light-emitting bodies were made by God **as actually existing**: . . . dicit enim [Augustinus] luminaria esse facta **in actu**, non in virtute tantum . . . *(Ibid.)*. One wants to observe, here, that if one takes heaven (or, the firmament) to be of the essence of the four elements, it can very likely be seen as having within itself (given to it in the beginning by God, of course) the power to produce the light-emitting bodies which adorn it.

[53] See above, p. 205, footnote 35. Any generation, it seems, whether of living things or of non-living things, requires an **agens univocum**, an **agens particulare**, i.e., an agent of the same species as the effect, in addition to an **agens universale**. Otherwise, there would be no adequate explanation for the fact that the effect is of the **particular sort or species** that it is.

etiam novae, si quae apparent, praeextiterunt in quibusdam
activis principiis, sicut et animalia ex putrefactione generata
producuntur ex virtutibus stellarum et elementorum quas a
principio acceperunt... (*S.T.,* I, q. 73, a. 1, ad 3).

. . . nothing which was made by God afterwards [i.e., after the
seventh day] is totally new; indeed all such things had preceded
in some way in the works of the six days. Some of them had
pre-existed materially, as the woman had in the rib of Adam out
of which God formed her. Others pre-existed in the works of
the six days *not only* materially, *but also causally,* as the
individuals which are now being generated; they were there
causally in the first individuals of their species. And new species
too, if any appeared, pre-existed in certain active principles, just
as the animals generated from putrefaction are produced from
the powers of the stars and of the elements, *which (powers) they
had received in the beginning* . . .

In q. 73, Aquinas asks: **Utrum** *completio* **divinorum operum debeat
septimo diei adscribi.** The Scriptures say **explicity** of the seventh day: *On the
seventh day God completed His work which He had made* (*Genesis,* 2, 2).
Here, as throughout his reflections on the initial production of things by God,
Aquinas proceeds with Augustine's teaching on scriptural interpretation in
mind, namely **this** teaching, which emphasizes **two** points:

. . . sicut Augustinus docet, in huiusmodi quaestionibus *duo*
sunt observanda. Primo quidem, ut veritas Scripturae
inconcusse teneatur. Secundo, cum Scriptura divina
multipliciter exponi possit, quod nulli expositioni aliquis ita
praecise inhaereat quod, si certa ratione constiterit hoc esse
falsum, quod aliquis sensum Scripturae esse asserere praesumat,
ne Scriptura ex hoc ab infidelibus derideatur, et ne eis via
credendi praecludatur... (*S.T.,* I, q. 68, a. 1, c.).

. . . as Augustine teaches, *two* things are to be observed in
questions of this kind. The first is this: to hold to the truth of
Scripture unwaveringly. The second is this, since divine
Scripture can be interpreted in many ways: not to adhere so

220

tenaciously to a given exposition of it as to presume to assert it as *the meaning* of Scripture, if it has been shown with certitude to be false; lest Scripture be ridiculed by those who do not believe, and obstacles be placed in the way of their becoming believers.

The truth to be held, here, without wavering is this, that God **did complete** his work of creative production on the seventh day, for this is **explicitly** stated in the Scriptures: *Complevit* **Deus die septimo opus suum quod fecerat** (*Genesis*, 2, 2). The question now becomes: How is this to be understood? Following Augustine's suggestion, one must not insist on taking this to mean something which is known for good reason(s), which has been shown with certitude, to be false : . . . si certa ratione constiterit esse falsum. This will open God's word to the possibility of ridicule by unbelievers, and become thereby an obstacle to their becoming believers. How then is this **completion** to be understood? In the body of this article, Aquinas points out that a thing can be said to be completed, or perfected, with respect to **what it is,** i.e., with respect to all that is required for its integrity, or wholeness, as the **substance** or **thing** that it is. This sort of completion, or perfection, is the "forma totius, quae ex integritate partium consurgit." But, a thing can also be said to be completed, or perfected, with respect to its **end.** This sort of completion, or perfection, might be   1) an end which is an **operation,** or **activity,** as the end of the citharist is **to play** the four-stringed musical instrument which is the cithara; or it might be an end which is   2) a **thing** which is attained by an operation or activity, as the end of the builder is **the house** which he makes by the activity of building. The first kind of completion brings about, i.e., causes, the second kind; for the form of a substance is the principle of its operation.

Now, the **ultimate (i.e., second)** completion, or perfection, or end of the whole universe is the perfect happiness of the Saints -- which **will come to be** in the final consummation of time. But, the **first** completion or perfection of the universe, which consists in its wholeness or integrity as the thing that it is, i.e., which consists in its "forma totius, quae ex integritate partium consurgit," **was already there** in the first production, at the first founding, of

221

things, i.e., "in prima rerum institutione," which took place over the six days. It is this completion which is attributed to the seventh day, and which is in its own way a cause contributing to the second completion. This is how Aquinas puts it:

> . . . ultima [sc. secunda] . . . perfectio, quae est finis totius universi, est perfecta beatitudo Sanctorum, quae erit in ultima consummatione saeculi. Prima autem perfectio, quae est in integritate universi, fuit in prima rerum institutione. Et haec deputatur septimo diei . . . (S.T., I, q. 73, a. 1, c.).

> . . . the ultimate [i.e., second] . . . perfection, which is the end of the whole universe, is the perfect happiness of the Saints, which will come to be in the final consummation of time. The first perfection, however, which lies in the integrity of the universe, was there in the first production of things. And it is this first completion which is attributed to the seventh day . . .

In his response to the third objection (quoted above, p. 218), Aquinas points out that nothing made by God after the seventh day is totally new. Some of these things pre-existed **materially** in the works of the six days; for example, observes Aquinas, the woman whom God formed out of the rib of Adam (*Genesis*, 2, 21-23), whom He had made earlier out of the slime of the earth (*Genesis*, 2, 7). Aquinas could have added that **all things** which came to be (and continue to come to be) after the seventh day, pre-existed **materially** in the four elements, and in certain appropriate mixed bodies produced out of the elements during the work of the six days. Certain other things, continues Aquinas, pre-existed in the works of the six days not only materially, but **causally** as well, i.e., as in the power of their agent causes. For example, all the individuals which are being generated now, were there in the first individuals of their species -- there, not only as in their matter, but also as in their agent causes. And if any **new** (interesting and surprising) species came into existence since the seventh day, continues Aquinas, these too were there in the works of the six days, in certain active (agent) causes, as well as in the matter of the four elements, and of certain appropriate mixed bodies. Similarly, adds Aquinas, all **animals** generated from putrefaction (like maggots, the legless larvae of the housefly), and even **new** (interesting and surprising) species of animals so generated, if any came to be, came to be from the powers of the stars (active powers) and of the four elements (active and material powers), which (powers) they (the stars and the elements) had received from God in the very beginning -- in prima rerum institutione. Indeed, one can add, the same can be said about **all** new species, **whether of animals or of plants.** Moreover, **every** new living thing, in any sense of "new," whether it be simply a new **individual** (of a species already in existence as a result of the work of the six days) or even a new **species** -- every new living thing came to be from the powers (active) of the heavenly bodies and of the four elements (active and material). And not only **living** things, one can add further, but **non-living** things as well. That is, even all new **elements** (beyond the original four, if one were to take the ancient and medieval four as truth, and if more than these four were possible; or beyond the original quarks and leptons, to take the **firmer** truth of what we know today), and all new **mixed bodies** as well, came to be out of the original elements, inasmuch as they (i.e., the original elements) had received from God -- in prima rerum institutione -- a nature such that they were to provide the **materials**, as well as the **agent powers** (can we today say: the **agent powers** of the strong nuclear force, the weak nuclear force, the electromagnetic force, and the force of gravity?), required for the orderly, developmental, unfolding, evolving production of all other physical things, out to the furthest reaches of space. In today's firmer view, the four forces could perhaps replace (as the required agent causes) the active power of the light and heat of the heavenly bodies of the older, and considerably less firm, view; indeed, a view which has been shown with good reasons, and with a high degree of certitude, to be just false.

Also from q. 73:

> ... in primis sex diebus productae sunt res in suis primis causis. Sed postea ex illis primis causis res multiplicantur et conservantur... (*S.T.,* I, q. 73, a. 3, ad 2).

> ... in the first six days, things were produced in their first causes. But after that, things were multiplied by these first causes, and conserved in being by them ...

In Aquinas' response to the second objection in a. 3 (just above), one finds an excellent summary of the longer statement in his response to the third objection in a. 1 (above, p. 220). The first causes, in whose powers things were produced in the course of the first six days, are the four elements (material and agent causes) and the heavenly bodies (the aiding and completing agent causes) of the ancient and medieval view. In today's firmer view, the first causes are the original quarks and leptons (material and agent causes) and their four forces (the aiding and completing agent causes).

From q. 74 the following:

> ... potest dici quod opus distinctionis et ornatus attenditur secundum aliquam mutationem creaturae, quae tempore mensuratur. Opus autem creationis consistit in sola divina actione in instanti rerum substantiam producentis. Et ideo quodlibet opus distinctionis et ornatus dicitur factum *in die,* creatio autem dicitur facta *in principio,* quod sonat aliquid indivisibile... (*S.T.,* I, q. 74, a. 1, ad 1).

> ... it can be said that the work of distinction and of adornment proceeds according to certain changes in creatures, and these changes are *measured by time.* But the work of creation consists in a divine action, and in that alone, and this action produces the substance of things *in an instant.* This is why each work of distinction and of adornment is said to have been done *in a day,* whereas creation is said to have been done *in the beginning,* which indicates something indivisible ...

From this response to the first objection (just above), it is clear that the four elements and the heavenly bodies were created on the first day out of absolute nothingness, and **in an instant** -- as to their substance, of course, and in many ways not yet fully formed. And that all else which was produced by God, in the course of the first six days, was produced by Him through distinction and adornment, in such a way that its production was through certain sorts of change out of prior materials, and so was produced **over a period of time.**

> . . . Deus creavit omnia simul, quantum ad rerum substantiam quodammodo informem. Sed quantum ad formationem quae facta est per distinctionem et ornatum, non simul . . . (*S.T.*, I, q. 74, a. 2, ad 2).

> . . . God created all things all together [i.e., at the same time], as regards their substance, but their substance in a way not yet fully formed. As regards their being more fully formed, however, which came about by distinction and adornment, this did not take place all together [i.e., not at the same time] . . .

Here, in his response to the second objection (just above), Aquinas explicitly states that the substance of **all** things (and not only of the heavenly bodies and the four elements) was created all together, though in some way -- quodammodo -- not yet fully formed. The substances of the heavenly bodies and of the four elements, of course, were there and **in actual existence,** but not yet with all their powers; whereas the substances of all other things were there only **potentialiter,** i.e., only in the power of the heavenly bodies and of the elements to produce them over time.

> . . . in die septimo cessavit Deus a novis operibus condendis, non autem a propagandis quibusdam ex aliis, ad quam propagationem pertinet quod post primum diem alii succedunt . . . (*S.T.*, I, q. 74, a. 2, ad 3).

> ... on the seventh day, God ceased from doing new works, but not from propagating certain things from other things [already made], to which propagation it belongs that after the first day there followed other days ...

This propagation from certain other things, things which had already been made, began with the **opus distinctionis** (days one through three), moved through the **opus ornatus** (days four through six), and continues into the present day.

> ... habet ... aqua praecipue vitalem virtutem, quia plurima animalia generantur in aqua, et omnium animalium semina sunt humida ... (*S.T.*, I, q. 74, a. 3, ad 4).

> ... water has a special life-giving power, because many animals are generated in water, and the seed of all animals is moist ...

Aquinas' response to the fourth objection (just above) raises the question: Do the other elements have special life-giving powers? Isn't it clear that living things need to be of a certain temperature (from the inclusion of fire?), but not too hot, nor too cold (from the inclusion of an appropriate measure of air and water and earth?)? Isn't it also clear that living things must be of a certain weight (from the inclusion of an appropriate measure of earth) in order to be kept close to the surface of our planet, and thus in an envirionment in which they can be provided with all that they need for nourishment, growth, and reproduction? And isn't it also clear that the food which they need must be heavy enough (earth) and wet enough (water) and porous enough (air) and warm enough (fire) to make possible the performance of the operations of life?

... [sunt aliqui qui posuerunt quod] in prima rerum productione materia erat sub formis substantialibus [quatuor] elementorum, ... [et] non fuerunt animalia et plantae in actu ... [et quod] post primam productionem creaturae, fuit aliquod tempus in quo non erat lux, item in quo non erat firmamentum formatum, item in quo non erat terra discooperta aquis, et in quo non erant formata caeli luminaria ... (*S.T.*, I, q. 74, a. 2, c.).

... [there are some who held that] in the first production of things matter existed under the substantial forms of the [four] elements, ... [and] that animals and plants did not actually exist ...; [and] that after the first production of created things, there was a period of time in which there was no light, in which the firmament had not been fully formed, in which the earth had not had its covering of water removed, and in which the light-emitting bodies of heaven had not been fully formed [either]...

Just after the instant of creation, the four elements were there, and the heavens with their light-emitting bodies were there, but far from fully formed, far from in possession of all their distinctive powers for producing particular effects. They were in process of being banged out of their previous non-dimensional existence in God. And then, in the very next instant, they were caught up in the process of expanding out of the initially unimaginably miniscule quasi-point of the first instant after creation, toward an unimaginably vast three-dimensional existence, and toward being more and more fully formed through the three days of distinction and the three of adornment, and beyond that into the present time. The heavenly bodies were caught up in the process of acquiring particular light-emitting powers, of moving away from one another, and of acquiring certain locations in relation to one another. The planet Earth was caught up in the process of developing its oceans, and its continents, and the primitive life forms out of which all the life forms which are now in existence emerged and evolved.

11. The elements and the eduction of substantial forms from the potency of matter

It is the view of Aquinas that substantial forms come to be neither by being generated, nor by being created; they come to be by being educed. This is so, he points out, because they neither exist as subsistent things, nor do they have matter as part of their natures. They come to be when the subsistent matter-form composites of which they are a component come to be, and they come to be as **that by which** these composites exist. They pre-existed in the matter of the thing(s) out of which the subsistent matter-form composite of which they are now a component is generated. Not actually yet hiddenly, notes Aquinas, as some maintained. Nor potentially in the sense that matter survives in them as part of what they are; but potentially in another sense, in the sense that matter, being disposed in a certain way by the substantial form which is now in it, can receive a **certain sort** of new substantial form, and **only** that sort, given of course the required attendant agent cause(s). Thus, to come to be at the generation of a matter-form composite, by the agent causality of another matter-form composite(s), **not** as a subsistent thing, **nor** as having matter as part of its nature, but as **that by which** the composite comes to be and continues to be, is to be educed from the potency of matter. The role of the elements in eduction is this. By its nature, matter first acquires the substantial forms of the elements, and is so disposed by these forms and the activities of their qualities, i.e., hot, dry, wet, and cold, that, given the sort of agent causes which exist in the natural world, and which act **from without,** in conjunction with the accompanying agent causality of the elements themselves, which act **from within,** matter can receive **only** such-and-such substantial forms, and **only** in such-and-such an order, from lower to higher.

To make the immediately preceding clear, it will be helpful to begin with the question: What exactly is a substantial form? For there are some, perhaps many, who would welcome a clear answer to this question. A substantial form is a differentiating factor of a certain sort. It is required to understand changes which can be called **radical** changes, i.e., changes in which something **goes out of existence** with the result that something else **comes into existence.** That is, a thing of one sort (or kind) goes out of existence, and its going out of existence is identically the coming into existence of a thing of another sort (or kind). For example, sperm and ovum go out of existence with the result that a human being comes into existence. That in the resulting human being by which the human being **differs from** the sperm and ovum is the human substantial form. According to Aquinas, the human substantial form is the human soul. A substantial form not only differentiates the result (the end term, or e.t.) of a radical change from that from which it came to be (the beginning term, or b.t.), but by its appearance accounts for the **beginning of the existence** of the thing which is the e.t.; and by its presence, for the **continued existence** of that thing. The substantial form of the e.t. is not the e.t. itself, but only one component of the e.t., the differentiating component. There is another component in the e.t., the surviving component, i.e., something which survives in the e.t. from the b.t. This surviving component is matter -- prime matter at least, when the e.t. is an element; prime matter plus the powers of certain required elements, when the e.t. is a mixed body.

The **substantial form** of a thing differs from the **essence** of a thing, though both are **differentiating** factors. Whereas the substantial form differentiates the e.t. of a radical change **from the b.t.**, the essence differentiates that e.t. **from nothingness.** Whereas the e.t. of a radical change differs from the b.t. by reason of the substantial form alone, since the matter of the b.t. has survived in the e.t.; the e.t. differs from nothingness by reason of its essence, i.e., by reason of the substantial form in conjunction with the matter which has survived in it from the b.t. The essence of a thing is **all** that within it by which it exists. The substantial form of a thing is but one component of that by which the thing exists, i.e., just one component of the thing's essence.

229

The substantial form of a thing is **not** something sense-perceivable. But it **is** real. It is as real as radical change. Clearly, what is real does not have to be sense-perceivable. Minds are real, but not sense-perceivable. Ideas are real, but not sense-perceivable. To be sure, a substantial form is neither a mind, nor an idea. We do, of course, form an idea of what a substantial form is, and we do this with our minds. But the substantial form is neither our idea of what it is, nor is it the mind with which we form that idea. The substantial form is **real,** and is found in the **real** e.t. of a **real** radical change as that by which the **real** e.t. differs from the previously **real** b.t. The substantial form is something perceivable by the mind, something intelligible -- like an idea or a mind, without itself being either an idea or a mind. The substantial form is an intelligible component of a sense-perceivable thing, the matter-form composite.

Though the substantial form itself is not sense-perceivable, because it is of itself without dimensions; it gives rise nonetheless to many features or characteristics or properties which **are** sense-perceivable. The most basic feature to which the substantial form gives rise is three dimensional quantity, which, though like substantial form also not sense-perceivable, is that in which sense-perceivable features (some of which are productively emitted by the substantial form) reside. The substantial form itself, as noted above (p. 166), is of itself both **like** and **unlike** a mathematical point; like, inasmuch as it is of itself without dimensions; unlike, inasmuch as it is **capable of physical causality** of various sorts, including an agent causality with respect to quantity, by which (agent causality) it causes the "**small**" **Big Bang** that gives size (dimensions) to the elements, and to all mixed bodies as well. Once dimensioned, the physical thing can take on sense-perceivable qualities of various sorts, like hot, cold; wet, dry; soft, hard; rough, smooth; heavy, light; short, long; some of which are caused **from within** by the substantial form itself, others **from without** by physical causes of various sorts in the surrounding environment.

The substantial form of a thing differs not only from the **essence** of that thing, but from the thing's **accidental forms** as well. A thing can have but one substantial form, but simultaneously many accidental forms. Moreover, whereas a substantial form is not itself a complete essence, since it is not a subsisting thing; it is nonetheless part of a complete essence, i.e., of the essence of the subsisting matter-form composite; the other part being either prime matter alone, in the case of something which is an element (the substantial form of an element needs prime matter as its appropriate subject); or prime matter plus certain elements (as virtual, dispositional, retrievable ingredients, which function as conjoined instrumental agent causes), in the case of something which is a mixed body (the substantial form of a mixed body needs both prime matter and a certain mix of elements as its appropriate subject). An accidental form, on the other hand, is neither a complete essence, since it itself is not a subsisting thing, but needs a subsisting thing as the subject in which it exists; nor is it part of a complete essence, for though it is **in** the subsisting thing, it is nonetheless not **of** the essence of, **not an ingredient of**, the essence of the subsisting thing, The three dimensions of a subsisting matter-form composite are among its accidental forms, as are features like its color, its weight, its being hot or cold, wet or dry, rough or smooth, soft or hard, and the like; each of which is properly said to be **of a being (entis),** rather than simply a **being (ens)**; i.e., not itself a subsisting thing, though real; but **of** a subsisting thing.

Having considered the question: What exactly is a substantial form?, it will be helpful to consider next why Aquinas maintains that substantial forms come to be **by being educed;** and neither by being created, nor by being generated, nor by being brought somehow out of a hidden actuality.

... sicut probat Aristoteles in *VII Metaph.*,[54] id quod proprie fit, est compositum. Formae autem corruptibilium rerum habent ut aliquando sint, aliquando non sint, absque hoc quod ipsae generentur aut corrumpantur, sed compositis generatis aut corruptis, quia etiam formae non habent esse, sed composita habent esse per eas. Sic enim alicui competit fieri, sicut et esse. (*S.T.*, I, q. 65, a. 4, c.).

... as Aristotle proves in Bk. VII of the *Metaphysics,* that which properly comes to be is the composite. The forms of corruptible things exist at times, and at times do not exist, without themselves being generated or corrupted, but rather at the generation and corruption of composites. For it is not these forms themselves which have existence; it is rather the composites which have existence through these forms. And coming into existence belongs to a thing in the same way in which existence belongs to it.

Aquinas notes just above, agreeing with Aristotle, that in the physical world, it is the composite of matter and form which subsists, and not its form. And so, it is the composite which is generated, and not its form. Its form comes to be when the composite comes to be, but only the composite subsists. The form is rather **that by which** the composite subsists. As Aquinas puts it just above, ". . . it is not these forms themselves which have existence; it is rather the composites which have existence through these forms."

... omnes qui non consideraverunt hoc quod philosophus supra ostendit, quod formae non fiunt, passi sunt difficultates circa factionem formarum. Propter hoc namque quidam coacti sunt dicere omnes formas esse ex creatione. Nam ponebant formas fieri, et non poterant ponere quod fierent ex materia, cum materia non sit pars formae. Unde sequebatur quod fierent ex nihilo, et per consequens quod crearentur. E contrario autem quidam posuerunt, propter hanc difficultatem, formas

---

54 Aristotle, *Metaphysics*, Bk. VII, ch. 8, 1033 a 24 - b 8; ch. 9, 1034 b 7-16. In Aquinas, see *In VII Metaph.*, lect. 4, nn. 1417-1423; lect. 8, n. 1458.

praeexistere in materia actu, quod est ponere latitationem formarum, sicut posuit Anaxagoras.

Sententia autem Aristotelis, qui ponit formas non fieri, sed compositum, utrumque excludit. Neque enim oportet dicere quod formae sint causatae ab aliquo extrinseco agente, neque quod fuerint semper actu in materia, sed in potentia tantum. Et quod in generatione compositi sint eductae de potentia in actum. (*In VII Metaph.*, lect. 7, n. 1430).

. . . all who did not take into account what the Philosopher showed above, that it is not forms which come to be [but rather composites], were beset with difficulties concerning the making of forms. For it was because of this that some were driven to say that all forms derive from creation. They held that forms come to be, but could not hold that they came to be out of matter, since matter is not a part of what a form is. Whence it followed that they came to be out of nothing, and consequently that they were created. There were others who, because of this difficulty, held on the contrary that forms pre-existed in matter in a state of actuality, which is to hold the hiddenness of forms, as Anaxagoras did.

Now the opinion of Aristotle, who holds that it is not forms which come to be, but rather the composite, excludes both creation and hiddenness. For it is not necessary to say that forms are caused by an extrinsic [creative] agent, nor that they have always existed in matter in a state of actuality, but rather only in a state of potentiality; and that they are educed from potency into actuality in the generation of the composite.

Just above, Aquinas is pointing out that it was puzzling to some to hold **both** that forms come to be, **and** that matter is not a part of their nature. For this seemed to mean that these forms did not come to be out of matter, and that hence they came to be out of nothing, and that therefore they must have been **created**. To others this seemed to mean, rather, that since these forms could not come to be out of a matter which would survive in them as a part of their nature, they must have **pre-existed** in their matter **in a state of hidden** actuality. So that they were generated, rather than created; but that generation was simply some sort of removal, or undoing, or unscrambling, of the hiddenness of their actuality. Now, if one attends to the fact, notes Aquinas, that it is not the form which comes to be, but rather that of which the form is a component (along with the appropriate matter), as Aristotle maintained, one can easily exclude both the need for creation and the need for hiddenness. For forms, as Arisotle sees it, pre-exist in matter, not in a state of actuality (though hidden), but rather in a state of potentiality, from which they **are** **educed** (not generated) when the composite is generated.

> . . . **formae . . . proprie non fiunt, sed educuntur de potentia** **materiae, in quantum materia quae est in potentia ad formam fit** **actu sub forma, quod est facere compositum. (***In VII Metaph.,*** **lect. 7, n. 23).**

> . . . **forms . . . do not properly come to be, but are educed from the** **potency of matter, inasmuch as matter which is potency to a** **form comes to be actually under that form; and this is to make** **the composite.**

Just above, Aquinas confirms the point made in the preceding passage, i.e., that it is not the form which properly comes to be, but the composite. And the coming to be of the composite is, one might add, **identically the** **eduction** of the form of the composite from the potency of the matter which survives in the composite as part of what the composite is.

> . . . **multis error accidit circa formas ex hoc quod de eis iudicant** **sicut de substantiis iudicatur. Quod quidem ex hoc contingere** **videtur quod formae per modum substantiarum signantur in** **abstracto, ut albedo, vel virtus, aut aliquid huiusmodi. Unde** **aliqui modum loquendi sequentes, sic de eis iudicant ac si essent** **substantiae. Et ex hinc processit error tam eorum qui posuerunt** **latitationem formarum, quam eorum qui posuerunt formas esse** **a creatione. Aestimaverunt enim quod formis competeret fieri**

234

sicut competit substantiis. Et ideo non invenientes ex quo formae generentur, posuerunt eas vel creari, vel praeexistere in materia, non attendentes quod sicut esse non est formae, sed subiecti per formam, ita nec fieri quod terminatur ad esse, est formae, sed subiecti. Sicut enim forma ens dicitur, non quia ipsa sit, si proprie loquamur, sed quia aliquid ea est; ita et forma fieri dicitur, non quia ipsa fiat, sed quia ea aliquid fit, dum scilicet subiectum reducitur de potentia in actum. (*Q.D., De Virt. in Comm.*, q. un., a. 11, c., in princ.).

. . . an error with respect to forms has befallen many, because they think about forms as they think about substances. And it appears that this happens because forms are designated in the abstract in the manner of substances, as whiteness, or virtue, or other things of this sort. Whence some, following a way of speaking, thought about forms as if they were substances. And from this comes the error both of those who held the hiddenness of forms, and of those who held that forms derive from creation. For they thought that coming to be belongs to forms as it belongs to substances. And so, not finding anything from which forms might be generated, they held either that forms are created, or that they pre-existed in matter, not paying attention that just as existence does not belong to form, but to the subject through the form, so too neither does coming to be which terminates in existence belong to form, but to the subject. For just as the form is said to be a being, not because it itself exists, if we speak properly, but because something [else] exists by reason of it; so too the form is said to come to be, not because it itself comes to be, but because something [else] comes to be by reason of it; and this, precisely when the subject is reduced from potency to actuality.

Just above, Aquinas gives an extraordinarily clear account of what happened to some when they allowed themselves to be mislead by a way of speaking. We speak of forms **in the abstract,** Aquinas notes, **as if** they were substances, e.g., whiteness, softness, hardness, virtue. And so, it seemed to them that coming to be belongs to forms as it belongs to substances. But, since matter is not a part of what a form is, there seemed to be nothing out of which forms could come to be. And so it seemed either that these forms were created (i.e., came to be out of nothing), or that they pre-existed in their matter in a state of (hidden) actuality. -- But again, forms do not come to be, in the proper sense of coming to be, since forms are not subsisting things. Rather, the subsisting composite comes to be; and the form is **that by which** the composite comes to be. Or, if the form can be said to come to be, this can be said only in an improper sense, meaning that it comes to be **not** as a subsisting thing, but **only** as **that by which** the subsisting thing subsists.

> . . . ex mixtione elementorum nedum intellectus, sed nec anima vegetabilis producitur. . . (*De Unitate Intellectus contra Averroistas*, c. 1, n. 47).
> . . . nulla anima [nec vegetabilium, nec animalium, nec hominum] ex commixtione elementorum causetur . . . (*Ibid.*).
>
> . . . it is not only the intellect which is not produced out of a mixing of elements, but neither is the vegetable soul . . .
> . . . no soul [neither of vegetables, nor of animals, nor of man] is caused out of a mixing of elements . . .

Just above, Aquinas observes that it is not only man's soul, the intellectual soul, which is not produced out of a mixing of elements, but neither is the vegetable soul, nor indeed any soul at all. What he means is that a mixing of elements -- with no living thing, no thing which has a soul, in attendance as an actively engaged **extrinsic** agent cause -- cannot produce a new living thing. A new living thing with a vegetable soul can indeed be produced out of a certain mixing of elements, but only if, along with the intrinsic **instrumental** agent causality of those elements and the extrinsic **universal** agent causality of some appropriate heavenly body(-ies), there is also the extrinsic **particular and univocal** agent causality of a living thing with that same sort of vegetable soul.[55] Similarly with respect to the production of a new living thing with an animal soul. But the human soul, the intellectual soul, can be produced **only** by God, by a direct act of creation.

---

55   See above pp. 206-207, with special attention to footnote 43.

To be sure, even the human soul needs a certain sort of matter in which to be created by God, i.e., a matter in which is found the appropriate mix of elements; and this mix is brought about, prior to God's creation of the human soul, by an appropriate conjunction of agent causes: not only certain required elements as intrinsic instrumental causes, but also certain heavenly bodies as extrinsic universal and analogical causes, and an already existing pair of human beings as extrinsic particular and univocal causes.

> . . . sicut totum esse earum [sc. formarum quae differunt ab anima intellectiva] est in concretione ad materiam, ita totaliter educi dicuntur de potentia materiae. Anima autem intellectiva, cum habeat operationem sine corpore, non est esse suum solum in concretione ad materiam; unde non potest dici quod educatur de materia, sed magis quod est a principio extrinseco. (*De Unitate Intellectus contra Averroistas*, c. 1, n. 46).

> . . . just as the whole being [of forms which are different from the intellectual soul] lies in their being bound to matter, so they are said to be *totally educed from* the potency of matter. But the intellectual soul, since it has an operation without the body, is not such that its existence consists only in being bound to matter. Whence it can*not* be said that it is *educed from* matter, but rather that it is from an extrinsic [and creating] principle.

Just above, Aquinas is pointing out a significant difference between the human soul, the intellectual soul, on the one hand, and all other types of soul, on the other hand. Man's soul has an operation **without** the body -- **habet operationem sine corpore** -- i.e., an activity which the soul **performs** independently of the body and all bodily organs, including the brain. All the activities of lower types of soul are **with** the body, i.e., completely dependent on the body **for their performance** -- dependent on the various elements, atoms, molecules, tissues, organs, etc., which are components of the body. From this it follows, as Aquinas sees it, that lower types of soul **can be educed from** the potency of matter, i.e., that they can be brought into existence by a

237

conjunction of the following, **without need of a direct and special creating act of God**: prime matter, properly disposed by an appropriate substantial form and by an appropriate mix of elements, along with the agent causality of certain heavenly bodies and certain particular matter-form composites. And so, the **receptive** and **agent** capacities which **reside in** the physical world can produce of themselves, i.e., **without a special creating act of God,** various lower types of soul. That is, these lower types of soul are totally educed from the potency of matter, since they are totally bound to matter in their existence and in their activities. But, the human soul is not bound to matter in its existence and activities, and so cannot be educed from the potency of matter, i.e., its production is wholly outside the receptive and agent capacities **which reside in** the physical world. The human soul, therefore, is derived from an **extrinsic** principle, i.e., extrinsic to the physical world, by which Aquinas means God. As Aquinas puts it in the passage just above: **Anima . . . intellectiva, cum habeat operationem sine corpore, . . . non potest dici quod educatur de materia, sed magis quod est a principio extrinseco.**

> . . . creari est quoddam fieri . . .   Fieri autem ordinatur ad esse rei. Unde illis proprie convenit fieri et creari, quibus convenit esse. Quod quidem convenit proprie subsistentibus, sive sint simplicia, sicut substantiae separatae, sive sint composita, sicut substantiae materiales. *Illi* enim proprie convenit esse, quod *habet* esse; et hoc est subsistens in suo esse. Formae autem et accidentia, et alia huiusmodi, non dicuntur entia quasi ipsa sint, sed quia eis aliquid est; ut albedo ea ratione dicitur ens, quia ea subiectum est album. Unde, secundum Philosophum, accidens magis proprie dicitur *entis* quam *ens*. Sicut igitur accidentia et formae, et huiusmodi, quae non subsistunt, magis sunt coexistentia quam entia; ita magis debent dici *concreata* quam creata. Proprie vero creata sunt subsistentia. (*S.T.,* I, q. 45, a. 4, c.)
>
> . . . being created is a kind of coming to be . . .   Now coming to be is ordered to the being of a thing.   Whence *coming to be* and *being created* belong properly to those things to which *being* belongs. Now, being belongs properly to subsisting things,

whether they are simple, like the separated substances, or composite, like material substances. For being belongs properly to that which *has* being; and this is something which subsists in *its own* being. Now forms and accidents, and other things of this sort, are not said to be beings as if they themselves exist, but rather because something [else] exists by reason of them. For example, whiteness is said to be a being, because its subject is white by reason of it. Whence, according to the Philosopher, an accident is more properly said to be *of a being* than a being. Therefore, just as accidents and forms, and the like, which do not subsist, *co-exist* rather than exist; so too, they ought to be said to be *co-created* rather than created. Things which are properly created are subsisting things.

Just above, Aquinas is noting that creation, like generation, is a kind of coming to be. So that creation, like generation, belongs properly only to that to which **existence** belongs. And that is the subsisting thing, whether it is simple, like a separated substance, or composite, like a material substance. Now, substantial forms and accidental forms are said to exist not because they are themselves subsisting things, but rather because they are either **that by which** a subsisting thing subsists (these are substantial forms) or **that by which** a subsisting thing is white, or tall, or virtuous, or something else of this sort (these are accidental forms). And so, since substantial forms and accidental forms do not subsist, they are co-existents (coexistentia), rather then existents (existentia). And this is why they ought to be said to be co-created (concreata) rather than created (creata). And, one can add, this is also why they ought to be said to be co-generated (cogenerata) rather than generated (generata). And for a substantial form to be **co-generated** is for it **to be educed** from the potency of matter.

> . . . quod creatur est ex nihilo. Composita autem non sunt ex nihilo, sed ex suis componentibus. Ergo compositis non convenit creari. (*S.T.,* I, q. 45, a. 4, obj. 2).
> . . . creatio non dicit constitutionem rei compositae ex principiis praeexistentibus; sed compositum sic dicitur creari, quod simul cum omnibus suis principiis in esse producitur. (*Ibid.,* ad 2).

> . . . what is created comes to be out of nothing. Now composites
> do not come to be out of nothing, but out of their components.
> Therefore it does not belong to composites to be created.
> . . . creation does not mean the putting together of a composite
> thing out of pre-existing principles. Rather the composite is said
> to be created in such a way that it is brought into being together
> with (at the same time as) all its principles.

Just above, Aquinas clarifies what it means for a composed thing to be created, in order to make clear that a composed thing, whether an element or a mixed body, **can be** created. The objection has it that composed things cannot be created, because they come to be out of their components, rather than out of nothing. Aquinas responds by emphasizing that the creation of a composed thing does not mean that it was constituted or put together out of component principles **which pre-existed** -- i.e., **prior** to its creation. It means rather that all of its component principles were brought into existence when it itself was brought into existence. In terms of the passage considered just prior to this one, the component principles of a composed thing are **co-created** when the composed thing itself is **created**. And these co-created component principles, one should point out, are prime matter and substantial form along with an appropriate mix of elements, in the case of a mixed body; prime matter and substantial form alone, in the case of an element. It should be clear that a co-created substantial form, precisely as co-created, was **not** educed from the potency of matter, for there was no pre-existing matter from which it could be educed.

*   *   *

And so, some sort of answer has been given to the following questions. 1) What exactly is a substantial form? A substantial form, briefly, is a certain sort of **real** differentiator, intelligible not sense-perceivable; it differentiates the **real** end term (e.t.) of a **real** radical change from the **real** beginning term (b.t.) of that **real** change. 2) Why does Aquinas maintain that when substantial forms come to be (**after** God's initial creative production of things) they come to be by being educed, rather than by being created, or by being generated, or by being brought somehow out of some sort of hidden actuality? Briefly, this is so because it is within the causal capacities, both receptive (forms pre-exist in matter **not** actually, but **potentially**) and agent, of things in the material world to bring these substantial forms into existence (as **that by which** subsisting things exist), **without need of a direct and special creative act of God.** 3) Why is it that the human soul, among substantial forms, cannot be educed from the potency of matter, but needs rather a direct and special creating act of God to bring it into existence? Briefly, this is so because the human soul has an operation which is **performed** independently of the body and all of its components, from the lowliest of quarks to the most sophisticated of bodily organs, like heart and brain. 4) What is the role of the elements in the eduction of lower souls and lower forms? Briefly, their role is that of a set of virtual, dispositional, retrievable, and instrumentally agent material ingredients.   5) What role, if any, do the elements have in relation to the creation of human souls? Briefly, an appropriate mix of elements is required to provide the sort of matter which even God needs as the matter in which He can create a human soul.

PART FOUR

THE ELEMENTS IN AQUINAS
AND THE ELEMENTS TODAY

The Elements in Aquinas
and the Elements Today

This part, PART FOUR, looks at an assortment of things from different sources, in an attempt to make clearer, as far as this can be done, **both** what Aquinas thought about the elements **and** what we today think about them. These two views, i.e., that of Aquinas and that of people today, might well, by appropriate comparisons and contrasts, illuminate one another in helpful and welcome ways.

It seems appropriate to begin this part with some thoughts on how quarks (which, along with leptons, are said today to be the elements of physical things) remain in the protons of which they are the constituents, thoughts patterned after the way in which, in the view of Aquinas, the four elements of **his** physical theory remain in the mixed bodies of which they are the constituents. These opening thoughts might be given the title **De Mixtione Quarcorum,** turning the English word "quark" into a second declension neuter Latin noun, "quarcum, -i," and inserting it into the title, **De Mixtione Elementorum,** in the place of the word "Elementorum."

1. How quarks remain in protons

An element of things in the physical world, as Aquinas understands it, and as we indicated above (pp. 103-104), has the following characteristics:

1. It is a simple body, out of which a mixed body is made, as out of a primary constituent, i.e., a constituent which itself has no prior bodily constituents.

2. It remains in some way in the mixed body, i.e., not by reason of its substantial form, but by reason of its powers, i.e., its qualitites: hot, cold, wet, dry. As remaining, it is not completely corrupted; neither is it completely

preserved. What is preserved are its powers, which, precisely because preserved, are retrievable. Its substantial form, too, is retrievable, and precisely via its powers, functioning as the appropriate dispositions (above, pp. 125-126).

3. It is indivisible in kind, i.e., it cannot be broken down so as to yield parts which are different in kind from its own kind.

4. It can exist separately, i.e., not as a constituent of a mixed body, both before and after having been such a constituent.

5. Elements can act upon, and be acted upon by, one another.

6. Elements become constituents of a mixed body only after they have been altered by one another, though not beyond retrievability.

The substantial forms of the quarks which enter the constitution of a proton are not actually present in the proton. Each proton has its own, and one, substantial form. And it is this substantial form which manifests **its** proper activities through **its** proper qualities, which had been the distinctive qualities, i.e., the extreme or excelling, qualities (now brought, or tempered, to a mean) of the formerly separately existing quarks. The mixed body which is the proton, like any bodily substance, can have actually **but one** substantial form, its own. Potentially, however, i.e., both virtually (in their power) and retrievably, it has as many substantial forms, in number and in kind, as the quarks which are required as its ingredients -- required by the **nature** of the proton, from which (nature), as employing the preserved powers of the constituting quarks, arise the **powers** for the performance of its (the proton's) **proper activities.**

If the substantial forms of the three quarks which make up a proton remained -- remained **actually** -- in the proton, the proton would be a proton throughout, yet simultaneously a u-quark in two of its parts, and a d-quark in the third of its parts; inasmuch as a proton is said to be made up out of two u-quarks and one d-quark. Which is quite clearly impossible, i.e.,

246

for a thing to be **of one sort** throughout, and at the same time **of another sort(s)** in different parts of itself. It must be the case then that, when two u-quarks and one d-quark become constituents of a proton, they cease being the u-quarks and the d-quark respectively. For a proton is a proton, and just a proton. Nonetheless, the u-quarks and the d-quark must remain in some way in the proton. For, all three are retrievable (which I shall assume, if they are really elements; since elements are retrievable). But, how exactly do they remain? Not actually; this is clear. For then, a proton would not be a proton, but just three juxtaposed quarks -- in addition to being **of one sort** throughout, and at the same time **of other sorts** in different parts of itself, as noted just above. Potentially, then? This seems the right thing to say; for what other alternative is there? But, what exactly does this mean? Shall we say, as Aquinas would, that what this means is that they (the quarks) remain by reason of their active and passive qualities (whatever these may be), but as altered somehow into a set of mean qualities of some sort, which are the qualities distinctive of, appropriate to, a proton (whatever these may be) -- altered by means of their (the quarks') proton-constituting interaction? And shall we take this to mean, as Aquinas would, that the substantial form of a proton is both brought into existence and (having been brought into existence) acts **through these mean qualities**, until such time as some external agent (or agents) "re-alters" the proton's mean qualities, i.e., nullifies the prior proton-constituting interaction between the u-quarks and the d-quark, releasing thereby the distinctive elemental qualities which belong to them as quarks, and thereby in turn bringing about their re-generation as actual, and separately existing and acting, physical entities?

Assuming that the generation of a proton is a **true** mixing, in the sense in which Aquinas understands a true mixing, the quarks do not survive with their respective substantial forms. What survives is their active and passive qualities, appropriately changed (constricted, contracted, restrained; imprisoned, so to say) by the required alteration into a set of mean qualities. These mean qualities serve as 1) the dispositions by which the proton (like any other mixed body) is brought into existence, 2) as that by which the proton acts, and   3) as that by the removal of which the quarks are released (as though from prison) to exist again as actual and separate and free physical realities. The required alteration affects the two u-quarks and the one d-quark which remain in the make-up of the proton. But, how are these quarks affected?   And by what?   Shall we say, as Aquinas might well have said, had he lived in the twentieth century, that they are affected by their respective electrical charges?   And by the gluons which carry the strong nuclear force which binds them together within their proton prison?

To make this clearer, one should keep in mind what is meant, as Aquinas sees it, by the **virtual, retrievable, dispositional and instrumental presence** of the lower in the higher, and apply it to what we know today about the make-up of physical things. Certain elements (the simplest and lowliest of bodily components, like quarks and electrons), and certain other bodily components as well (complex and higher ones, like the chemical elements of the periodic table, and the molecules made out of these) are required as ingredients in the make-up of progressively more and more complex bodily things, all the way up to, and including the most complex bodily thing which we know, i.e., man. That is, one should keep in mind Aquinas' view 1) that prime matter is in potency to forms in a certain order, and relate this to his view   2) that whereas a mixed body can have **actually** only one substantial form, its own; **potentially,** nonetheless, it **can** have -- indeed **must** have -- at least as many substantial forms, in number and in kind, as the **elements** (as well as the lower kinds of **mixed bodies**) which are required as its ingredients, i.e., without which it could not **be** or **act.**

What, one may ask, is to be said about characteristic 4?   It has been pointed out that "quarks are never free,"[1] that "there can be no such thing as

1   Lederman, Leon (with Dick Teresi), *The God Particle: If the Universe is the Answer, What Is the Question?* New York: Houghton Mifflin Company, 1993; p. 305. --   The subtitle of this book might make more sense, it seems, if it read the other way around, i.e.: If the Universe is the **Question,** What is the Answer? Don't we confront the universe, and ask: What is the universe? And, why does the universe exist? And don't we propose the following as possible answers? What the universe is, is precisely this: something

a free quark."[2]   If quarks cannot exist separately (i.e., by themselves all alone, as opposed to as constituents of a proton, both before and after having been such constituents), doesn't this make it difficult (**at least** difficult, maybe even impossible) to accept them as true elements? Unless, of course, it is just **too cold** now, **not hot enough** now, to sustain a free quark.

And what about characteristics 5 and 6? If quarks cannot exist alone, in separation from the protons of which they are said to be the constituents, how can we come to understand how they can act upon, and be acted upon by, one another, so as to enter into the composition of a proton?   That is, how can we come to know what their active and passive qualities (powers, or properties) are -- **before** they become constituents of a proton?   If quarks cannot be free, how can their "before" properties be determined? Are quarks retrievable from their imprisonment within the confines of a proton? Can our particle accelerators produce the heat, the energy, required to retrieve them?   Is it possible to construct such an accelerator? An accelerator which is capable of producing heat, energy, of an intensity to match the heat "just after" the Big Bang, i.e., infinitesimally minisculely beyond it,[3] when the world is said by

---

made up out of quarks and leptons, arranged in certain specific ways. And, the reason why (or at least, **one** reason why) the universe exists, is precisely this (the very same reason): because it is something made up out of quarks and leptons, arranged in certain specific ways.   Moreover, strictly speaking, **things, i.e., real things like the universe,** are not, cannot be, **answers** to questions, any more than they can be the **questions** themselves. Answers, like questions, are not **real** things. They are things of a **grammatical** or **logical** or **mental** sort. They are sentences, or propositions, or ideas. Both questions and answers are **about** things.   They are not those things themselves.

2   Lederman, *op. cit.*, p. 318.

3   Prior to 10^{-43} seconds after the Big Bang? Gerald L. Schroeder, physicist and theologian, points out :   "While the conditions that existed prior to the appearance of energy and matter [i.e., prior to the Big Bang] are not known, we can attempt to describe them at the briefest instant following the beginning, at about 10^{-43} seconds after the start." (*Genesis and the Big Bang*, New York: Bantam Books, 1992; p. 65). Is it possible, in principle, to construct a particle accelerator which can re-create the conditions of the newly beginning universe prior to 10^{-43} seconds after the start?, even though "physics and mathematics, as we know them today, cannot deal with times earlier than 10^{-43} seconds after the beginning," because "prior to that time, the temperatures and densities of matter exceeded those that can be described by the laws of nature as we now understand them." (Schroeder, *ibid.*, p. 66).

some to have been a sea of free quarks (and perhaps of free leptons as well), i.e., a sea of separately existing and acting quarks (and leptons)?

2. A quark, like any element, is an agent cause of a special sort, besides being a material cause of a special sort

It is the view of Aquinas that all types of non-living things, reaching down to and including the elements, are related to the substantial forms of all higher types of things, living as well as non-living, as that which can be their matter (subject) and their instrument, i.e., as that in which these substantial forms can exist (their matter, or subject) and that through the surviving powers of which (their instrument) they can perform their proper or distinctive activities.

To make this clearer, one should keep in mind, as noted above (pp. 140-141) that an instrument can be either a **separated** instrument, i.e., one whose form is a form different from that of the principal agent, like the pen (instrument) with which I (the principal agent) write; or a **conjoined** instrument, i.e., one whose form **is** the form of the principal agent, like a hand, or a vital organ (e.g., the liver), or a molecule of carbon dioxide, or an atom of oxygen, or a proton, or a quark, or a lepton; all of which are in various ways parts or components of mixed bodies, however lowly (the lowly proton is composed of quarks), or however exalted (man is composed of quarks, and protons, and atoms, and molecules, and vital organs, and hands, etc.).

Now quarks, Aquinas would say, are related to the form of a proton as matter (**elemental** matter, not prime matter) and as **conjoined** instrument. That is, not only do quarks enter into the proton as ingredients (matter) of what the proton is, but they do (agent) what quarks, as put together into a

250

proton, have the power to do; and thereby enable (as instrument) the proton to do what a proton, as proton, does. That is, the quarks are a **conjoined** instrument; their form is the form of the proton. Protons, in turn (along with the quarks which are their ingredients), are similarly related to the form of an atom, i.e., as matter (**quasi-elemental**[4] matter, not prime matter) and as **conjoined** instrument. That is, not only do the protons (and their ingredient quarks) which compose the atom (along with some electrons and neutrons) enter into the atom as ingredients (matter) of what the atom is, but they do (agent) what protons and quarks and electrons and neutrons, as put together into an atom, have the power to do; and thereby enable (as instrument) the atom to do what an atom, as atom, does. Protons (along with their brother atomic components) are a **conjoined** instrument; their form is the form of the atom. Molecules, in their turn (through the **conjoined** instrumentality of their **ingredient** quarks and electrons and protons and neutrons) are related to the forms of progressively higher bodily things, up to and including man, as their quasi-elemental matter and conjoined instrument. So that in man we have a highly complex entity which can do, has the power to do, what man does, precisely because of a serial ordering of quasi-elemental matters which are also conjoined instruments: his component bodily organs, like heart and liver, use their component molecules, like carbon dioxide, which use their component atoms, like oxygen, which use their component electrons and protons and neutrons, the last two of which (i.e., protons and neutrons) use their component quarks, to do what they, as put together into man can do, thereby enabling man to do what man, as man, does. Thus, quarks (along with protons, atoms, molecules, etc., on up to vital bodily organs) are all of them, each in its own way, **not only** material causes of a special sort (i.e, **capable of agent causality**, because of certain remaining powers, as distinct

---

4   The term "quasi-elemental" is being used to mean: like, or **resembling** (quasi), an element, without being an element. That is, just as an element, e.g., a quark, remains (as ingredient) in the proton with its powers, though without its substantial form (it is by those remaining powers that the quark functions as a conjoined instrument of the proton); so too the proton remains (as ingredient) in the atom with its powers, though without its substantial form (it is by those remaining powers that the proton, in its turn, functions as a conjoined instrument of the atom).

from prime matter which is a **purely passive or receptive** potentiality), **but also** agent causes of a special sort, i.e., **conjoined instrumental** agent causes. -- And this is why it can be said that quarks, along with these other components, from the lowest to the highest, have, all of them, a **virtual, retrievable, dispositional, and instrumental presence,** the lower in the higher; and why the higher cannot exist and act without the lower, though the lower can, and does, exist and act without the higher.[5]

3. Ingredients in the definitions of quarks and leptons

Atoms today are defined in terms of the protons, neutrons, and electrons which compose them; protons and neutrons, in terms of the quarks which compose them. But what about the quarks themselves? And their sister elements, the leptons, e.g., electrons? How are they to be defined? What are **their** intrinsic components (if that is the right question)? What are the ingredients of **their** essences? That is, what is that **within them** which accounts for the fact 1) that they have come into existence (their becoming), and 2) that they are now in existence (their being), and 3) that they do what they do (their activities)?

It will be helpful to begin here with a reminder of what is meant by an element. This will be to begin as we did earlier (pp. 180-181) with respect to the four elements in the physical theory of Aquinas; an eminently appropriate way to begin, since that meaning of "element" is as applicable to the quarks and leptons of today (because, as far as we know, but **only** as far as we know,[6] they are **ultimate** particles) as it was to the the four elements of days gone by. And with that firmly in mind, one would be in a position to

---

[5] For Aquinas on the material and agent causality of the four elements, see above, pp. 137-143, section 3, **Is an element in any way an agent cause, in addition to being a special sort of material cause?**

[6] See below, pp. 286-287, on the **rishon.**

proceed more profitably in pursuing the questions: What is a quark? What is a u-quark? A d-quark? And all other types of quarks? What is a lepton? What is an electron? An electron neutrino? And all other types of leptons? We shall not pursue all these questions, just those which will suffice for our purposes.[7]

What then, as a reminder, is an element? An element is a simple body, i.e., something composed out of prime matter and a substantial form (but **not** out of any prior bodies, since there are no prior bodies), which (substantial form), as efficient cause, not only extends the element three-dimensionally (and keeps it so extended),[8] but also causes it to have certain proper accidents by which it can both affect, and be affected by, the other elements, so as to undergo **the substantial changes** in which it is transformed into other elements (can a quark of one type be transformed into a quark of another type,[9] or into a lepton; can a lepton of one type be transformed into a lepton of another type, or into a quark?), and **the alterations** by which it becomes an ingredient in the make-up of mixed bodies (like protons, neutrons, atoms, molecules, and the like, ascending to ever more complex entities, up to and terminating in man, the most complex).

Fire, suggests Aquinas as we saw above (pp. 168-169), can be defined as **a simple body, hot and dry.** Now bodies are either **simple** (the elements themselves) or **mixed** (made out of elements). A mixed body is doubly composed: not only 1) out of prime matter and substantial form, but also 2) out of simple bodies, i.e., out of elements. These elements are put together not by simple aggregation, in the way in which a **heap** is made out of, say, bricks and stones; nor by a composition which **not only** puts them together in

---

7   See below, p. 256, the paragraph beginning with the words: "Quarks and electrons . . ."

8   This is a kind of **"small" Big Bang,** as we noted earlier (p. 166) -- **small** since it occurs **within,** and is **limited to,** the confines of the element. Any substantial form does this for the body of which it is the substantial form.

9   See Lederman, *The God Particle,* pp. 325-326, where he points out that a quark of one type **can be** transformed into a quark of another type, e.g., a u-quark becomes a d-quark, and vice versa.

some given order, in the way in which a **house** is made out of an orderly arrangement of wood and bricks and stones, **but also** holds them together by certain joining or binding materials, like nails and glue and mortar; but by a **mixing (per mixtionem)** in which the elements affect and alter one another so as to remain in the mixed body in a special way, i.e., virtually, or with their powers (as well as retrievably, dispositionally, and instrumentally), though not actually (i.e., not with their substantial forms). -- A simple body, on the other hand, is composed out of prime matter and substantial form indeed, but **not** also out of simple bodies. A simple body is not doubly composed. It has **no** composing **bodily** ingredients, in addition to its composing prime matter and substantial form. There are no prior bodily things out of which simple bodies could be composed. Simple bodies, i.e., elements, are the **ultimate** bodily constituents of all other bodily things. The expression "simple body," it is quite clear, functions as a **genus** in this definition of fire. That is, **all** elements have this in common that they are simple bodies. The expression "hot and dry," by way of contrast, functions as a **specific difference.** Hot and dry are proper accidents of fire, caused by, and manifesting, the substantial form of fire.

A quark (and a lepton), like any element (assuming that each is, indeed, an element), is a **simple body,** i.e., composed out of prime matter and substantial form, but **not** also out of prior bodily components. Assigning this **genus** is an easy matter. For anything which comes to be in change is composed of prime matter and substantial form; quarks and leptons come into being in change. And any element is such that it cannot be composed out of prior bodily things; there are no prior bodily things.

But, what is to function as the **specific difference?** Hot and dry, as Aquinas sees it, are proper accidents of fire, caused by, and manifesting, the substantial form of fire; this is why the expression "hot and dry" functions as expressing the specific difference. What, now, are the proper accidents, i.e., the substantial-form-manifesting characteristics or properties or attributes, of quarks and leptons? To identify these is, clearly, to identify

254

what will be expressed in their specific differences. And physicists have already identified them.

In his *The God Particle*, which he sees as a kind of play or drama, Leon Lederman, experimental physicist and Nobel laureate, begins with a page entitled DRAMATIS PERSONAE. Some of the actors in his play are **matter** particles (e.g., quarks, electrons), others are **reaction** particles (e.g., neutrinos), still others are **force carrying** particles (e.g., gluons, photons). From his list of performers in this atomic-cosmic drama:

Atomos or a-tom: Theoretical particle invented by Democritus. The a-tom, invisible and indivisible, is the smallest unit of matter. Not to be confused with the so-called *chemical* atom, which is merely the smallest unit of each of the elements [in the periodic table] (hydrogen, carbon, oxygen, and so on).

Quark [a matter particle]: Another a-tom [but a contemporary one, as opposed to an a-tom of Democritus]. There are six quarks -- five discovered, one still sought after (in 1993). Each of the six quarks comes in three colors. Only two of the six, the up and the down quark, exist naturally in today's universe.

Electron [a matter particle]: The first a-tom discovered, in 1898. Like all modern a-toms, the electron is believed to have the curious property of "zero radius." It is a member of the lepton family of a-toms.

Neutrino [a reaction particle]: Another a-tom in the lepton family. There are three different kinds. Neutrinos are not used to build matter, but they are essential to certain reactions. They win the minimalist contest: zero charge, zero radius, and very possibly zero mass.

Photon, graviton, the W^+, W^-, and Z^0 family, and gluons [force carrying particles]: These are particles, but *not* matter particles like quarks and leptons. They *transmit* the electromagnetic [transmitted by photons,] gravitational [by gravitons], weak [by

255

the W$^+$, W$^-$, and Z^0 family], and strong [by gluons] forces, respectively. Only the graviton has not yet been detected. (Lederman, *The God Particle*, p. ix).

Quarks and electrons (electrons are one of the leptons) are **matter** particles, as different from **reaction** particles and **force transmitting** particles. The attempt at this point is to describe, with help from Lederman and others, some of the intrinsic properties (i.e., the proper accidents, or substantial-form-manifesting properties, as Aquinas would put it) which physicists have identified as belonging to the **three fundamental matter particles,** i.e., 1) the up quark (u-quark), 2) the down quark (d-quark), and 3) the electron -- since a) this will more than suffice for our purposes (i.e., to try to understand how u-quarks and d-quarks combine to form protons and neutrons, how protons and neutrons combine to form the nucleus of an atom, and how electrons combine with the nucleus to form an atom), and b) since, as Lederman explains to Democritus, "almost everything in the universe **today** is composed of only two quarks -- the up and the down -- and the electron. The neutrino [another of the leptons, but a **reaction** particle] zings around the universe freely and pops out[10] of our radioactive nuclei, but most of the other quarks and leptons must be manufactured in our laboratories."[11]

Before describing the proper accidents, i.e., the substantial-form-manifesting properties, of the u-quark, the d-quark, and the electron, one should perhaps consider whether an **elementary** particle -- **any** elementary particle -- can be something **without** dimensions. For Lederman, as well as others, points out many times that quarks are thought to be **without dimensions.**   And this seems difficult to accept, since dimensions (three

---

10   Does "pops out" imply that the neutrino was an ingredient or component, in some sense of "ingredient" or "component, " of those nuclei? But, isn't a neutrino a lepton? Can leptons be ingredients of the nucleus of an atom??   Mustn't leptons be **extra**-nuclear ingredients of atoms? Are leptons ever subject to the strong nuclear force?
11   Lederman, *op. cit.*, p. 51.   Lederman is speaking to Democritus, in one of many very clever, entertaining, and most instructive dialogues, scattered throughout the book.

256

dimensions) belong to anything which has a substantial form.

Quarks, physicists say, have no size at all; they are **like** geometrical **points;** they are there, i.e., have a location or a place, but take up no space. This may sound "real crazy," Lederman apologizes. But it makes sense, some philosophers might want to note, at least in a way. That is, an explanatory principle (or cause) must be in some significant way **unlike** what it explains. For, if the **explanans** and the **explanandum** are alike in every way, no explanation has been given. To say that **what has dimensions** is made up out of components each of which **has dimensions**, and to stop there, is not to have explained why **what has dimensions** has the dimensions that it has. And so, it seems, the dimensions of **what has dimensions** must be explained by components which do **not** themselves have dimensions. The dimension-**ed,** as such, is quite appropriately explained by the dimension-**less.** But this dimensionless component, the quark, must be **unlike** a geometrical point, as well as like one. A quark is after all a **physical** reality, a **physical** point, **not** a mathematical point. As physical, a quark has something dimensionless within it which enables it to account for the dimensions of the whole, the proton or the neutron, of which it is an ingredient. As Aquinas would insist, it has a substantial form, which, as efficient cause, does exactly that, i.e., accounts for the dimensions of the whole. But, this must be properly understood. Since a quark is said to be an element, it itself must have dimensions,[12] however small they may be; it itself must be something **bodily,** for elements are ultimate **bodies.** That is, elements are the **bodily**

---

12   **It itself** must have dimensions, or one or other of its properties. Is it its **mass** that has these dimensions? Is it its **charge**? Is it some other of its properties? To what exactly does the word "it" refer, in the expression "it itself;" or the word "its," in expressions like "its mass"? -- And an additional and related question: Are mass and charge and spin, and the other properties which are attributed to particles -- are these properties such that **only** things with dimensions can have them? Or is Lederman right when he notes that if you ask questions like, "What is it that's spinning?," when scientists tell you that particles have spin (which question seems to imply that what has spin is **something which has dimensions**); then "you expose yourself as one who has not yet been cleansed of impure prequantum thinking . . . " (Lederman, *The God Particle,* p. 344).

constituents of all other bodies, they themselves having **no** bodily constituents.[13] Nonetheless, since a quark comes to be in change, it must have prime matter and a substantial form as its basic constituents; and both of these are, in themselves, dimensionless. And so, it is **not** the quark **itself** which is without dimensions, even though it is said to be pointlike -- a pointlike a-tom.[14] It is **prime matter** (and the substantial form as well which actualizes it) which is without dimensions. And this is why, it appears, Lederman says **at times** that quarks have **no** dimensions[15] (recognizing dimensionless prime matter in some implicit and unwitting way, though wrongly attributing its dimensionlessness to quarks themselves) and **at times** that they, i.e., quarks, **do** have dimensions, but dimensions which are so incredibly small that quarks are "as good an approximation to points as you can get."[16] It is not the quark itself which is point-like; it is rather the prime matter within it which is point-like.[17] Quarks themselves have the dimensions which they have because of the on-going **efficient** causality of their dimensionless substantial forms and the on-going **receptive** causality of their dimensionless prime matter; but the proton, of which the quarks are constituents, has the dimensions which it has, because of the dimensions of its constituent quarks, which (dimensions), though they survive in the

---

13 See above, p. 159, for a brief discussion of the question: How is it that an element is a **bodily** thing, i.e., something three-dimensional, since an element is composed **only** out of prime matter and substantial form, and neither of these components is a body? See also above, pp. 165-167, on the description of the birth of an element, for more details with respect to this question.

14 This is said to be the case as regards leptons, too : ". . . [there are] two classes of **pointlike** a-toms -- the quarks and **the leptons**." (Lederman, *op. cit.*, p. 309).

15 Lederman writes: "And here's Boscovich [Roger Joseph Boscovich, eighteenth century scientist] putting forth the proposition that matter is composed of particles that have no dimensions! We found a particle just a couple of decades ago [Lederman is writing in 1993] that fits such a description. It's called a quark." (Lederman, *op. cit.*, p. 103). See also Lederman, *ibid.*, p. 55: "The quarks -- they're all pointlike, dimensionless; they have no real size."

16 This is said about leptons as well: "The radius of a quark is less than an incredibly small 10^{-21} centimeters. As far as we can tell, quarks **and leptons** are as good an approximation to points as you can get." Lederman, *op. cit.*, p. 405.

17 See above p. 253, the paragraph beginning with the words: "What then, as a reminder, is an element?" See also p. 166.

proton which is generated out of their conjunction (though not as dimensions of the quarks, since the quarks do not survive with their substantial forms), are maintained in existence by the substantial form of the proton. That is, the dimensions (which **were** the dimensions of the just corrupted quarks) survive in the newly generated proton (though the quarks themselves do not), and are kept in existence by the conjoined on-going efficient causality of the dimensionless substantial form of that proton and the on-going receptive causality of its dimensionless prime matter (thereby becoming the dimensions of the proton itself), which (prime matter) has survived in it (i.e., in the newly generated proton) from the just corrupted quarks.

It seems clear, from the immediately preceding, that any and every **elementary** particle, i.e., anything at all which is said to be an **element**, must have dimensions, i.e., **three** dimensions. For elements are ultimate **bodies**. It may be difficult, perhaps even impossible (in some sense of "impossible") to determine whether **its** dimensions are the dimensions of its **mass,** or of its **charge,** or of its **spin,** or of some other of its properties. It may even be that it (i.e., the elementary particle) has several sets of dimensions, one set for its mass, another for its charge, another for its . . . , etc. But it must have dimensions. **These are conferred on it, as they are on anything which is composed of prime matter and substantial form, by its substantial form.** In addition, one wants to ask whether particle properties like mass, charge, spin, etc., are such that something without dimensions can have them; and whether, if something without dimensions can have these properties -- whether these properties themselves can exist without having dimensions of their own. This is like asking whether something without dimensions can be soft or hard, rough or smooth, red or blue. And if it can, whether softness, hardness, etc. themselves can exist without having dimensions of their own. -- Consider, moreover, a world in which there is matter, but this matter is **without** dimensions. Could there be, in such a world, a numerical plurality of things composed out of matter and form, things which come into existence in change? If matter were not quantified, if it did not have dimensions; there would be no possibility of dividing this matter, and so no possibility of a numerical plurality of things made of matter. If matter were not quantified, it would be like a mathematical point. If matter were not quantified, there could not be a plurality of elementary particles, whether quarks, or leptons, or particles of any other sort. Nor could there be a plurality of things made up out of elementary particles. If matter were not quantified, the physical universe -- **as a whole** -- would be like a mathematical point.

Having seen that any **elementary** particle must have three dimensions, we turn now to define the three fundamental **matter particles**, i.e., the u-quark, the d-quark, and the electron -- in terms of a listing of the intrinsic properties (i.e., the proper accidents, or substantial-form-manifesting attributes) which physicists have identified as belonging to them. This will be followed by a brief description or definition of each of these intrinsic properties. And this, in turn, will be followed by a definition of the **force transmitting (or messenger) particles**, i.e., gluons (for the strong force), photons (for the electromagnetic force), W^+ and W^- and Z^0 particles (for the weak force), and gravitons (for the force of gravity) -- these definitions, too, in terms of a listing of the intrinsic properties which physicists have identified as belonging to them.

Matter particles:

A **u-quark** is a simple body **(genus)**, with a radius of less than 10^{-21} centimeters, a mass of 10 (in terms of the mass of the electron, taken as unity), a rest energy of 5 MeV, an electric charge of +2/3, a color charge (chromodynamic charge) of either red, or yellow, or blue (some physicists call the yellow one **green**, still others call it **white**), a spin of 1/2, and a baryon number of +1/3 (these intrinsic properties taken together constitute the **specific difference**).

A **d-quark** is a simple body **(genus)**, with a radius of less than 10^{-21} centimeters, a mass of 20 (in terms of the mass of the electron, taken as unity), a rest energy of 10 MeV, an electric charge of -1/3. a color charge of either red, or yellow, or blue (some physicists call the yellow one **green**, still others call it **white**), a spin of 1/2, and a baryon number of +1/3 (these intrinsic properties taken together constitute the **specific difference**).[18]

An **electron** is a simple body **(genus)**, with a radius of less than 10^{-18} centimeters, a mass of 10^{-30} kilograms (i.e., of about 9.107 x 10^{-28} gram; or 1/1837 that of a proton), a rest energy of .511 MeV, an electric charge of -1 (i.e., a negative electric charge of about 1.602 x 10^{-19} coulomb), a spin of 1/2, and a baryon number of 0, i.e., **no** baryon number (these intrinsic properties taken together constitute the **specific difference**).[19]

It is to be noted, and emphasized, that the above definitions of the u-quark, the d-quark, and the electron are being patterned after Aquinas' definition of the element fire as a simple body **(genus)**, hot and dry **(specific difference)**.

---

[18] It is to be noted that **no one alone** of the intrinsic properties of the u-quark and of the d-quark functions as the cause which initiates, and sustains, the exchange of gluons which binds the quarks together to form a proton and a neutron -- but rather, **all** of them taken together. That is, **all** of these properties, taken together, enable quarks to combine with other quarks (and with anti-quarks) to form baryons and mesons. And this is so, because **all of them taken together** constitute the **specific difference**.

[19] Similarly, **all** of the intrinsic properties of an **electron,** taken together, initiate and sustain the exchange of photons which binds the electron to the nucleus. And all of the intrinsic properties of the **nucleus,** too -- taken together -- contribute to initiating and sustaining this binding exchange of photons. Similarly, again, **all** of the intrinsic properties of particles subject to the weak nuclear force initiate and sustain the exchange of W^{+} and W^{-} and Z^{0} particles, which (exchange) causes certain processes, like the conversion of a neutron into a proton, or vice versa. Lastly, **mass** is the **only** intrinsic property of physical bodies which initiates, and sustains, the exchange of gravitons causing bodies to attract one another.

*   *   *

To make the preceding definitions at least minimally understandable to those of us who are not physicists, it will be helpful to give some sort of definition of radius, mass, rest energy, electric charge, color charge, spin, and baryon number (and of certain related things like diameter, chord, weight, density, and others).

Radius: the distance in a straight line from the center of a spherical or circular physical object to its outer edge.

If the dimensions of particles are given in terms of the diameter, then:
Diameter: a **chord** through the center of a spherical or circular physical object; the radius times two.

Chord: the distance in a straight line between two points on a curve.

Mass: the amount of "stuff" in a physical object. Mass is neither the size, nor the weight, nor the density of the physical object.   Mass is that characteristic of a body which relates that body to other bodies by pulling on them, and to imposed forces by resisting them.   Mass is a scalar quantity, as opposed to a vector quantity, i.e., it has magnitude but no direction.   When physicists say, "mass," without specifying whether they mean **inertial** mass or **gravitational** mass, (see below, p. 263, for the difference), they mean **inertial** mass.

Weight: the force that pulls a physical body directly toward a nearby celestial body, e.g., the planet Earth.   This force is due to the gravitational attraction between the two bodies.   Weight is not mass.   A body of a given (i.e., same) mass weighs more on Earth than it does on the Moon.   Weight is a vector quantity, i.e., it has magnitude and direction.

262

Density: the mass of a physical body **in a given volume,** or per unit of volume.   Density is a scalar quantity.

Gravitational mass: the amount of stuff in a physical object **which pulls on another physical object.**   Gravitational mass is a scalar quantity.

Inertial mass: the amount of stuff in a physical object **which resists a force,** and determines the resulting motion.   It is that property of matter which is measured by the response of a physical object to a force.   Inertial mass and gravitational mass are two quite different attributes of matter.   But, the gravitational stuff of a physical object is precisely equal to its inertial stuff, i.e., to the stuff (inertial mass) which appears in Newton's second law, i.e., F=ma: **force** is equal to the **mass** multiplied by the **acceleration.**   Acceleration is the rate at which the speed of a motion changes (increases).   Mass (inertial) is equal to the **force** divided by the **acceleration.**   Inertial mass is a scalar quantity.

Rest mass: the amount of stuff in a physical object **prior to** any increase of mass which a body takes on, according to the theory of relativity, because of an acquired motion, or acceleration thereof.   Rest mass is a scalar quantity.

Relativistic mass: rest mass **plus** any increase of mass which a body takes on, according to the theory of relativity, because of an acquired motion, or acceleration thereof.   Relativistic mass is a scalar quantity.

Energy: the capacity for doing work, e.g., for bringing to rest a body which was in motion, or for putting into motion a body which was at rest, or for changing the direction of the motion of a body, or for accelerating the motion of a body.   Energy is a scalar quantity.

Rest energy : the rest mass of a physical object, converted into energy, and expressed in terms of the electron volt (eV). Rest energy is a scalar quantity.

It is to be noted that "rest energy," "rest mass," and "inertial mass" have the **same referent,** but they are **conceptually different**. Their conceptual differences are clearly expressed in their definitions, above.

Electric charge: a non-gravitational force which arises when two different bodies such as glass and a silk cloth are rubbed against each other, and which is either positive (+) by arbitrary convention, like that on the glass, or negative (-) by arbitrary convention, like that on the silk. Positive charges **repel** one another; negative charges **repel** one another. A positive charge and a negative charge **attract** one another, e.g., the **negatively charged** electrons of atoms and their **positively charged** nuclei **attract** one another, thereby binding them into the physical unit which is the atom. Electric charge is the source of the electromagnetic force, which is infinite in range and is transmitted by photons. Electric charge is a scalar quantity.

Color charge (or, **color force**): a non-gravitational force which arises out of the color of a quark. Just as electric charge is the source of the electromagnetic force, so too color charge, which arises out of quark color, is the source of the strong nuclear force which binds quarks into hadrons, and quarks and antiquarks into mesons. The strong nuclear force has been named the chromodynamic force, from the Greek word **"chroma,"** meaning color. The chromodynamic force is transmitted by particles called gluons (from the word **"glue"**). Whereas the electromagnetic force is infinite in range, the strong nuclear force is limited to the confines of the nucleus of the atom. Color charge is a scalar quantity.

Spin: the rotation of a physical object on its axis, in addition to other motions it might have; e.g., the rotation of the Earth on its axis, causing night and day, in addition to its orbital motion around the Sun. With respect to particles, spin was first found in the electron, later on in other elementary particles. Spin is a fundamental intrinsic property of a particle, along with its electric charge and its mass. In relation to elementary particles, it is more accurate to say that the particle has an intrinsic angular momentum (of a given quantity), called spin, *as if* it were rotating about its axis, rather than really rotating about that axis. Spin is a vector quantity, with an *axis* of rotation, and a *direction* of rotation as well (i.e., either right-handed or left-handed).

Baryon number (or **baryonic charge**): an **intrinsic** property of certain particles (i.e., of baryons and anti-baryons), along with other intrinsic properties like mass, charge, and spin. It explains the **stability of the proton** (i.e., prevents its decay), among other things, e.g., it **prevents** mesons from being the **sole** products of a collision between two protons, and **permits** mesons to be the **sole** products of an interaction between a proton and an anti-proton. All three-quark particles, i.e., baryons, e.g., the proton, the neutron, the lambda, have a baryon number of +1. All anti-baryons, e.g., the anti-proton, the anti-neutron, the anti-lambda, have a baryon number of -1. All particles of other types have a baryon number of 0. Baryon number is a scalar quantity

Force transmitting (messenger) particles:

A **gluon** is a simple body **(genus)**, which transmits the strong nuclear force, has zero mass, zero charge, and a spin of 1 **(specific difference)**.

A **photon** is a simple body **(genus)**, which transmits the electromagnetic force, has zero mass, zero charge, and a spin of 1 **(specific difference)**.

A **W⁺** particle is a simple body **(genus)**, which transmits the weak nuclear force, has a rest mass (expressed as rest energy) of 80 GeV, a charge of +1, and a spin of 1 **(specific difference)**.

A **W⁻** particle is a simple body **(genus)**, which transmits the weak nuclear force, has a rest mass (expressed as rest energy) of 80 GeV, a charge of -1, and a spin of 1 **(specific difference)**.

A **Z⁰** particle is a simple body **(genus)**, which transmits the weak nuclear force, has a rest mass (expressed as rest energy) of 91 GeV, zero charge, and a spin of 1 **(specific difference)**.

"But why," one wants to ask, as Leon Lederman himself does, "**three** [weak force] carriers? Why three messenger particles [for the weak force]...?" (*The God Particle*, p. 325).   Experimental data, Lederman answers, gathered by the 1970s "insisted that the weak force had to be carried by **three** massive messenger particles . . . -- one positively charged [the W⁺], one negatively charged [the W⁻], and one neutral [the Z⁰] -- . . . to propagate the field that induces the changes" (*op. cit.*, p. 325) which result in the decay of unstable hadrons. These changes are "really manifestations of the constituent quarks undergoing [multiple and complex] reactions [with a number of intermediate stages] -- for example, an up quark changing to a down quark or vice versa." (*op. cit.*, p. 325).   It is the multiplicity and complexity of these reactions, with their many intermediate stages, which require **three** different force carriers.

A **graviton** is a simple body **(genus)**, which transmits gravitational force, i.e., the force of gravity, has zero mass, zero charge, and a spin of 2 **(specific difference)**.

The following definitions will be helpful at this point.

Force: in classical physics, force is defined as something capable of affecting the **motion** of a body (stopping its motion, starting it up, speeding it up, slowing it down, changing its direction, and so on), or of **distorting the shape** of a body. In particle physics, force is the cause of every change, reaction, creation and disintegration. For example, when two particles collide, resulting in the creation of new particles, a certain force is responsible. When particles decay into other particles, there is a force which is responsible, and it may be seen as acting between the original particle (even though it no longer exists) and the decay products, after they have begun to exist. Forces are vector quantities.

Gravitational force (the force of gravity): the first force to be identified by physicists. It is the force by which **every** piece of matter, however large or small, in the universe **attracts** **(never repels)** every other piece of matter. Under certain circumstances, gravity can cause black holes. Gravitational force acts on **all** particles; indeed, on **all** pieces of matter, however large or small.

The electromagnetic force: identified by physicists after the force of gravity. It is a combination of the **electrostatic force** and the **magnetic force.** Unlike gravity which is always an attracting force, the electromagnetic force can either **attract** (when one charge is positive and the other is negative) or **repel** (when both are either positive or negative). Electromagnetic force acts on **all charged** particles.

The electrostatic force: the force acting between two **stationary** charges. One of the aspects of the electromagnetic force.

The magnetic force: the force which arises between **moving** charges. Another of the aspects of the electromagnetic force. Since the magnetic force between moving charges has been shown to be a direct consequence of the electrostatic force, it has become customary to speak of a unified electromagnetic force.

The strong nuclear force: the short range **attracting** force between nucleons (i.e, protons and neutrons), which binds together protons and neutrons to form nuclei. It has come to be seen as a kind of residual overflow of another and more fundamental strong force, i.e., the strong force (color charge, or color force; see above p. 264) which binds quarks together within nucleons. The strong nuclear force acts only on **some** particles, i.e., only on hadrons, e.g., protons, neutrons, and pions; and on the quarks (and anti-quarks) which compose them. The strong force does **not** act on **leptons**.

The weak nuclear force: the force, arising from within particles, which causes certain conversions, e.g., the conversion of a neutron into a proton (beta decay), or vice versa, of a pion into a muon, of a muon into an electron. The weak nuclear force and the electromagnetic force combine to become the **electroweak force,** in a way which is much like the way in which the electrostatic force combines with the magnetic force to become the **electromagnetic force.** The weak nuclear force acts on **all** particles.

*　　　　*　　　　*

From the preceding definitions (pp. 260-268), one may be able to understand (if he has been a diligent and attentive reader) how u-quarks and d-quarks combine to form protons and neutrons, how protons and neutrons combine to form the nucleus of an atom, and how electrons combine with the nucleus to form an atom. Nonetheless, these things will become clearer (and more understandable, it is hoped) below, at a more suitable and helpful point, on pp. 281-284, beginning with: "Physicists say that the strong nuclear force is generated by an exchange of gluons . . ."

4. Is there such a thing as a mixing?   Are protons mixings of quarks?

C. J. F. Williams' book on Aristotle's *De Generatione et Corruptione* [20] offers a translation which is very clear, appropriately ascetic yet easy and pleasurable to read, and followed by a copious, hard-thinking and challenging commentary, which he most modestly calls Notes.   His comments on what Aristotle says about **mixis** (**mixtio**, in Aquinas), the topic of Bk. I, ch.10, begin with a reference to Harold H. Joachim's translation:[21]

> The word translated here [i.e., by Williams] as 'mixing' is rendered by Joachim 'combination'. He [i.e., Joachim] thus assimilates the distinction between mixing *(mixis)* and composition *(synthesis)* -- cf. 328 a 6 -- to the modern distinction between chemical combination and mechanical mixture.   The analogy is good in so far as chemical combination is a more intimate union of substances than is mechanical mixture, as mixing is than composition; but the word 'combination' by itself does not have this sense, and the complete phrase 'chemical combination' imports too much modern theory.   Moreover, the modern theory is alien to Aristotle's thinking on the subject; for in chemical combination the atoms of the combining substances remain intact and change only in respect of their relation to each other.   For Aristotle this would be a case of mere 'composition'. Modern chemistry is, after all, atomistic.[22]

Joachim, notes Williams, is in effect likening what Aristotle calls **mixis** to what we nowadays call chemical combination, and what Aristotle calls **synthesis** to what some nowadays call mechanical mixture. This likening is both good and bad, continues Williams. It is good inasmuch as a chemical

---

20   Williams, C. J. F., *Aristotle's De Generatione et Corruptione,* Translated with notes (in the Clarendon Aristotle Series), New York: Oxford University Press, 1982.
21   Joachim, Harold H., translation of *De Generatione et Corruptione* in *The Basic Works of Aristotle,* edited and with an introduction by Richard McKeon, New York: Random House, 1942; pp. 470-531.
22   Williams, *op. cit.,* p. 142.

combination is **a more intimate union** of things than a mere mechanical mixture, just as a **mixis** is a more intimate union than a mere composition (synthesis). In the result of a mere mechanical mixture, the ingredients do not interact with one another so as to cause changes which affect them intrinsically; they are simply moved about so as to be intermingled in the way in which grains of wheat, for example, might be intermingled with, mixed together with, grains of oats or grains of barley, each of the grains surviving as, each continuing to be just, the grain that it was; or in the way in which stones and bricks might be thrown together into a heap, each continuing to be just the stone and just the brick that it was. It is bad inasmuch as the word "combination," used by itself, does not convey the meaning which Aristotle intends by mixis, and the whole phrase "chemical combination" carries with it too much modern scientific theory. Besides, continues Williams, modern scientific theory is alien to Aristotle's way of thinking about mixis. For Aristotle, the combining ingredients in a mixis do **not** remain **intact,** though they do remain **in some way,** since they are retrievable. In chemical combination, urges Williams, the combining ingredients **remain intact,** which seems to mean that they undergo no changes which affect them intrinsically; they "change only in respect of their relation to each other." But Williams does not specify what he has in mind when he notes that they "change only in respect of their relation to each other."

One must note that when hydrogen and oxygen combine chemically, i.e., interact, to form water, the resulting water is neither hydrogen nor oxygen; each molecule of water is just water, and throughout. To be sure, the hydrogen and the oxygen are retrievable, and so they survive in the newly formed water **in some way.** But it is clear that they do not survive intact, i.e., that they undergo some sort of change which affects them intrinsically; that something of them does survive, but that they, as they, intact and intrinsically unchanged, do not.

Similarly, when two u-quarks and one d-quark combine to form a proton, the resulting proton is neither a u-quark nor a d-quark; the proton is a proton throughout. The quarks are retrievable, and so they survive in the newly formed proton **in some way.** But it is also clear that they do not survive intact, i.e., that they undergo some sort of change which affects them intrinsically; that something of them does survive, but that they, as they, intact and intrinsically unchanged, do not.

For Aristotle, states Williams in the end, the case in which the combining ingredients "remain intact and change only in respect of their relation to each other" (by which William seems to mean that the **only** thing which has changed is **where** each ingredient is) would be a case of mere composition, a case in which the ingredients **have been simply juxtaposed, put next to or alongside one another,** and **only** that. Modern chemistry is, after all, atomistic, adds Williams, by way of explanation. Atomistic changes are changes in which each of the combined ingredients undergoes no intrinsic change of any sort, whatever other sorts of changes, locational or other, and however many, each might be said to have undergone. But **mixis,** for Aristotle, continues Williams,

> is what gives rise to homoeomers, and the nature of a homoeomer, as the word itself indicates, is to be such that every smallest part of it is of the same character as every other and as the whole.[23]

But this means, one must be reminded, that a **mixis** is a change in which the ingredients about to be combined **act upon, and are acted upon by,** one another (and by certain required extrinsic agents, as well) in such a way that the result is a thing which is **different in kind** from any of its ingredients. Water is **different in kind** from the oxygen and the hydrogen which have interacted to generate it. Similarly, the proton is **different in kind** from the u-quarks and the d-quark which have interacted to generate it. It may just be,

---

23   Williams, *Aristotle's De Generatione et Corruptione,* p. 142.

one wants to say, that the chemical combination of the mutually interacting hydrogen and oxygen, as they become water, is not atomistic, after all; that the generation of a proton out of mutually interacting quarks is not atomistic either; and that modern scientific theory is just wrong when it "denies that anything occurs which can properly be so described [i.e., as a **mixis**]".[24]

A mixing **(mixis, mixtio)**, as we indicated above (p. 250), results **neither** in something which is like a **heap,** e.g., of bricks and stones, in which its constituents are simply thrown together; **nor** does it result in something which is like a **house,** i.e., something which is not simply thrown together, but carefully put together out of constituents, e.g., wood and bricks and stones, arranged in an orderly way, and held together by certain joining materials, e.g., nails and mortar and glue. It results rather in something, i.e., a mixed body (like a molecule of water, or a proton), which **differs in kind** from any and all of its constituents, and in which the constituents, having undergone a mutual interactive alteration, remain in a special way, i.e., **virtually, though not actually** -- **virtually,** meaning: with their powers, but these powers appropriately altered by means of their preceding interactive alteration (as well as retrievably, dispositionally, and instrumentally); **though not actually,** meaning: not with their substantial forms, because a substance (e.g., a molecule of water, or a proton) can have **actually** but **one** substantial form, **its own**.

The point to be stressed here is this, that a mixed body **differs in kind** from all of its constituents, and so must have a substantial form **of its own** to account for this difference in kind. And this is why the constituents of a mixed body do not survive therein with **their** substantial forms. If they did, then a molecule of water would be water **(actually** water) throughout, and at the same time hydrogen **(actually** hydrogen) in these two parts, and oxygen **(actually** oxygen) in that third part. Similarly, a proton would be a proton **(actually** a proton) throughout, and at the same time a u-quark **(actually** a

---

24   Williams, *ibid.*

u-quark) in these two parts, and a d-quark (**actually** a d-quark) in that third part.

To make it clearer that modern scientific theory may be just wrong when it "denies that anything occurs which can properly be so described [i.e., as a **mixis**]," it will be helpful to consider the following summary of what Aristotle has to say about **mixis** (**mixtio**, in Aquinas) in Bk. I, ch. 10 of his *De Generatione et Corruptione:*

> Deinde ... recapitulat [Philosophus] quae dicta sunt de mixtione ..., dicens manifestum esse ... et quod est mixtio, et quid est, et quare est: quia propter passionem et actionem contrariorum.
>
> Et dictum est etiam quae sunt miscibilia: quando ista [sunt] passiva ad invicem, et bene terminabilia; et talia sunt bene divisibilia.
>
> Dictum est etiam, quod ad hoc quod sit mixtio, necessarium est quod miscibilia non sint simpliciter corrupta, nec sunt simpliciter eadem ut prius. Sunt enim corrupta quantum ad formas, et remanent quantum ad virtutem, ...
>
> Adhuc etiam ostensum est quod mixtio non est compositio minimorum secundum naturam, sicut dicebat una opinio, nec minimorum secundum sensum, ut dicebat alia. Talia enim minima non sunt miscibilia. Sed illud est miscibile, quod cum sit bene determinabile, est activum et passivum; et illud quod admiscetur cum tali miscibili, est miscibile ad homiomerum, idest facit cum alio mixtum quod est ejusdem rationis in toto et in partibus.
>
> Patet etiam quod mixtio est miscibilium alteratorum unio. Quae quidem alteratio solum est intelligenda in virtutibus sive qualitatibus eorum. Sed, si etiam alteratio sumatur improprie, mixtio est miscibilium alteratorum et corruptorum secundum formas unio.[25]

---

[25] *In I De Gen. et Corrupt.*, lect. 25, in fine. This summary is not the work of St. Thomas Aquinas, whose commentary on Aristotle's *De Gen. et Corrupt.* is unfinished, terminating with Bk. I, lect. 17. The rest was written by Thomas Sutton and others (see above, p. 172, footnote 11).

Then . . . he [Aristotle, the Philosopher] recapitulates what he had said about mixing, noting that it is clear . . . that there *is* such a thing as mixing, and *what* mixing is, and *why* mixing takes place, namely because of the passivity and activity of contraries.

He had also pointed out what sorts of things are mixables, namely things that can be acted upon by one another, and can be easily bounded, and such things are things which can be easily divided.

He had also said that for mixing to take place, it is necessary that the mixables be neither simply corrupted, nor remain simply the same as before. For they are corrupted with respect to forms, and remain with respect to power, . . .

He had also pointed out . . . that mixing is not [just] a composition of particles of the smallest sort according to nature, as one opinion had it; nor of particles of the smallest sort according to sense, as the other had it. For it is not the smallness of the particles that makes them mixables. Rather, only that is a mixable which can be easily bounded, is both active and passive, and when reacting with another mixable produces something homoeomerous, i.e., a mixed body which is of the same nature in its totality as it is in each of its parts.

Lastly, it is clear that a mixing is a uniting of altered mixables; this alteration being understood as an alteration in their powers or qualities only. But, if alteration be taken in an improper sense, a mixing is a uniting of mixables, altered and corrupted with respect to forms.

Is there such a thing as a mixing? This question raises a prior one, namely, what exactly does the word "mixing" mean? As indicated just above, the word "mixing" means: a uniting of altered mixables. Now, mixables, notes Aristotle and the author of the just-above quoted summary as well, are things which can be easily bounded, such things being things which can be easily divided, or parted. Liquid-like things (a not uncommon example of the ancients and medievals), say, water at room temperature, and air-like things, say, water in the form of steam, can be easily divided, or parted. But easy divisibility, partibility, is not enough. Mixable things must also be capable of acting upon, and being acted upon by, one another, and in such a way that they alter one another without totally corrupting one another: " . . . it is necessary that the mixables be neither simply corrupted, nor remain simply the same as before . . ." That is, the mixed body which is generated from their interaction must be such that the interagent mixables survive in it (i.e., in the mixed body) **in some way**. The mixables are **there**, i.e., in the mixed body, in a way, and **not there,** in a way: **there** with their powers (". . . [they] remain with respect to power . . ."), appropriately altered of course, and these powers function as instruments of the form of the mixed body, and thus also as ingredients without which the mixed body could not exist; **not there** with their substantial forms (". . . they are corrupted with respect to forms . . ."),** since the mixed body exists as a thing **different in kind** from any of its ingredient mixables. The mixed body is **through and through** of a given kind, and this kind is not the kind of any of its ingredients.

Now a proton, being a **mixed body,** could not exist and perform as a proton does, without its constituent **elements,** i.e., its three constituent quarks, two u-quarks and one d-quark. But a proton is not a quark, neither as a totality nor in any of its parts; not a u-quark in these two parts of itself, nor a d-quark in that third part of itself. A proton is a proton through and through. This means that the quarks which have interacted, and, having interacted, have survived in the newly generated proton, have not survived with their substantial forms, though they **have** survived, though they are there in some way. They have been corrupted with respect to **what they actually are,** as determined by their substantial forms. But they have not been corrupted with respect to **what they can actually do,** i.e., with respect to their powers. Their powers, appropriately altered by the preceding proton-generating interaction[26] among the required quarks, have been preserved, by the substantial form of the newly generated proton, in order to function as instruments through which the newly generated proton does what protons do. The quarks are there, in the sense that the proton has certain quark-enabled powers. But the quarks themselves, as things with their own substantial forms, are not there. What is there now is a proton, **different in kind** from any of the quarks which are said to have survived as its constituents.

Aristotle, and the author of the above summary as well, speak of **easy** divisibility. How is this to be understood? An element, unlike a mixed body, cannot be divided, or resolved, by a required alteration of an appropriate sort (as opposed to being divided by a simple act of cutting, as with a saw)[27] into **bodies** which are more simple than the element itself. There are no such more simple bodies. Only prime matter and substantial form are more simple than an element, and neither one nor the other is a body. When the ancients and the medievals spoke of the **easy divisibility** of an element, say of water, they were speaking of what one might describe today as a "sea of free particles of water," i.e., a **quantity** of water in its liquid state (**not** a single molecule of H_2O), as opposed to water in its frozen state, patterning this description after the way in which people today often speak of the "sea of free quarks" which (quarks) , they say, whizzed about just after the Big Bang. One can think of these free quarks as slipping by and around, over and under, to the left of and to the right of, one another, much as molecules of water do in a churning river. And just as a sea of particles of water, the ancients and the medievals would say, could be mixed, **and with ease,** with a sea of particles of

---

[26] Can this preceding proton-generating interaction be said to be, or at least include in some way, the exchange of gluons which generates the strong nuclear force? And is this exchange of gluons a **continuing** interaction within the proton, required to account for the **continued** existence of the proton? Is this what Lederman has in mind when he talks about "how quarks whirl about each other in their proton prison"? (Lederman, *The God Particle*, p. 209). That is, is this "whirling about each other" connected in some way with the quark to quark exchange of gluons?

[27] See above, pp. 53-54, on how an element's **indivisibility according to species** is to be understood.

air, or a sea of air with a sea of fire, because each of these seas is very easily partible or divisible, thus enabling these particles, in contact with one another, to interact by means of their distinctive powers or qualities, i.e., hot, cold, wet, dry, in order to produce mixed bodies of various sorts; so too a sea of free u-quarks, we today might say, can be mixed, **and with ease,** with a sea of free d-quarks, or s-quarks, or free quarks of any other flavor, because each of these seas is very easily partible or divisible, **if they are in heat as intense as it was just after the Big Bang** -- but now in the relative cold of 15 billion years later, only with the greatest difficulty -- thus enabling them (the quarks), in contact with appropriate others, to interact with one another by means of their distinctive powers or qualities, e.g., mass, charge, spin, baryon number, strangeness, **both** in order to be transformed into one another, **and** in order to produce mixed bodies of various kinds, e.g., protons and neutrons.[28] Easy divisibility yields easy mixability, as a kind of contactual prelude to the mixing which comes about by way of appropriate alteration, and which results in the generation of a mixed body. "Mixable," thus, has two senses in this context: 1) mixable, because easily partible or divisible, in the sense in which a sea of free quarks of one flavor is mixable with a sea of free quarks of another flavor, and 2) mixable, as in the definition of mixing, i.e., a uniting of altered mixables. The first sense applies to a **sea** of particles, and **prior to** the alteration which results in a mixed body(-ies). The second sense applies to **single** particles, e.g., to single u-quarks or d-quarks, and **posterior to** this alteration

Moreover, it is not the smallness of mixable particles (in both senses of "mixable") that makes them mixable things, though the ultimate mixables are of the smallest possible sort, and of this sort **in themselves** (i.e., ". . . **according to nature** . . ."), as opposed to being particles of the smallest possible sort **in relation to our sensory perception of them** (i.e., ". . .

---

28   There is a quark to quark exchange of gluons in the production of protons and neutrons, inasmuch as it is this exchange of gluons which generates the strong nuclear force, which binds the quarks to one another.   What, if anything (if this is an appropriate question), is exchanged in the transformation of one sort of quark into another sort?

according to sense . . ."). Indeed, it is often said today that quarks and leptons have no dimensions at all, that they are absolutely point-like. Which is very difficult, very difficult indeed, to understand and accept; and perhaps even untrue. Rather, what makes mixable particles mixable things is 1) their easy partibility or divisibility as ingredients of a sea, and 2) their having mutually interactive powers or qualities by which they can generate (by way of exchanging the appropriate force-carrying particles, whether gluons, or photons, or the weak-force-carrying particles of the W^+ and W^- and Z^0 family, or gravitons?) something homoeomerous, i.e., a mixed body, like a proton, which is of the same nature in its totality as it is in each of its parts.

As a last point in commenting on the summary, the recapitulation, which appears above (pp. 273-274), it should be noted that **alteration** belongs **properly** to **qualities or powers, corruption** to **things (substances).** When a mixing occurs, i.e., when a mixed body comes into existence out of the required pre-existing mixables, the powers or qualities of the mixables are **altered,** being brought thereby to an appropriate mean or middle (or, if to speak of "an appropriate **mean or middle**" turns out to be unacceptable, for some convincing reason, one could perhaps speak of "an appropriate **state**") -- appropriate to the mixed body about to come to be; but the mixables themselves, as things or substances with their own substantial forms, are corrupted. They, as they, do not survive. What survives is their altered, and thereby brought to an appropriate mean or **state,** powers or qualities.

Returning now to the question asked above, at the top of p. 269: Is there such a thing as a mixing?, one must note that the answer is: **Yes.** But accepting this answer depends on the prior acceptance of substantial change **as a fact,** and in particular on the prior acceptance that there are things (substances) which **differ in kind** from the previously existing elements which survive in them as their constituents. And so, if there are **such** substances, there must be mixings.

Now, will the physicist deny that protons **differ in kind** from the quarks which survive in them as their constituents?   A substance can have **actually** only **one** substantial form, **its own**.   And so, if protons differ in kind from the surviving quarks which are their components, the quarks cannot survive with their own substantial forms.   They do, nonetheless, survive with their powers, altered (by means of an exchange of gluons?), of course, to a proton-appropriate mean or state;   otherwise a proton could neither be, nor behave as, a proton.   The generation of a proton comes about, therefore, by way of a mixing.   The conclusion follows, therefore, that since there are protons which come to be out of quarks, there must be mixings.

Someone might say that a proton is certainly **not** like a **heap of things,** e.g., of bricks and stones, in which the bricks and stones which are its constituents are simply thrown together;   but that it **is** just as certainly like a **house,** i.e., not just thrown together, but carefully put together out of constituents, e.g., wood and bricks and stones, which are arranged in an orderly way, and which are held together by certain joining materials, e.g., nails and mortar and carpenter's glue.   For, isn't a proton carefully put together out of two u-quarks (one green, the other blue), and one d-quark (red) -- green, blue and red being needed to get something white or colorless[29] -- arranged in an orderly way, and held together by the strong

---

29   Lederman, *The God Particle,* p. 335.   " [The color of a quark] has nothing to do with color as you and I recognize it.   Color explains certain experimental results and predicts others.   For example, it explained how a proton could have two up quarks and a down quark, when the Pauli principle specifically excluded two identical objects in the same state.   If one of the up quarks is blue and the other is green, we satisfy Pauli's rule.   Color gives the strong force the equivalent of electric charge.

"Color must come in *three* types, said Gell-Mann and others who had worked in this garden.   Remember that Faraday and Ben Franklin had determined that electric charge came in two styles, designated plus and minus.   Quarks need three.   So now all quarks come in three colors.   Perhaps the color idea was stolen from the palette because there are three primary colors.   A better analogy might be that electric charge is one-dimensional, with plus and minus directions, and color is three-dimensional (three axes: red, blue, and green).

nuclear force, i.e., the quark-quark force carried by the appropriate gluons?[30]

How, one might ask, is the joining or binding function of the gluons within a proton **different, if it is, from** that of the nails and the mortar and the carpenter's glue in a house?   Is the whole or totality which is a proton different, in some significant way, from the whole or totality which is a house?   Do quarks exist as quarks **before** they enter the constitution of the proton which is generated out of their conjunction, in the way in which wood and bricks and stones exist as wood and bricks and stones **before** they enter the make-up of the house which comes to be out of their conjunction?   And if they do, what accounts for this prior existence?   And what about gluons?   Do they have a **pre-**proton existence?   Or do they come into existence with the proton itself, emerging somehow out of the combining interaction of the quarks (and of other necessary agents, if there are any others) which ushers the proton into existence?

Color explained why quark combinations are, uniquely, either quark plus anti-quark, (mesons) or three quarks (baryons).   These combinations show no color; the quarkness vanishes when we stare at a meson or a baryon.   A red quark combines with an antired antiquark to produce a colorless meson.   The red and antired cancel.   Likewise, the red, blue, and green quarks in a proton mix to make white (try this by spinning a color wheel). Again colorless.

"Even though these are nice reasons for using the word 'color,' it has no literal meaning. We are describing another abstract property that the theorists gave to quarks to account for the increasing amount of data." (Lederman, *ibid.,* pp. 334-335).

"And what about the messenger particles? How do we describe the color-force-carrying particles?   What emerged was that gluons carry *two* colors -- a color and another anticolor -- and, in their emission or absorption by quarks, they exchange the quark color. For example, a red-antiblue gluon changes a red quark to an antiblue quark.   This exchange is the origin of the strong force, and Murray [i.e., Murray Gell-Mann] the Great Namer dubbed the theory quantum chromodynamnics (QCD) in resonance with quantum electrodynamics (QED). The color-changing task means that we need enough gluons to make all possible changes. It turns out that eight gluons will do it. If you ask a theorist, 'Why eight ?' he'll wisely say, 'Why, eight is nine minus one.' " (Lederman, *ibid.,* pp. 335-336).

[30]   ". . . we define it [i.e., the strong nuclear force] as the quark-quark force carried by gluons.   But what about the 'old' strong force between neutrons and protons?   We now understand this as the residual effects of the gluons, sort of leaking out of the neutrons and protons that bind together in the nucleus.   The old strong force that is well described by exchange of pions is now seen as a consequence of the complexities of quark-gluon processes." (Lederman, *ibid.,* p. 338).

Physicists say that the strong nuclear force is generated by an exchange of gluons among quarks. This seems to imply that the gluons derive somehow from the quarks themselves; that the quarks are **interacting** with one another, and in some way **altering** one another, by transmitting these gluons to one another, or in some way drawing them out of one another (or both) -- in order to absorb them, and then to re-exchange them, in a continuing and repetitive process. Can this be taken as a sophisticated 20th century scientific account of what Aristotle and the medievals called a **mixtio** -- i.e., a **miscibilum alteratorum unio?** -- Moreover, when it is said that the electromagnetic force is generated by an exchange of photons between the electrons of an atom, on the one hand, and the nucleus of the atom, on the other, is it being said that the photons derive somehow from within the electrons and the nucleus themselves? That the electrons and the nucleus are **interacting** with one another, and in some way **altering** one another, by transmitting these photons to one another, or in some way drawing them out of one another (or both) -- in order to absorb them, and then to re-exchange them, in a continuing and repetitive process? And can this be, again, a sophisticated and detailed 20th century account of the inner workings of a **mixtio?** -- When it is said that the weak force is generated by an exchange of the W^+ and W^- and Z^0 particles, is it being said that these bosons derive somehow from the particles between (among) which they are being exchanged, that these latter particles are **interacting** with one another, and in some way **altering** one another, by transmitting these bosons to one another, or in some way extracting them out of one another (or both) -- in order to absorb them, and then to re-exchange them, in a continuing and repetitive process? And can this be, again, a detailed 20th century account of the viscera of a **mixtio?** -- When it is said that the force of gravity is generated by an exchange of gravitons, is it being said that these gravitons derive somehow from within the bodies themselves between (among) which they are being exchanged, that these bodies are **interacting** with one another, and in some way **altering** one another, by transmitting these gravitons to one another, or in some way extracting them out of one another (or both) -- in order to absorb them, and then to re-exchange them, in a continuing and repetitive process?   To be sure, the exchange among gravitons cannot be seen as a 20th century account of the inner workings of a **mixtio.**   Unlike what happens in the exchange of gluons, and of photons, and of the weak-force-carrying bosons, i.e., the generation of a mixed body(-ies); there is no mixed body which results from an exchange of gravitons.   The result here is, rather, simply bringing the bodies spatially closer together.   And this is significant, for it can be seen as a result which is necessary to enable the other three forces to do their work.

A thought experiment may be of some help to make this last comment understandable.   Imagine a universe in which there are **only** the following elementary particles: two u-quarks, one d-quark, and one electron -- and nothing else.   Imagine further that these particles are motionless.   That they are very far apart from one another, at the outer edge of a universe as large as a grapefruit (if a grapefruit is too large, let it be as large as a mustard seed), on the circumference of that mustard seed, and in a same plane (to make this consideration more simple).   That they are located at points on that circumference which (points) divide that circumference into four more or less equal parts.   Can it be said that there will be first of all an exchange of gravitons to bring these particles closer and closer together?   And then, when appropriately close together, that there will be an exchange of gluons among the quarks to generate a proton, followed by an exchange of photons between the proton and the electron to form a hydrogen atom?   And then, when the right time comes, that there will be an exchange of whatever weak bosons are there to be exchanged, so as to cause the proton to decay (if this be possible)?   And that this decay will somehow send the original four particles back out to the outer edge of our mustard-seed universe, where gravitons will again begin their exchanging work,   which will enable the gluons to do their exchanging work, which will in turn enable the photons to do their exchanging work, thereby generating again a hydrogen atom, which will again decay, and so on **ad infinitum cyclicum.**   --   Gravity, thus, would bring the elementary particles close enough together to enable the strong force, the electromagnetic force, and the weak force to do their respective jobs. And the weak force would initiate the decay (could this, too, be **some sort** of "small" Big Bang? -- see above, p. 166, and p. 253, footnote 8) which would send the particles out to the outer edges, where gravity would again take over. If this could be the case, then it seems that all force-carrying particles derive somehow out of the mass of physical things, and that mass therefore would be the originating source of all physical forces.

From the preceding, it is quite clear that the binding function of the gluons within a proton is radically different from that of nails and mortar and carpenter's glue in a house.   For the gluons **emerge out of the nature of the quarks themselves** which compose the proton, whereas nails and mortar and carpenter's glue do **not** emerge out of the nature of the composing wood and bricks and stones.   Quarks are such **by their nature** that they emit gluons to, and extract them from, other quarks, thereby generating protons (and neutrons; as well as mesons of various sorts in conjunction with the appropriate antiquarks).   Protons and neutrons, in turn, along with electrons, are such **by their nature** that they emit photons to, and extract them from, one another so as to form atoms, which in turn are such **by their nature** that they emit the appropriate force carrying particles to, and extract them from, other atoms to form molecules; and so on, to higher and more complex types of physical bodies, up to and including man, the most complex.   What is important here is that these particles are such **by their nature.**   And this is exactly what Aquinas has in mind when he points out that the **elements** (in his day, earth and water and air and fire) were given (by God) at the very beginning, i.e., when they were first brought into being at creation, **a nature, both active and material, such** that **all terrestrial** physical things could be derived from them **as from their primary material constituents.**[31]   The

---

[31]   See above, p. 217, the paragraph beginning with the words: "What is **most particularly** interesting and instructive about the response of Aquinas . . ."

quarks and the leptons of today's physics were given at the very beginning, i.e., when they first came into being out of the fires of the Big Bang, **a nature, both active and material, such** that **all physical** things, **celestial** as well as terrestrial, could be derived from them **as from their primary material constituents.**

5. Particle physics and prime matter

The neutrino

A neutrino is, in a way, like prime matter. Whereas prime matter has **no** properties (**no** forms) at all, a neutrino has **very few** of them. The neutrino is just a convenient example; many of the particles of today's physics are **almost** property-**less.**

Reflecting on the agonies of the status of the Standard Model in 1993, one of which (agonies) is **not knowing** whether neutrinos have any rest mass, Lederman looks at one of the neutrinos, i.e., the electron neutrino, "the garden-variety, first generation neutrino -- since it has the lowest mass. (Unless, of course, all neutrino masses are zero)."[32] The electron neutrino, Lederman points out, has **no** electric charge, **no** strong force, **no** electromagnetic force, **no** size (**no** spatial extent, zero radius), and it **may not** have a mass. "Nothing has so few properties . . . as the neutrino. Its presence is less than a whisper."[33] But the neutrino, continues Lederman, **does have** "a sort of location -- a trajectory, always heading in one direction with a velocity close (or equal) to that of light [depending on whether or not

---

32   Lederman, *The God Particle*, p. 343.
33   Lederman, *op. cit.*, p. 344.

it has a rest mass]."[34]   It has spin, too; and this spin is always left-handed.[35] "This handedness [i.e., chirality] is one of the few properties the poor little fellow has."[36]   The word "chirality," or handedness, derives from the Greek word, *chiros*, which means **hand**.   "The neutrino is said to have left handedness or [left] chirality, while the anti-neutrino has a right handedness [or right chirality]."[37]   The neutrino, lastly, has the weak force.[38]

A neutrino, some philosophers might want to say, is as close to prime matter as one can get; and if not that, very close indeed.   That "whisper" of a particle, as Lederman fondly calls it, with almost no properties to its name, quite naturally brings to mind Aquinas' comment (following Aristotle) that prime matter of itself, considered as such, is neither a substance, nor a quantity, nor a quality, nor anything else which is found in any of the ten categories:

> [Dicit Aristoteles] materiam esse "quae secundum se," idest secundum sui essentiam considerata, nullatenus est "neque quid," idest substantia, "neque qualitas, neque aliquid aliorum generum, quibus ens dividitur, vel deteminatur." (*In VII Metaph.,*   lect. 2, n. 1285).

> [Aristotle says that] matter is that "which according to itself," i.e., considered in its essence, is in no way a "thing with a what [or essence]," i.e., a substance, "nor is it a quality, or anything else of the other genera by which being is divided, or determined."

Prime matter, the ultimate matter, the ultimate subject, the matter prior to which there is no matter --   this matter is such in itself that it is not only absolutely matterless, but absolutely formless as well; such in itself that

---

34   Lederman, *ibid.*
35   Lederman, *op. cit.,* p. 345.
36   Lederman, *ibid.*
37   Ne'eman, Yuval and Kirsh, Yoram, *The   Particle   Hunters*   (second edition), Cambridge, England: Cambridge University Press, 1996; p. 175.
38   Lederman, *The God Particle,*   p. 345.

no forms at all are intrinsic ingredients of its nature, neither substantial forms nor accidental forms. It is such by its nature that it **can acquire** all these forms (in a certain order, of course, beginning with substantial forms, moving on to accidental forms); it is **pure potentiality** for all these forms. Of itself, it is absolutely without any properties at all.

The rishon

The rishon model proposed by Haim Harari (which is a model attempting to go beyond the Standard Model, in which quarks and leptons are taken to be really elementary) has it that "both quarks and leptons [have an inner structure, i.e., that they] are constructed of . . . two types of 'ultimate' particles which Harari called rishons. (*Rishon* in Hebrew means first or primary.) The two rishons are designated T and V for *Tohu* and *Vohu*. (These mean 'formless' and 'void' [like prime matter, one wants to note] in Hebrew. This is the description of the universe in its initial state, according to the first chapter of Genesis.)"[39] The only property which the rishons seem to have is electric charge; at any rate, this is the only property which Ne'eman and Kirsh mention in their brief account of the rishon model.[40] The T rishon has an electric charge of +1/3, and the V rishon is neutral. But there are also anti-rishons, the anti-T rishon with a charge of -1/3, and the anti-V rishon with a charge of 0. Quarks and leptons come to be out of certain combinations of T and V and anti-T and anti-V.[41]

---

[39] Ne'eman and Kirsh, *The Particle Hunters*, pp. 276-277.
[40] Ne'eman and Kirsh, *ibid.*
[41] "In Harari's model any three rishons and any three anti-rishons may be combined together, but rishons and anti-rishons do not intermingle. This rule allows 8 combinations which correspond to the 8 quarks and leptons of the first generation and their anti-particles." (Ne'eman and Kirsh, *op. cit.,* p. 277). Three T rishons combine to generate a positron, and three anti-T rishons combine to form an electron. Three V rishons constitute the neutrino, and three anti-V rishons the anti-neutrino. Other allowed combinations yield fractionally charged quarks, e.g., two T's and one V make up the u-quark, one anti-T and two anti-V's make up the d-quark. (Ne'eman and Kirsh, *ibid.*)

So far, however, although Harari's model accounts nicely for **certain** properties of quarks and leptons, it **has failed** to account for **all** of their properties; and a good model, of course, ought to account for all of them. Nonetheless, it is interesting to notice that as particle physics makes its way toward particles which are hoped to be **the truly elementary** particles, i.e., such that there are no prior particles out of which they themselves are structured, the particles have fewer and fewer properties, they are seen to be more and more like prime matter -- i.e., like matter which is both matterless and formless, "formless" meaning without properties. And this brings to mind what Aquinas points out in a context in which he is grading forms from the highest to the lowest. Just as there are forms, he notes, **above** the human soul, so too there are forms **below** it. And just as forms **above** it have more actuality than the human soul, and are thus further removed from the potentiality of matter, so too the forms **below** it have more potentiality than the human soul, and thus come closer and closer to the potentiality of matter. The grading here is from the sensitive, through the vegetative and the non-living mixed bodies, down to the forms of the elements, whose operations or activities are simply those which are required for preparing matter for its tranformations from element to other element, and for the eduction of the forms of mixed bodies, i.e., of things composd out of the elements. Aquinas writes:

> . . . post istam formam, quae est anima [humana], inveniuntur aliae formae plus de potentia habentes et magis propinquae materiae, intantum quod esse earum sine materia non est. In quibus etiam invenitur ordo et gradus usque ad primas formas elementorum, quae sunt propinquissimae materiae; unde nec aliquam operationem habent, nisi secundum exigentiam qualitatum activarum et passivarum, et aliorum quibus materia ad formam disponitur. (*De Ente et Essentia*, cap. 5, n. 87).

> . . . posterior to this form which is the [human] soul are found other forms which have more potency, and which are still closer to matter, so close that they do not exist without matter. Among these forms, too, is found an order and a grading, down to the first forms, the forms of the elements, which are the closest to

matter, so close indeed that they have no activities other than those which arise out of their active and passive qualities, and others, by which matter is made ready, or disposed, for form.

6. Eddington's two tables

I have settled down to the task of writing these lectures and have drawn up my chairs to my two tables. Two tables! Yes; there are duplicates of every object about me -- two tables, two chairs, two pens . . .

One of them [i.e., of my two tables] has been familiar to me from earliest years. It is a commonplace object of that environment which I call the world. How shall I describe it? It has extension; it is comparatively permanent; it is colored; above all it is *substantial*. By substantial I do not merely mean that it does not collapse when I lean up on it; I mean that it is constituted of "substance," and by that word I am trying to convey to you some conception of its intrinsic nature. It is a *thing*; not like space, which is a mere negation;[42] nor like time, which is -- Heaven knows what! But that will not help you to my meaning because it is the distinctive characteristic of a "thing" to have this substantiality, and I do not think substantiality can be described better than by saying that it is the kind of nature exemplified[43] by an ordinary table. . .

Table no. 2 is my scientific table. It is a more recent acquaintance and I do not feel so familiar with it. It does not belong to the world previously mentioned -- that world which spontaneously appears around me when I open my eyes, though how much of it is objective and how much subjective I do not

---

[42]   Space is **not a mere** negation. Democritus' understanding of space (the void) as a real, three-dimensional, empty, penetrable receptacle, in which things or substances (the atoms) can move about, is more plausible. On Democritus' view, to call space a **negation** would be to point only to its intrinsic **emptiness**.

[43]   When a **description,** or **definition,** of **what a thing is** is not forthcoming (for whatever reason), it is always helpful, in a way even necessary, to turn to **examples.**

here consider. It is part of a world which in more devious ways has forced itself on my attention. My scientific table is mostly emptiness. Sparsely scattered in that emptiness are numerous electric charges rushing about with great speed; but their combined bulk amounts to less than a billionth of the bulk of the table itself. Notwithstanding its strange construction it turns out to be an entirely efficient table. It supports my writing paper as satisfactorily as table no. 1; for when I lay the paper on it the little electric particles with their headlong speed keep on hitting the underside, so that the paper is maintained in shuttlecock fashion at a nearly steady level. If I lean upon this table I shall not go through; or, to be strictly accurate, the chance of my scientific elbow going through my scientific table is so excessively small that it can be neglected in practical life. . .

There is nothing *substantial* about my second table. It is nearly all empty space -- space pervaded, it is true, by fields of force, but these are assigned to the category of "influences," not of "things." Even in the minute part which is not empty we must not transfer the old notion of substance . . .   . . . our scientific information is summed up in measures . . . [of] an external world; but the attributes of this world, except insofar as they are reflected in the measures, are outside scientific scrutiny . . .[44]

The commonplace table can be described, notes Eddington, as having extension, as being comparatively permanent, as being colored, etc., but above all, as being **substantial.** But he experiences some difficulty in explaining what he means by the word "substantial." He means, he says, not only that the table does not collapse when he leans on it, but that it is a **thing,** as opposed to space which, he observes, is a kind of **no**-thing, or **nothing,** i.e., a "mere negation," as he puts it. Nor is the table like time, which is -- and here he falters, not knowing what to say about time. He means, perhaps, that time is not something permanent (he had said that the table is comparatively permanent), i.e., time is moving from the past, into the present, then into the future; or the other way around, the future of time slips somehow into the

[44]   Eddington, Sir Arthur S., *The Nature of the Physical World* (The Gifford Lectures, 1927), Cambridge, England: Cambridge University Press, 1929; Introduction, pp. ix-xi.

present, which in turn slips somehow into the past. Perhaps, also, that the table is there altogether, with all its parts, all at once; whereas time is not.

The scientific table, by way of contrast, observes Eddington, is **mostly emptiness**. And throughout this emptiness there are numerous, but sparsely scattered, electric charges, rushing about with incredibly great speed. This table supports his writing paper as satisfactorily as the commonplace table, for the little electric charges with their great speed keep hitting the bottom side of the paper, and by their shuttlecock action keep the paper at a relatively steady level. When he leans his **scientific elbow** on his **scientific table,** there is hardly a chance that it will go through. For ordinary purposes, both tables seem to be on a par. But there is **nothing substantial** about the scientific table. It is **not a thing**. It is mostly a no-thing, mostly a negation, mostly empty space; but an "empty" space which is also "full" -- full of force fields. It is empty in one way, full in another. These fields, like the scientific table, however, are not things either; they are **influences.** Better still, he notes, they are just numbers resulting from measurements. Whereas the commonplace table is substantial, i.e., solid or full, and impenetrable, ". . . it being the intrinsic nature of substance to occupy space to the exclusion of other substances . . . ;" the scientific table is not, except perhaps, but only questionably, in the thinly scattered tiny specks which are its intrinsic electric particles. Whereas the commonplace table is a substance throughout, the scientific table is a substance only here and there, if at all.

How, now, are these two tables connected? Or, more generally, how are the commonplace and the scientific worlds connected? They may well be "one and the same world," observes Eddington, though differently described, differently interpreted.[45] "It is true," writes Eddington, "that the whole scientific inquiry starts from the familiar world and in the end it must return to the familiar world; but the part of the journey over which the physicist has

---

45   Eddington, *ibid.*, p. xii.

charge is in foreign territory."[46]   Foreign territory? What does Eddington mean by "foreign territory"? As though to answer this question, Eddington adds that "there is a familiar table parallel to the scientific table, but there is no familiar electron . . . parallel to the scientific electron . . ."   And there is no desire or attempt to find a familiar counterpart to the scientific electron, which could be used to **explain**[47] that scientific electron.   For it is the scientific which explains the commonplace, and not the other way around. The electron -- along with force fields, and other scientific measures --   is the unfamiliar foreigner in the land of the scientific table which is used to explain substantiality -- and other familiar properties -- in the land of the commonplace table.   Scientific inquiry "starts from the familiar world," moves into a foreign world in quest of an explanation, then returns "to the familiar world" to explain that world.

But what sort of explanation is this? It is an explanation of a most interesting sort, indeed. Explanations, one must note, identify causes.   But these causes -- electrons, force fields, quanta, and the like --   are only a different way of describing "one and the same world," one and same table. The commonplace world, with its tables and chairs and papers and pens, is the "world which spontaneously appears around me **when I open my eyes**."[48] It is the world given to me in my ordinary sensory perceptions.   The scientific world is that same world, but at a different level. It is not given to me in my ordinary sense perceptions; it does not appear around me spontaneously "when I open my eyes."   It is, in a way, invented by me; but also, in a way, discovered by me.   Today's physics assures me that "my scientific table is the only one which is **really** there . . .;"[49] and that it **explains** my commonplace table. Its electrons, force fields, etc., explain why it is that my commonplace table is said by me, on the basis of my open eyes and ears and

---

46   Eddington, *ibid.,* p. xiii.
47   "We do not even desire to manufacture a familiar counterpart to these things [i.e., electrons, quanta, potentials, Hamiltonian functions, etc.] or, as we should commonly say, to "explain" the electron." (Eddington, *ibid.,* p. xiii).
48   Eddington, *ibid.,* p. x.
49   Eddington, *ibid.,* p. xii.

the touch of my fingers, to be a thing (a substance), to have extension, to be impenetrable, to be comparatively permanent, to be colored, etc. The unfamiliar (the uncommon, the unperceived by ordinary means) is that **deep within** the familiar (the common, the perceived by ordinary means) which explains why the familiar is the sort of thing that it is. Although it is the unfamiliar which **causes** the familiar, the unfamiliar is at the same time the same as the familiar, though only in a way, i.e., at a different level. This table is at once commonplace and scientific; has at once scientific features and commonplace features; and the scientifc features **cause, and thereby explain,** the commonplace ones. The table is at once, and most interestingly, this collection of effects (commonplace) **produced by** that collection of causes (scientific), and that collection of causes (scientific) **producing** this collection of effects (commonplace).

*   *   *

Can one say, now -- moving beyond Eddington (1928) to the present day (1997) -- that this commonplace table is this extended, somewhat permanent, colored, etc., thing (or substance) -- **as caused by** that scientific collection of u-quarks, d-quarks, neutrons and electrons which reside deep within itself? And that it (i.e., this commonplace table) is also that scientific collection of u-quarks, d-quarks, neutrons and electrons -- but **as causing,** from deep within itself, the extended, somewhat permanent, colored, etc., thing (or substance) which it is? Or, perhaps better, that this commonplace table is **nothing but,** i.e., **identical with,** these scientific u-quarks, d-quarks, neutrons and electrons arranged and interacting in a given way -- though differently described, i.e., either **as a cause** (the scientific) producing an effect or **as an effect** (the commonplace) being produced by a cause.

Can one say, further -- moving back into the past of the medievals, in particular to that of Aquinas -- that the commonplace table (as a **mixed body**)

292

is just what it is because of the special sort of material and agent causality being exercised by its ingredient **mixables**?, i.e., by its component quarks, protons, neutrons, electrons, atoms, molecules; which are **not only** material causes of a special sort, i.e., capable of **agent** causality (because of certain surviving **active** potentialities or powers, as different from prime matter which is a **purely passive or receptive** potentiality), **but also** agent causes of a special sort, i.e., **conjoined intrumental** agent causes (see above, section 2, **A quark, like any element, is an agent cause of a special sort, besides being a material cause of a special sort,** pp. 250-252).

Can one say, further still -- again moving back to Aquinas -- that to speak of the commonplace characteristics of things **as caused by** the scientific components within them is to speak in some way -- though without intending it and without being very clear or explicit or complete -- about why substantial forms other than the human soul **are educed from the potentiality of matter,** rather than being created, or generated, or brought out of some sort of hidden actuality? These substantial forms (i.e., all forms with the exception of the human soul) can be so educed, i.e., brought into existence **without** need of a direct and special creative act of God (since this eduction is **within** the causal capacities, both receptive and agent, of things in the physical world) by a conjunction of the following: prime matter, properly disposed by an appropriate substantial form and by an appropriate mix of scientific components, like quarks, protons, neutrons, electrons, atoms, molecules, along with physical agent causes of certain appropriate sorts. The same scientific components which **actively** cause, and **passively** retain (within the **mixed bodies** which arise out of their conjunction), the commonplace features of our ordinary sense-perceivable world, provide the complex of **disposing receptive** ingredients required for the eduction of their educible physical forms. Their role, thus, in such eductions, is that of a set of virtual, dispositional, retrievable, and instrumentally agent material ingredients (see above, section 11, **The elements and the eduction of substantial forms from the potency of matter,** pp. 228-241).

7.   Searle on micro-properties and macro-properties

What Sir Arthur Eddington said (in 1928) in terms of his two tables has been said more recently (1984), and perhaps more clearly and instructively, by John R. Searle, in terms of micro-properties and macro-properties:

> A common distinction in physics [today] is between micro- and macro-properties of systems -- the small and large scales. Consider, for example, the desk at which I am now sitting, or the glass of water in front of me. Each object is composed of micro-particles. The micro-particles have features at the level of molecules and atoms as well as the deeper level of subatomic particles. But each object also has certain properties such as the solidity of the table, the liquidity of the water, and the transparency of the glass, which are surface or global features of the physical systems. Many such features or global properties can be causally explained by the behaviour of elements at the micro-level. For example, the solidity of the table in front of me is explained by the lattice structure occupied by the molecules of which the table is composed. Similarly, the liquidity of the water is explained by the nature of the interactions between the H_2O molecules. Those macro-features are causally explained by the behaviour[50] of elements at the micro-level.
>
> . . . we have no difficulty at all in supposing that the surface features [like solidity, liquidity, and transparency] are *caused by*

---

[50]   Searle speaks of properties, features, structures, interactions, and behaviours, as though they were the same.   But, they seem to be different, and Searle does not point out the differences.   "Feature" and "property" seem to be words with a sort of **general** meaning, so that a feature (or property) can be either a structure, or an interaction, or a behavior.   Does it make sense to call a **lattice structure a behavior?**

the behaviour of elements at the micro-level, and at the same time we accept that the surface phenomena *just are* features of the very systems in question. I think the clearest way of stating this point is to say that the surface feature is both *caused by* the behaviour of micro-elements, and at the same time is *realised in* the system that is made up of the micro-elements. There is a cause and effect relationship, but at the same time the surface features are just higher level features of the very system whose behaviour at the micro-level causes those features.

. . . someone might say that liquidity, solidity, and so on are identical with features of the micro-structure. So, for example, we might just define solidity as the lattice structure of the molecular arrangement, just as heat is often identified with the mean kinetic energy of molecule movements. This point seems to me correct . . . It is a characteristic of the progress of science that an expression that is originally defined in terms of surface features, features accessible to the senses, is subsequently defined in terms of the micro-structure that causes the surface features. Thus, to take the example of solidity, the table in front of me is solid in the ordinary sense that it is rigid, it resists pressure, it supports books, it is not easily penetrable by most other objects such as other tables, and so on. Such is the commonsense notion of solidity. And in a scientific vein one can define solidity as whatever micro-structure causes these gross observable features. So one can then say either that solidity just is the lattice structure of the system of molecules and that solidity so defined causes, for example, resistance to touch and pressure. Or one can say that solidity consists of such high level features as rigidity and resistance to touch and pressure and that it is caused by the behaviour of elements at the micro-level.[51]

The desk at which I am now sitting, points out Searle, the drinking glass in front of me, and the water within it, all three, are objects composed of micro-particles. And these micro-particles have features or properties at various levels, e.g., at the level of the molecule, at the level of the atom, at

[51]   Searle, John R., *Minds, Brains and Science*, Cambridge, Mass.: Harvard University Press, 1984; pp. 20-22.

the level of the subatomic. But physical objects, such as my desk, also have certain other properties or features, like solidity (the desk) or liquidity (the water) or transparency (the drinking glass, and the water). These features are surface features, global features, i.e, "features accessible to the senses," "gross observable features." Now many of these surface features, continues Searle, can be causally explained by certain molecular, or atomic, or subatomic features, in brief, by certain **micro-features,** of the particles which make up the very objects which have these surface features. The commonplace (Eddington) or macro (Searle) can be causally explained by the scientifc (Eddington) or micro (Searle). The solidity of the table, exemplifies Searle -- that is, the fact "that it is rigid, it resists pressure, it supports books, it is not easily penetrable by most other objects such as other tables, and so on" -- can be "explained by the lattice structure occupied by the molecules" of which the table is composed. The liquidity of the water can be explained by the sort of interaction which takes place among H_2O molecules, i.e., they move freely among themselves without any tendency to separate. The transparency of the drinking glass (and of the water) can be explained (my guess) by the fact that the quarks and leptons which compose it are so arranged that they permit light to pass between them (and so, through the glass), thereby making the glass see-through-able by our eyes.

Having noted that the macro can be explained by the micro, Searle points out the interesting aspect of this sort of explanation. The macro is both **caused by** the micro and **realized in** the object that is made up of the micro. "I think," emphasizes Searle, "the clearest way of stating this point is to say that the surface feature is both *caused by* the behaviour of the micro-elements, and at the same time is *realised in* the system that is made up of the micro-elements. There is a cause and effect relationship, but at the same time the surface features are just higher level features of the very system whose behaviour at the micro-level causes those features." Indeed, continues Searle, one can even say that solidity, liquidity, transparency, etc., are **identical with** features of the micro-structure. Thus, for example, solidity is **nothing but, is identical with,** the lattice structure of the arrangement of the molecules; liquidity is **nothing but, is identical with,** the free movement of molecules among themselves without any tendency to separate. It can be said, thus, **either** that solidity is nothing but the lattice structure of a collection of molecules (micro), and that, so defined, it is **the cause** of rigidity, resistance to pressure, impenetrability, etc. (macro); **or** that solidity consists of rigidity, resistance, impenetrability, etc. (macro), and that, so defined, it is **the effect** of the lattice structure (micro). Macro-features are both **caused by,** and **retained in** (realized in) one and the same object -- caused by certain features of micro-particles, and at the same time retained in the object that is composed of these micro-particles. In the language of Aquinas, the object (desk, drinking glass, water) is just what it is because of the special twofold causality being exercised by the **mixables** which enter into its make-up, i.e., by its component micro-particles (quarks, protons, neutrons, electrons, atoms, molecules), which are not only 1) **material** causes of a special sort, i.e., capable of **agent** causality, but also 2) **agent** causes of as special sort, i.e., **conjoined instrumental** agent causes. As conjoined instrumental **agents,** the micro-particles **cause** the macro-features, and as **material** causes, they **retain** these macro-features. Macro-features are both caused by, and realized in, this physical object, just because this physical object is the sort of **mixed body** which it is -- just because it is the intimately conjoined (by mixing, i.e., **mixtio**) collection of micro-particles which it is.

8. Nahmanides' thirteenth century theological Big Bang

> Nahmanides' account of the first seconds of the universe reads like this: At the briefest instant following creation all the matter of the universe was concentrated in a very small place, no larger than a grain of mustard.[52] The matter at this time was

---

[52] From the words "a very small place," and "no larger than," it is clear that matter, at this briefest instant following creation, was already corporeal, i.e., already had **dimensions.**

so thin, so intangible, that it did not have real substance.[53] It did have, however, a potential to gain substance and form and to become tangible matter. From the initial concentration of this intangible substance in its minute location, the substance expanded, expanding the universe as it did so. As the expansion progressed, a change in the substance occurred. This initially thin noncorporeal[54] substance took on the tangible aspects of matter as we know it. From this initial act of creation, from this ethereally thin pseudosubstance, everything that has existed, or will ever exist, was, is, and will be formed. [Nahmanides, *Commentary on the Torah*, Genesis, 1, 1].

Nahmanides' reference to a grain of mustard is the traditional way of saying, "in the language of man,"[55] the tiniest imaginable speck of space. Nahmanides taught that at the beginning, all that is on and within the Earth and all the heavens, in fact all the universe, was somehow packed, compressed, squeezed into this speck of space, the size of a mustard grain. (Schroeder, Gerald L., *Genesis and the Big Bang*, New York: Bantam Books, 1990; pp. 64-65).

Nahmanides, or Moses ben Nahman (1194-1270), was a contemporary of St. Thomas Aquinas (1225-1274); but neither, it seems, knew of the work of the other;[56] quite unlike Maimonides, or Moses ben Maimon (1135-1204),

---

[53] "To have real substance" seems to mean, here, to be tangible, i.e., to be something one can get a hold of -- solid, rigid, resisting pressure, impenetrable by other bodies, capable of supporting other bodies.

[54] "Noncorporeal" here cannot mean **without dimensions**. It means **ethereally thin,** as Nahmanides himself explicitly indicates just two lines below. For ethereally thin, can we say: fire-like, or air-like, mist-like, fog-like, smoke-like, vapor-like, steam-like, in that it is easily partible, easily penetrable?

[55] "In the language of man," i.e., ordinary, everyday language, but as given a certain precision for theological purposes -- as opposed to "in scientific terms." See Schroeder, Gerald L., *Genesis and the Big Bang*, New York: Bantam Books, 1990, p. 57, where he writes: "Old Testament theology talks **in the language of man,** while current cosmology makes its statements **in scientific terms.**"

[56] Is there any explanation for this? Is it just that there was not enough time for their works to be copied, and then to be brought to one another -- by foot or by donkey or by horse, or by whatever other, clearly slow, means of transport available at that time? Nahmanides was in Spain prior to 1263, when he engaged in Barcelona (his opponent was

whose work Aquinas knew very well, and admired very much.

What is to be made of Nahmanides' account of the state of the universe just the briefest instant after its creation by God? In the beginning, the matter of the physical world was called into being out of nothingness by God's creative act. And at the briefest instant after creation, points out Nahmanides, all this matter was somehow concentrated, packed, squeezed, compressed into a "very small place, no larger than a grain of mustard." At this time, matter was a very thin, intangible, ethereal (again we ask, can one say, fire-like, air-like, mist-like, fog-like, vapor-like, smoke-like, steam-like?) pseudo-substance. It had no real substance (tangibility); but it did have a potential to take on substance and form (differentiation), to become a tangible and differentiated matter. And then, **just after** the briefest instant **after** creation, continues Nahmanides, this matter began to expand (under God's creative direction, no doubt), causing that initial very small place to begin to expand as well, so as to become the space of the universe as we know it, in all its immensity, a universe in which, "as the expansion progressed," that "initially thin noncorporeal substance took on the tangible aspects of matter."

In pursuing the question, What is to be made of Nahmanides' account?, it will be helpful to consider what Schroeder has to say about it (if only because it is from Schroeder that I first heard of Nahmanides); then to consider what Aquinas would have (might have) said about it, if he had had the good fortune of having heard of Nahmanides, and of having known his work, *The Commentary on the Torah*.

---

the apostate Jew, Pablo Christiani) in perhaps the most famous of all the medieval Jewish-Christian debates. This debate was held in the presence of the Spanish king, James of Aragon, and Nahmanides was assured by the king that he could speak without fear of censorship or retribution. Nonetheless, in spite of all of King James' assurances and good intentions, Nahmanides decided that it would be prudent for him to leave Spain. When the debates were over, Nahmanides emigrated to Palestine. (SeeTelushkin, Rabbi Joseph, *Jewish Literacy*, New York: William Morrow and Company, Inc., 1991; pp. 187-188). From Spain to France or Germany or Italy, and the other way around, before 1263; and from Palestine after that -- too far away, and too little time, during the lifetime of each of them?

But first, a point to clear up about the meaning of the word "creation." It is used both scientifically, notes Schroeder, and theologically: scientifically, to designate the event known today as the Big Bang, and theologically, to designate the event described in *Genesis* 1, 1: In the beginning, God created heaven and earth. But these two events, one must point out, are not one and the same event; and Schroeder does not make this clear. Indeed, what he writes on pp. 56-57 -- while considering the question he had just raised, namely, What was happening **before** the beginning, i.e., before creation?, -- seems to take these two creation events to be one and the same thing. He talks about events "that **preceded** the beginning, that is the creation" of Genesis 1, 1; and then refers to these same events as "events **prior to** the Big Bang," seeming thereby to identify the creation of Genesis with creation by the Big Bang. Schroeder is concerned here to point out that events **before** the creation event, if there are any,[57] are **not** accessible to human investigation; unlike events which occur **after** the creation event, which are.

Before creation in the **theological** sense, one must hasten to point out, there was nothing in existence but God; thus no physical matter. And thus no possibility of any sort of physical event at all. But before creation in the **scientific** sense, i.e., before the Big Bang, something **did** exist, i.e., the **pre**-Big Bang particle, which contained the original materials out of which the whole physical universe was to expand. Or, is that a misunderstanding of what science says? Is it, rather, the view of science that the **original particle** and the **Big Bang** came on the scene **together,** so that the original particle did **not** exist before the explosive instant of the Big Bang? In any case, whereas creation in the theological sense is **creatio ex nihilo materiae,**[58] and by the

---

57   Schroeder wonders about this explicitly, i.e., about whether there were any **pre**-creation events, as he asks, "But what was happening **before** the beginning? Can we study, either theologically or scientifically, what there was **before** the beginning, **if anything?**" (Schroeder, Gerald L., *Genesis and the Big Bang*, p. 56). Notice the last two words. i.e., **if anything.**
58   Although Schroeder does not, on pp. 56-57, make it clear that the creation event described in Genesis 1,1, is not the same thing as the creation event we designate today as

infinite power of God; creation in the scientific sense is **creatio ex particula materiae,** and the power of God is irrelevant. What then, one wants to ask, accounts for the existence of that particle of matter? Is one to say that it **always** existed, since something must always have existed because something exists right now (and it might as well be that particle which always existed, as anything else, e.g., God, some might want to say)?

9. Schroeder on Nahmanides' account of the beginning and expansion of the universe

Having pointed out that both science and theology have come to the same conclusion (though from different directions, i.e., for different reasons)[59] about events **before** the creation event, i.e., about **pre-**beginning

---

the Big Bang, he does recognize that the former is a creation **out of absolute nothingness.** He writes: "The creation of the heavens and the Earth from absolute nothing is at the root of biblical faith . . . The Hebrew word used for creation, **barah,** is the only word in the Hebrew language that means the creation of something from nothing. Biblically it is applicable only to the actions of God. It is the second word of the Bible." (Schroeder, *op. cit.,* p. 62).

[59] As regards the reason of theological tradition, Schroeder writes: "Because the Bible begins with a letter [the Hebrew letter **beth**] that is bounded on all sides except the forward, so the events that occur **after** 'the beginning' are those that are accessible to human investigation. Similarly, those that **preceded** the beginning, that is the creation, are not open to investigation." Schroeder, *op. cit.,* p. 57) -- As regards the reason of science, Schroeder writes: "This melee of random high-energy collisions [among particles of **matter,** i.e., quarks and electrons, and the packets of **energy** we call photons, behaving according to Einstein's $E=mc^2$, at the earliest instant after the Big Bang about which scientists can theorize, i.e., about 10^{-43} seconds after the start] precluded any possibility of order in the energy of particles present, order that would have contained information related to what preceded that instant. Without order, information cannot be transferred across a sequence of time, a temporal interface, separating the 'before' from the 'after'." (Schroeder, *ibid.,* pp. 57-58). "The matter and space of this moment [i.e., of the earliest instant about which we can theorize] were so tightly packed, so dense, that the violent collisions among the particles of **matter** and those packets of **energy** we refer to as photons were continually shattering each other into and out of existence. Energy and matter were in a fluid interchange, just as Einstein's most basic statement of relativity implies: $E = mc^2$ and, equally true, $mc^2 = E$. At this early time, the E, that is the energy, of the photons was converting into the m, the mass, of mc^2, and equally rapidly, this very m of the mc^2 was reconverting to E. " (Schroeder, *ibid.,* p. 57).

(pre-creation, **pre**-Big Bang) events -- namely, the conclusion that these events are not accessible, not open, to human invesitigation; Schroeder moves on to point out what science and theology have to say about events **after** the creation event; in particular to point out that the "parallel between the opinion of present-day cosmological theory and the biblical tradition that predates it by over a thousand years is striking, almost unnerving . . .,"[60] -- the tradition that began with Nahmanides in the thirteenth century.

According to Nahmanides, the creation of the **matter** of the physical universe, points out Schroeder, brought with it both **time** and **space**. Prior to the creation of the physical universe, there was neither time nor space. And this makes sense, one wants to note, for time is the measure of the various motions or changes of material things; and space is the real, penetrable, three-dimensional emptiness in which material things exist, and in which their various motions or changes take place. No matter, therefore no motion or change, therefore no time. No matter, therefore no space, i.e., no real penetrable emptiness which, though different from matter, is that precisely in which matter exists and changes. Both science and the theology of the biblical tradition agree on this.

But, according to science, the matter present at the very beginning "is pressed into a space of zero size[61] and infinite density," whereas according to biblical tradition, matter at the beginning was contained "in a tiny but finite speck of space, about the size of a grain of mustard."[62] **No** size (science), as opposed to **some** size, though very small (biblical tradition).

---

[60] Schroeder, *ibid.*, p. 67.
[61] **Zero size** is very difficult to accept, unless it is taken to refer to the existence which matter, and the space which is its receptacle, had in God before God's creative act; for a dimensionless matter and a dimensionless space **in the physical world** seems an impossibility. More likely, talk of **zero size** at the very beginning is required by the **mathematics** which physicists use in their attempt to describe the condition of our universe at that very early time.
[62] Schroeder, *ibid.*, p. 63.

According to Nahmanides -- whose insight depends on three things, as Schroeder sees it, namely 1) on what has been revealed in the Bible, 2) on a study of the natural sciences, and 3) on having received what Nahmanides calls a "hidden wisdom," which appears to be some sort of "grace" or free gift from God as one studies the Scriptures[63] -- this beginning matter was very tiny, as well as very thin (i.e., intangible, without substance, ethereal). It had nonetheless, a potential to expand, and at the same time to take on, somehow, substance (tangibility) and form (differentiation), and to give rise to everything which was, is, and ever will be.[64] God created (**barah**) this tiny speck of thin matter, this tiny speck of super-rarefied matter, out of nothing (**creatio ex nihilo materiae**); and gave it this explosive, expanding, condensing or substance-acquiring, and differentiating potential (or nature).

What today's cosmologists say about the physical universe, emphasizes Schroeder, is very much like what Nahmanides had said -- there is a beginning matter which is very small and very rarefied and undifferentiated, followed by an expansion which condenses this matter into multiple and differentiated forms. But unlike Nahmanides, today's cosmologists add **many details,** mathematically expressed and with incredible precision, which Nahmanides, in the thirteenth century (no telescopes and no particle accelerators), quite understandably could not have done. Schroeder presents some of these details in what he calls cosmology's "description . . . for that same early time in our evolution," i.e., the time of Nahmanides' grain of mustard **at the briefest instant following creation:**

---

[63]   Schroeder, *ibid.,* p. 64. This free gift from God might be a special sort of **crowning supernatural** power of insight, added to the **natural** power of insight which theologians develop **because of a long familiarity** with their field. Long familiarity with a given field -- whether theology or philosophy or science, or whatever -- produces in the faithful and diligent investigator, as is well known, a **natural** power of insight of a very special and extraordinary sort.
[64]   Schroeder, *ibid.,* p. 65.

The present universe, according to current cosmological understanding, is the result of a Big Bang, a massive expansion from a single point . . .   . . . at the briefest instant following the beginning, at about 10^{-43} seconds after the start , . . . the universe was . . . the size of a speck of dust . . .

At this early time, all matter was concentrated into one miniscule core location.   The temperature was 10^{32} K (100 million million million million million degrees Kelvin) . . .

. . . Physics and mathematics, as we know them today, cannot deal with times earlier than 10^{-43} seconds after the beginning. Prior to that time, the temperatures and densities of matter exceeded those that can be described by the laws of nature as we now understand them . . .

As the study of events following the Big Bang is extended mathematically to earlier times, the size of the universe shrinks toward zero and, inversely, the temperature and density increase toward infinity. The actual instant of the beginning envisions, for physicists, a moment when an infinitely small[65] point of space was packed with matter squeezed to an infinitely high density.[66] This conditon of infinities is referred to as a singularity, and singularities cannot be treated by conventional mathematics . . .

In very early times, matter was not matter as we know it. The high pressure and temperature in this core had reduced all matter to its form as pure energy.[67] The concept of matter, even of the tiny theoretical fundamental particles called quarks, has no meaning for the temperature, pressure, and spacial dimensions that are speculated to have existed at this very early time. There was exquisitely hot energy and very little else. Within the initial core location,   an explosion or inflation occurred that forced the energy-matter out in all directions. The

---

65   Does "infinitely small" mean **zero size**?
66   Does "infinitely high density" imply   **zero size**?
67   Does "pure energy" imply **zero size**? Did the high pressure and high temperature in this core have the effect of squeezing all the dimensionality out of matter -- out of all the fundamental particles, like quarks and leptons?

cause of this inflation is not clear.[68] Some scientists posit that mutual repulsion among all that was present occurred, something akin to a force of antigravity.[69] The term inflation is used deliberately. It implies that the forces[70] that pushed back the boundaries of space to the size of a grapefuit[71] came from within. There was no without. There was and is the universe and the space it occupies. That was and is the totality of all physical existence.

Concurrent with the expansion there was a lowering of pressure and temperature. At these more moderate, expanded conditions (a mere billion billion billion degrees Kelvin), energy could now condense into the tiniest of particles, the theoretical quarks and the known electrons. This took place in accord with Einstein's law, $E = mc^2$, which states that energy and mass are actually different states of a single energy-matter continuum, just as water, steam, and ice are all composed of a single entity, H_2O. Energy is matter in its intangible form; matter is energy in its tangible form.

As this expansion progressed out, away from the core, pressures and temperatures fell. Conditions became less harsh. The transition of energy to the more substantive forms of tangible matter continued. The material universe as we understand it came into being. The entire process is referred to as the Big Bang. Thus far, the cosmological description of the early universe. [72]   (Schroeder, *Genesis and the Big Bang*, pp. 65-67).

---

[68]   Not clear? Why not? Because this explosion or inflation cannot be caused except by God's creative act? Is this **intrinsically** caused inflation, i.e., caused by forces **from within** the initial core, simultaneous with the exit of this core from within God, at His creative act?

[69]   Is antigravity even a possibility? Is it a force in the realm of antimatter? And does this imply that matter, as we know it, is derived from antimatter; and that antimatter is therefore more fundamental than matter?

[70]   Are these forces in some way connected with what Lederman calls **the God Particle**?

[71]   How many seconds old was the universe when the boundaries of space had expanded from the size of a grain of mustard to that of a grapefruit? How much older than 10^{-43} seconds?

[72]   Does "early universe" here mean: from zero size to grapefruit size? And how long did it take the universe to become the size of a grapefruit?

Schroeder ends his reflections on Nahmanides' theological Big Bang account by noting that "revelation, at least as we have it today, did not provide details" (p. 68) for our understanding of the creation and development of our physical universe. Physics and cosmology provided these details. Nonetheless, revelation did provide, for its diligent and patient and prayerful students, the truth about creation and expansion, a truth accepted not on the basis of discovery and proof, but on the basis of faith -- "faith in the accuracy of revelation even when it precedes the advances of science that eventually come to confirm it." (p. 68).

Study the Bible, counsels Nahmanides -- diligently, patiently, prayerfully. Study the sciences, he continues -- perseveringly, painstakingly, deeply. Have faith, he adds -- humbly, sensitively, unswervingly. The Bible will give us truth about the physical world. The sciences will confirm this truth; and, we today might hasten to note, add a wealth of mathematically expressed details. Faith confirmed, and given detail, by the sciences. St. Augustine? **Fides quaerens intellectum?** Faith seeking understanding -- understanding from the sciences, from mathematics, from philosophy, from all that the **natural** powers of the human mind can discover and prove. Like revelation, one must acknowledge with Nahmanides (and with Aquinas), the human mind, too, is from God.

10. What Aquinas might have said about Nahmanides' account

What, now, might Aquinas have said about the universe of Nahmanides, a universe which, in all its present immensity and diversity, **expanded out of** the tiniest imaginable speck of space, no larger that a grain of mustard, into which, at the beginning, all of its matter had been somehow compressed? Would Aquinas have accepted such an account?

One might begin here by making two points: 1) that the creation event described in *Genesis* 1, 1 is, for Aquinas as it is for Nahmanides, a creation **ex** nihilo materiae, a creation out of absolutely no matter, by the infinite power of God, and that alone; and 2) that, according to Aquinas, the four elements and the heavenly bodies were brought into existence **on the first** of the six days, and in the **first** of the three works, i.e., in the work of **creation**, and **in an instant** -- as to their substance, of course, and in many ways far from fully formed; and that everything else that was produced by God during the first six days was produced by Him in the second and third of the three works, i.e., in the work of **distinction** and **adornment,** and in such a way that the production of these things was by means of certain sorts of **changes** out of prior materials, and so was produced, **not** in an instant, **but over a period of time**.

The **implications** of the first point, together with what Aquinas says **explicitly** about the second point (already described in some detail, above in sections 8-10, on pp. 192-227) make it quite clear that Aquinas would have accepted Nahmanides' "expanding grain of mustard" account. Or, if that is too strong, that what Aquinas says, both implicitly and explicitly, about the creation, distinction, and adornment of the first six days is **compatible with** Nahmanides' account, or at least **not in**compatible with it.

The first point: Creation as described in *Genesis* 1, 1 is creation out of absolutely no matter

What does this sort of creation imply? It implies that in the beginning instant of the existence of the physical universe, just after the first now of time, just after it had been created by God -- everything which came into existence must have been in some way all together, all together in the minutest possible particle of matter. The universe, in that first instant of time, must have been so small that it could not possibly have been any smaller. Indeed, it must have been even smaller than Nahmanides' grain of mustard; unless, as Schroeder suggests, the expression "grain of mustard" be taken to mean **the tiniest imaginable speck,**[73] and even so, **not** the tiniest imaginable **to us,** but the tiniest imaginable **in itself,** i.e., such **in itself** that it could not possibly have been any tinier.

To clarify the immediately preceding. -- Within their cause, "before" they were brought into being (i.e., within God, and only God, since there was no pre-existing matter), the things that came into existence in that first instant of time, i.e., the four elements and the heavenly bodies, must have been gathered together as though within a mathematical point, since God is a pure spirit, a thing without dimensions. There within God, these things took up no space at all; there was no space for them to take up. They were there, within God's infinite power to call them into existence, but not as within some pre-existing matter, nor therefore as with dimensions, nor therefore as taking up any space. There was then only God, nothing but God; no matter, no dimensions, no space, nothing at all **outside of God** as distinct from God, for God had not yet created. Nor was there **within God** any matter, or dimensions, or space, as part of His nature, for God is a pure spirit. As soon as God uttered His creating word, **Fiant (Let them come to be),** the infinite power of these words hurled these things, i.e., the four elements and the heavenly bodies, out from within Himself, hurled them out **into their own existence,** and in all directions, with an emerging motion which began to accelerate into a space which came to be with them, and which (space) began to expand in all directions with an accelerating speed which equalled the accelerating speed of their motion. But "before" this, these things had been within God, from forever, without motion and without dimensions. And so, when they emerged into their own existence, the motion with which they emerged was a motion which **had to begin,** and the dimensions which they took on **had to begin to be taken on.** Now, the acceleration of motion **takes time;** and taking on dimensions **takes time,** too. In the beginning instant of its existence, therefore, the material universe -- a universe just emerging out of its **prior dimensionless** existence in God -- must have been as small as it could

---

73   Schroeder, *Genesis and the Big Bang,* p. 65.

possibly have been, the tiniest possible **in itself**, as noted just above; and the motion by which it began to exit its **prior motionless** existence within God must have been as slow as it could possibly have been. In that beginning instant, these things must have been **in some way** all together in a particle of matter so small (and this particle in a space just as small) that it could not in principle have been any smaller (or any bigger); and the emerging motion of each of these things must have been so slow that, though it was on its way to acceleration, it could not in principle have been, in that first moment of time, any slower (or any faster). This was the moment of Nahmanides' grain of mustard. But then, i.e., in the very next moment, and continuing in all succeeding moments right up to the present time, the ethereal matter in that tiny place "expanded," as Nahmanides put it, "expanding the universe as it did so, . . . [and from it] everything that has existed, or will ever exist, was, is and will be formed." (above, p. 298). Quite clearly, Aquinas and Nahmanides are quite in accord. This brings us to the second point.

The second point: The four elements and the heavenly bodies were created on the first day, out of absolutely no prior matter, and in an instant; all other physical things which came to be during the first six days, and after those days to the present, were produced, not in an instant, but over a period of time, and out of prior matter

A brief recap of what Aquinas says explicitly about this second point (already seen above at some length, on pp. 192-227) will be a convenient and helpful way to proceed.

> . . . it belongs to the *work of creation* to produce the substance of the elements, whereas it belongs to the *work of distinction* and *of adornment* to form certain things out of the already existing elements . . . (above, p. 207)

> . . . three things were mentioned [in the Scriptures] in the *work of creation,* namely heaven and water and earth. And these

> same three things were given some form during the three days
> of the *work of distinction*...   ...And similarly [these same
> three things were adorned] in [the three days of] the *work of
> adornment*...   (above, p. 208)

Three things, note the Scriptures, were brought into being as pertaining to the **opus creationis,** namely heaven and water and earth. Water and earth, taken together, are being contrasted with **heaven,** notes Aquinas, and thus quite obviously include in some way **all terrestrial bodies,** mixed bodies as well as elements. And so, since "it belongs to **the work of creation** to produce the substance of the elements," one can conclude that all mixed bodies were **in some way** (i.e., as in their pre-existing matter, and in their partial agent cause) there **in the substance of the four elements,** when these elements first began to exist. With heaven and the four elements, effects of the **opus creationis,** already in existence on the first day, the **opus distinctionis** was begun, and on that same first day; continuing on the second and third days, followed by the **opus ornatus** on days four through six.

> ... the work of distinction and of adornment proceeds according
> to certain changes in creatures, and these changes are *measured
> by time.*   But the work of creation consists in a divine action,
> and in that alone, and this action produces the substance of
> things *in an instant*...   (above, p. 224)

The four elements and the heavenly bodies, products of the **opus creationis,** were created by God on the first day out of absolute nothingness, and **in an instant.** But the things made by God as products of the **opus distinctionis** and the **opus ornatus,** were made by Him by means of **certain sorts of changes** out of already existing materials (basically the four elements), and so were produced **over a period of time,** namely that of the six days.

> . . . God created all things all together [i.e., at the same time], as
> regards their substance, but their substance in a way not yet fully
> formed. As regards their being more fully formed, however,
> which came about by distinction and adornment, this did not
> take place all together [i.e., not at the same time] . . . (above,
> p. 225)

The substance of **all** things (and not only of the heavenly bodies and
the four elements) was created all together, though in some way --
quodammodo -- not yet fully formed. The substances of the heavenly bodies
and of the four elements were there **as actually existing,** but not yet with all
their powers; whereas the substances of all other things were there only
potentialiter, i.e., only in the power of the heavenly bodies and of the
elements to produce them over time.

> . . . nothing which was made by God afterwards [i.e., after the
> seventh day] is totally new; indeed all such things had preceded
> in some way in the works of the six days. Some of them had pre-
> existed materially, as the woman had in the rib of Adam out of
> which God formed her. Others pre-existed in the works of the
> six days *not only* materially, *but also* causally, as the individuals
> which are now being generated; they were there causally in the
> first individuals of their species. And new species too, if any
> appeared, pre-existed in certain active principles, just as the
> animals generated from putrefaction are produced from the
> powers of the stars and of the elements, *which (powers) they had
> received in the beginning* . . . (above, p. 220)

None of the things made by God after the seventh day is totally new,
points out Aquinas. Some of these things pre-existed **materially** in the works
of the six days; for example, observes Aquinas, the woman whom God
formed out of the rib of Adam, whom He had made earlier out of the slime of
the earth. Aquinas could have added that **all things** which came to be (and
continue to come to be) after the seventh day, pre-existed **materially** in the
four elements, and in certain appropriate mixed bodies produced out of the

four elements during the work of the six days. Certain other things, continues Aquinas, pre-existed in the works of the six days **causally**, i.e., in the power of their agent causes to produce them, as well as materially. For example, all the individuals which are being generated at the present time, were there in the first individuals of their species -- there, not only as in their matter, but also as in the productive power of their agent causes. And if any **new** species came into existence since the seventh day, continues Aquinas (this reference to **new** species is quite interesting, and in a way surprising), these too were there in the works of the six days, in certain active (agent) causes, as well as in the matter of the four elements and of certain appropriate mixed bodies. Similarly, adds Aquinas, all **animals** generated from putrefaction (like maggots, the legless larvae of the housefly) and even **new** (interesting and surprising) species of animals so generated, if any came to be, came to be from the powers of the stars (active powers) and of the four elements (active and material powers), which (powers) they (the stars and the elements) had received from God in the very beginning -- in prima rerum institutione. Indeed, one can add, the same can be said about **all** new species, **whether of animals or of plants.** Moreover, **every** new living thing, in any sense of "new," whether it be simply a new **individual** (of a species already in existence as a result of the work of the six days) or even a new **species,** came to be from the powers (active) of the heavenly bodies and of the four elements (active and material). And not only **living** things, one can add further, but **non-living** things as well. That is, even all new **elements,** if any came to be, and all new **mixed bodies** as well, came to be out of the original elements, inasmuch as they (the original elements) had received from God -- in prima rerum institutione -- a nature such that they were to provide the materials, as well as the agent powers, which are required (in conjunction with the agent powers of the heavenly bodies) for the orderly, developmental, unfolding, evolving production of **all other physical things, in the whole of the physical universe,** out to the furthest reaches of space.

312

*   *   *

Thus -- from what Aquinas says, both implicitly and explicitly, about the creation, distinction, and adornment of the first six days -- it is quite clear that in the beginning instant of the existence of the physical universe, all bodily things were there **in some way,** and all together, in a particle of matter so small that it could not possibly have been any smaller. The first three, i.e., heaven and water and earth,[74] were there **in one way** -- i.e., they were there as actually existing substances, but far from fully formed; and the light of the sun was there, and of other heavenly bodies as well,[75] coming to be later on during the work of the first day, but still to acquire, on a later day (i.e., on the fourth day), their **special** powers for producing **particular** effects. The firmament, too, was there, and the waters which came to be both above it and below it (coming to be as the work of the **second** day), but **in another way** -- i.e., as in their agent and material causes. And **in that same way,** the sea too was there, and the dry land (emerging as the work of the **third** day); **in that same way,** the light-giving bodies (or at least their special powers) which were to adorn heaven, were there[76] (emerging as the work of the **fourth** day); **in that same way,** the birds and the fishes, which were to adorn the air and water, were there (emerging as the work of the **fifth** day); **in that same way,** the animals, and man's body as well, which were to adorn the earth, were there (coming to be as the work of the **sixth** day). All these things were there -- in the material and the agent causality of the four elements, in part; and in other part, in the agent causality of the heavenly bodies. But the human soul was not there in any way at all. Man's soul came to be in man's body on the **sixth** day, indeed, but by a direct and special creative act of God.

---

74   See above, pp. 208-209.
75   See above, p. 209, especially footnote 45;   also p. 213, with special attention to footnote 49.
76   See above, pp. 211-212, for two views on the production of heavenly bodies other than the sun.

And so, as a final comment for this recap (begun above on p. 309). --
Just after the instant of creation, according to Aquinas, the four elements (the
aqua et terra of the first three)[77] were there; and the heavens, too, with their
light-emitting bodies (the **caelum** of the first three) were there -- as actually
existing substances, but far from being fully formed, far from being in full
possession of all their distinctive powers for producing particular effects.
They were beginning to emerge, beginning to be hurled out of, banged out of,
their former motionless and dimensionless existence within God. And then
in the very next instant, they (the first three) were taken up into a process of
expanding out of that unimaginably small quasi-point of the first instant
after creation into a three-dimensional existence which was becoming
unimaginably ever more vast; they were moving toward becoming more and
more fully formed, and toward becoming more and more fully empowered to
produce particular effects -- throughout the three days of distinction and the
three days of adornment, and beyond that into the present time. The
heavenly bodies were taken up into a process of acquiring particular light-
emitting powers, of moving away from one another, and of acquiring their
various locations in relation to one another. And the planet Earth was taken
up into a process of developing its oceans, and its continents, and the few
primitive life forms out of which the multiple and complex life forms which
are now in existence emerged and evolved.[78] -- Thus Aquinas. Penning

---

77   See above, pp. 208-209.

78   It ought to be noted that Darwin, **at least in word** if not in truth, takes pleasure, at the
end of his *Origin of Species,* in the "grandeur," as he puts it, of the way in which the
Creator breathed the several powers of life into a few forms or into one, and how from so
simple a beginning endless most beautiful and wonderful forms of life have been, and
continue to be, evolved. -- "It is interesting to contemplate a tangled bank, clothed with
many plants of many kinds, with birds singing on the bushes, with various insects flitting
about, and with worms crawling through the damp earth, and to reflect that these
elaborately constructed forms, so different from each other, and dependent upon each other
in so complex a manner, have all been produced by laws acting around us. These laws, taken
in the largest sense, being Growth with Reproduction, Inheritance . . . , Variability . . . , a
Ratio of Increase . . . , a Struggle for Life . . . , Natural Selection . . . , Divergence of
Character . . . , Extinction of less-improved forms. Thus, from the war of nature, from
famine and death, the most exalted object which we are capable of conceiving, namely, the
production of the higher animals, directly follows. **There is grandeur in this view of life,**

details remarkably in accord with Nahmanides. Details which provide a striking **complement** to, a striking filling out of, Nahmanides' simple and undetailed account. Considerably more than just **not in**compatible with that account. Considerably more than simply **compatible with** it. Indeed, details which fill out Nahmanides' account as though Nahmanides himself had written them.

---

with its several powers, having been originally breathed by the Creator into a few forms or into one; and that, whilst this planet has gone cycling on according to the fixed law of gravity, from so simple a beginning endless forms most beautiful and most wonderful have been, and are being evolved." (Darwin, Charles, *The Origin of Species* (Abridged and Introduced by Philip Appleman), New York: W.W. Norton and Company, 1975; p. 123).

Index of Names

Index of Subjects

definition of, 267
magnetic force,
    definition of, 268
origin of forces in subatomic particles,
    281-283
photon, as transmitter of electro-
    magnetic force, 264-265
strong nuclear force, 264, 265
    definition of, 268
weak nuclear force, 266
    definition of, 268

Form, 10, 17, 18
actuality of matter, 7
as one of the three principles of
    nature, 2, 34-36, 39-41
as *per se* principle, 15-19, 21-23
accidental form, 6-8, 10-11, 114, 115
how accidental form differs from
    substantial form, 231
artificial forms as accidental forms,
    10-11
distinguished from matter and
    privation, 23-25
priority and posteriority of, 65
sameness and difference of, 90, 91
sensible form, 149-151
substantial form, 6-8, 54, 55, 105-126,
    129-133, 136, 163, 166, 167
    as source of actual existence and
      knowability, 28
    account of what a substantial form
      is, 228-231
    its eduction from matter, 228, 231-
      241
    grades of, 164, 165
    how it differs from accidental
      form, 231
    how it differs from essence, 229
    incorruptibility and ingenerability
      of, 29, 30
    in relation to three dimensionality
      and the "small" Big Bang, 166,
      224, 253, 283

Generation.
    See Change

The heavens and the heavenly bodies,
causality of, 205-219, 223
circular motion of, 203
classification of the heavens, 199
incorruptibility and ingenerability of,
    185, 200-205
matter of, 200
nature of, 199-205
three basic characteristics of, 202, 203

Incorruptibility and ingenerability,
of the heavens and the heavenly
    bodies, 185, 200-205
of prime matter and substantial form,
    29, 30
Indivisibility,
in form, 47, 48, 50
in kind, 103, 104-106
in quantity, 30, 31, 47, 48, 52
in species, 47, 48, 51, 53
into parts, 53
of elements, 53, 54
Ingredient,
actual ingredient of the essence, 133
matter and form as ingredients, 17
of the essence, 42, 99, 131, 132
virtual ingredient of the essence, 133
Instrument,
conjoined instrument, 142, 143
separated instrument, 142

Macro-properties, 294-297
Man,
definition of, 153
Mass,
definition of, 262
gravitational mass,
    definition of, 263
inertial mass,
    definition of, 263
relativistic mass,
    definition of, 263
rest mass,
    definition of, 263
Matter, 10, 17, 19, 108-110,

photon,
  definition of, 265
  general description of, 255
proton,
  as a mixed body, 247, 275, 276
quark,
  as agent and material cause, 250-252
  as element, 250-252
  dimensions of, 256-269
  dispositional presence of, 250-252
  general description of, 255
  genus of, 254
  instrumental presence of, 250-252
  retrievable presence of, 250-252
  specific difference of, 254
  virtual presence of, in a proton, 246, 247, 250-252, 275, 276
  d-quark,
    definition of, 260
  u-quark,
    definition of, 260
  reaction particle, 255, 256
  rishon, related to prime matter, 286-288
  W^+ particle,
    definition of, 266
    general description of, 255
  W^- particle,
    definition of, 266
    general description of, 255
  Z^0 particle,
    definition of, 266
    general description of, 255
Passive quality.
  See Quality
Per accidens reduced to *per se*, 39-43
Per se existence, 31-33
Potentiality, 17, 20, 63, 64
  potential existence, 1-5, 7, 31-33
  priority and posteriority of, 65
  pure potency, 55
Power, 122
  active power, 55
Predication,
  analogical, 91-94

  equivocal, 92, 93
  of universals, 79, 80
  univocal, 92, 93
Presence,
  dispositional presence, 140, 250-252
  instrumental presence, 140, 141, 250-252
  retrievable presence, 250-252
  virtual presence, 133, 246, 247, 250-252, 275, 276
Prime matter.
  See Matter
Principle, 56, 99
  distinguished from cause, 39-41, 43-46
  principles of nature: matter, form and privation, 2, 34-36, 39-41
Priority and posteriority,
  in completeness, 63-65
  in existence, 64
  in generation, 63-65
  in perfection, 63-65
  in substance, 63-65
  in time, 63-65
  of actuality, 65
  of cause and effect, 63-67, 75-79
Privation,
  as concomitant to matter, 18
  as one of the three principles of nature, 2, 10, 34-36, 39-41, 99
  as *per accidens* principle, 15-19, 21-23
  as principle of generation, 8, 15-23
  distinguished from form and matter, 23-25
Property,
  macro-properties, 294-297
  micro-properties, 294-297
Proton,
  as a mixed body, 247, 275, 276

Quality,
  active quality, 105, 106, 108, 112, 121, 123
  of a mixed body, 122
  of a simple body, 122
  of an element, 123-125
  passive quality, 105, 106, 108, 112, 121, 123